POLITICAL CONCEPTS

IDIOM INVENTING WRITING THEORY

Jacques Lezra and Paul North, series editors

POLITICAL CONCEPTS

A CRITICAL LEXICON

J. M. BERNSTEIN, ADI OPHIR, AND
ANN LAURA STOLER, EDITORS

Fordham University Press *New York* *2018*

Fordham University Press also publishes its books in a variety of electronic formats. Some content that appears in print may not be available in electronic books.

Visit us online at www.fordhampress.com.

Library of Congress Cataloging-in-Publication Data available online at https://catalog.loc.gov.

Printed in the United States of America

20 19 18 5 4 3 2 1

First edition

CONTENTS

POLITICAL CONCEPTS

INTRODUCTION. POLITICAL CONCEPTS: A CRITICAL LEXICON

We live in a time of fast-moving social and economic change combined with ever-growing political gridlock. Nonetheless, the overwhelming bulk of work in political theory travels along well-trodden and safe academic pathways. Perhaps the reason for this is that in our academic and intellectual culture there is tacit consensus that political thinking should remain within the confines of agreed-upon disciplinary practices. Creating a space where the rules governing this consensus could be questioned, and where different, sometimes unsafe, sorts of political thinking could flourish was, from the beginning, at the center of the "political concepts" project. Thinking about the meaning of a political concept should at the same time be a means of thinking about, and of making possible ways of intervening in, the political realities of the present. Such were the colloquia (held at the New School for Social Research, Columbia, New York University, and Brown) at which the concepts that make up this volume were presented, debated, and reframed. In this respect, the present volume presents a welcome break with academic conventions. Although each piece is signed by a single author who bears the ultimate responsibility for the position taken, all the pieces carry the mark of an openly contentious and public plurality of thought, question, and collaboration.

This book is a lexicon in the making. It seeks to revive our common political vocabulary, both everyday and academic, and to do so critically. Its entries do not seek to present a definitive history of a concept or an idea, nor do they attempt to summarize or exhaust a range of views regarding certain concepts. The volume's contributors, although well versed in the history of the concept on which they write and the role it plays in various theoretical discussions, seek to present their own original reflection on the question of *what is* that concept and thereby what sort of work a rethinking of that concept can do for us now. Each addresses a concept posed in the traditional Socratic question format, "What is X?," "What is that thing about which we speak?" Our orienting intuition is that the explicitness of a radical questioning of this kind gives authors both the freedom and the authority to engage, intervene, critique, and transform the conceptual terrain they have inherited. By addressing a concept in the "What is X" format, authors take the position of a questioning subject and assume a more direct and personal responsibility than is the academic norm for the answer they give and for the very act of providing such an answer.

Each of the entries, either implicitly or explicitly, attempts to reopen the question "What is political thinking?" Each is an effort to reinvent *political writing.* In this setting *the political* as such may be understood as a property, a field of interest, a dimension of human existence, a set of practices, or a kind of event. But deciding what is and what is not political is a fraught, perhaps intractably opaque, matter. Just *who* decides the question, on what grounds, to what ends—these seem like properly *political* questions themselves. But can a properly political question be formulated *before* we know what is or is not political? Deciding what is political and what is not can serve to contain and restrain struggles, make existing power relations at once self-evident and opaque, and blur the possibility of reimagining them differently. Alternatively, the decision as to what is political can disclose the work that politics entails in thought and action, and to make it possible on those grounds to interrogate and to intervene in contemporary struggles and power relations. Lexical writing as here conceived does not stand upon a decided concept of the political but returns in practice and in concern to the question "What is the political?" by submitting the question in a field of plural contention. To that extent, and on a basic level, lexical writing is a political act.

This sort of lexical writing reopens the question "What is a concept?," whether through the critical investigation of common concepts (such as "liberal," "archive," "development," "crisis," and "concept" itself), the suggestion of new concepts ("enough," "like"), or the addition of ones that would not normally appear in a political lexicon ("blood," "translation," "colony"). The concepts in this book do not represent a list of "key concepts" that the editors privilege over others left in the margins. The essays collected here represent their authors' sense of political urgency as it bears down on a concept in the field in which it appears (or fails to appear), and thus their critique of a prevalent notion of urgency and the priorities it entails. Hence, this lexicon holds refounded concepts up to the test of their possible actualization in concrete circumstances, which exceed not only the disciplinary capacities but even the original conceptions of the lexicographers themselves.

This effort to redefine fundamental concepts of political thinking, to invent new uses for existing concepts, or to introduce new concepts into circulation, whether through import or innovation, seeks to transform the scholarly discourse and the scholarly writing of the humanities and social sciences. This sought-for transformation takes place on two levels. First, any inquiry into fundamental concepts does not stop at disciplinary boundaries nor presuppose the limitations set by research schools and methodologies; rather, it turns those concepts into objects of inquiry in their own right. It is an inquiry that is inherently critical. It is so just by virtue of asking the Socratic question, with its built-in suspicion toward the common use of concepts, its puzzlement over the implicit presuppositions of such use, and its awareness of the *locality*, the historicity and cultural and linguistic specificity, of these uses. In this sense, conceptual thinking and the productive doubt it entails is an invitation to reinvigorate what critical inquiry involves. Second, conceptual inquiry can uncover the political dimension of the common use of concepts, thereby sharpening the political attentiveness of knowledge producers and consumers.

The driving force behind this effort is a distress and a demand stemming from a standard political theory that neither tries nor seems capable of dealing with the deep transformation of the human condition and emergent practices that mark our time. Nor does it engage the demands that existing conceptual practices exert upon us. Common political discourse—that is, politics as represented via most forms of media—seems only to dwindle our reflection on the human condition, encouraging epistemic blindness and emotional distance, if not outright alienation. The intellectual resources suggested by the various strands of critical theory also are no longer satisfactory. Contributors to this lexicon thus share in an effort to address a contemporary demand—not merely for a renewal of political theory, but for a new vocabulary with which to speak about the political.

The contributors to this first volume of a lexicon in formation seek to restore the momentum and inspiration of critical thought and to reorient it toward the fundamental questions of contemporary political reality. They seek to reexamine the basic terms of that discourse and the practices it invites and allows—critique, power, the political, subversion, minority, resistance—which have petrified into clichés and code words. Critical writing is destined to be reflective and resistant to that which seeks to constrain it through well-trodden linguistic formulas. At the same time, it must take care not to be overly preoccupied with itself, with its own rhetoric, and with the metaphors that both guide and constrain its scholarly imagination. It must not give up its orientation toward the world and the era it seeks to describe, explain, and transform. The lexical form of writing, with its insistence on Socratic questioning that isolates a single issue whose concept it pursues, is meant to restore this orientation.

Focusing on a single concept is not meant to undo the fact that concepts always appear alongside many others, arranged in more or less structured constellations and that none of them can be understood without its relations to others. Like the focusing of a camera lens, this gesture is designed to frame the discussion so as to draw our attention to actions, events, occurrences, or constitutive contexts that have as yet failed to be articulated, having no appropriate expression in an existing language. To focus on a single concept means to sharpen our sensitivity to the way language hides not only that which is happening or acting or being enacted, not only what should not necessarily happen or might yet happen, but also that language in use cannot give an expression to all of that. Focusing on a single concept further leaves open the question of whether that concept needs to be undone or whether it can be renewed; whether what is required is to uncover its contingent genealogy and arbitrary application, its ideological functioning and the underlying interests it serves. Or is it also possible to reconstruct or refound the concept, along with the rest of the conceptual apparatus to which it relates, motivated by the effort to gain a more adequate perception of the political potentialities that this concept can either suppress or unleash? *Political Concepts* is a lexicon in formation that invites recurrent reformulations that respond to those concepts already entrenched and that makes room for new formulations and diverse responses to them.

1

ARCHĒ

Stathis Gourgouris

I can say, perhaps a little playfully but not altogether inaccurately, that I have chosen to engage with the very first political concept—certainly in name, if nothing else. But as you will see, my reading is precisely to demonstrate how, from its initial invocation (from its *archē*, as it were), this concept renders any notions of the first, or of the one, impossible, indeterminable, *an-archic*. In this sense, though the word I am examining is *archē*, the political concept I substantially engage with and care about is "anarchy," whose elemental significance, I argue, is actually inherent in the archaic conceptualization of *archē*. It is this archaic conceptualization that interests me here; hence, I do not engage with some important treatments of this notion in Heidegger, Derrida, or Reiner Schürmann. So I will merely weave a thread around four instances of the notion in the Greek philosophical vocabulary, two phrases in Aristotle, one in Herodotus, and the famous passage known as the Anaximander fragment.

Let us look at a well-known assertion in Aristotle's *Politics*:

> Ἔστι τις ἀρχή καθ' ἣν ἄρχει τῶν ὁμοίων τῷ γένει καὶ τῶν ἐλευθέρων (ταύτην γαρ λέγομεν εἶναι τὴν πολιτικήν ἀρχήν), ήν δεῖ τὸν ἄρχοντα ἀρχόμενον μαθεῖν.[1]

This phrase encapsulates not only the paradoxality of democracy but also the deeper significance of what it means for a society to constitute *on its own and for itself* a mode of political life without fixed norms and without guarantees.

This mode of life is political par excellence, and democracy is its name. It is a mode that animates political life: the essence of human being as *zōon politikon*. If the human animal is a political animal, it is because it refuses to consider the *archē* of things as natural and subjects it to interrogation. Aristotle's particular stipulation about rulers learning by being ruled has drawn voluminous commentary on its significance as political science. But as always there is more to the Greek language than might be immediately comprehensible.

We must not forget that *archē* means both origin and rule, much in the sense that, in the English language, we understand rule to pertain both to matters of governance and to matters of principle, indeed first principles, the essential rules of the game, of proposition, of foundation, of order. The ruler, after all, is a primary figure (even in cases articulated as *primus inter pares*), the premier in a constitutive mechanism of ruling that presupposes him to be the primary guardian of the set of rules he represents. In any archaic configuration of power, the *archon* commands authority not only over the domain of rules that govern a society. He also embodies the point of departure of whatever trajectory such rules are to have in their implementation, whether they are to be enforced in principle or not, safeguarded for future generations (of rulers and ruled), or dismantled in favor of another course of rule, another beginning. Such is obviously the essence of the figure of the *patriarch*, which is why even when the primordial parricide takes place, according, let us say, to Freud's tales—when, in fact, the singular origin of principle and rule is to be multiplied and distributed (in Freud's analysis, institutionalized) in the hands of the many murderous sons—the patriarchic order is hardly abolished. On the contrary, in its multiplication, the authorial origin is consolidated.

But when Aristotle demands that the *archon* must also be *archomenos*, something else entirely takes place. The singular notion of *archē* is deconstituted by a corresponding alterity. In order to know how to rule, one must know how to be ruled: this is the quintessential element of autonomy. Knowledge of being ruled does not mean mere experiential accounting from the standpoint of the (always) ruled. In a direct sense, it means knowing the other side of rule, enabling an affirmative investment in the object of rule from a subject-position that is not consumed in the typical objectification suffered by those ruled. In this respect, being ruled provides the sort of knowledge—achieved explicitly as a result of learning (*mathein*)—that relativizes a ruler's presumed monopoly over the authority to determine what rule means and, in effect, abolishes the presumed epistemic distinction between rulers and ruled in producing a subject of authority, of power, in the double sense.[2] Aristotle's phrasing is perfectly apt:

τὴν τῶν ἐλευθέρων ἀρχήν ἐπίστασθαι ἐπ΄ ἀμφότερα: "the rule of the free is known from both sides."[3]

This *co-incidence* can be considered from two standpoints. On the one hand, the ruled authorize their own position as ruled; that is, they are not ruled in the simple sense of submitting to the authority of the ruler, an authority predicated on the assumption that the ruler is also the origin of rule. They are ruled by virtue of their own decision to be ruled, which is to say, they hold the reins of interrogation (and thus signification) over the terms of ruling—who rules, why, and how?—the very mode of interrogation of the rule of law. This is why this notion has nothing to do with the debilitating paradox of "voluntary servitude" that Étienne de la Boétie so brilliantly exposed several centuries ago, which nonetheless continues to characterize most of today's societies of consensus. The ruled who hold the reins of interrogation over the signifying framework of rule can never become servile by definition; they are motivated by a principle of self-limitation that safeguards their autonomy, their self-determination. That is why in the Athenian polis slaves are not ruled, strictly speaking; they just execute commands. For this reason, the police work was assigned to slaves, the famous Scythian archers.[4] It is similar in the case of women and children, whose existence within the *oikos* bears its own economy. As Hannah Arendt argued, Athenian democracy makes the political independent of the social and the economic; the necessity of entwining these two domains is a problem of modernity. Whatever the conditions of power within the *oikos* and the specific variations of patriarchical society pertinent to the Greeks, *archē* in the political sense exists only in the public space of male citizens. All others are altogether outside the realm of ruling, not only because to be ruled means to participate in ruling but also because ruling does not mean issuing commands within a hierarchical structure. Rather, ruling becomes a condition shared by the free and the equal, which is as such—Aristotle is unequivocal on this—*political rule* (πολιτική ἀρχή). By this logic, a ruler who has never known how to be ruled—*a ruler who has not known the autonomy of being ruled*—cannot possibly rule without abusing autonomy in favor of ruling in its name. Aristotle's injunction against such a ruler opens the way toward considering the project of autonomy as an interminable exercise of self-rule even in the political domain of being ruled.

On the other hand, Aristotle's configuration of *archē* also subverts the signification of ruler as primordial authority, which is why it is pertinent only to a democracy and not a monarchy. If, concurrently to rule, *archē* signifies origin, the requisite knowledge of *archomenos* forbids the ruler's singular occupation of the origin of authority, thus introducing a difference at the origin, a foundational *différance*. As *archomenos*, a ruler can never claim to be the first and only. At most he can acknowledge the position of *archon* as a transitory moment in the process of ruling, which is a process whose ultimate beginning is unknown and irrelevant and whose ultimate endpoint is incomprehensible as such—a process undertaken by society as a whole, provided that society recognizes and enacts its autonomy.[5] For an *archon* to recognize the *archomenos* as a subject-position means to recognize an alterity within, which by traditional logic is impossible. What makes this possible—the capacity for *self-alteration*—is even more farfetched, logically speaking. It signifies a process by which alterity is internally produced, dissolving the very thing that enables it, the very thing whose existence derives meaning from being altered, *from othering itself*.[6]

If knowing how to be ruled is essential to ruling, no ruler can claim self-authorization, and *archē* can no longer constitute itself as a singular origin. Authority begins already cleft and differential, open to question at the point of its constitution, by virtue of the fact that both subject and object of power are in a position of *co-incidence*. Although nominally, at a specific point in time, someone rules and someone is being ruled, these positions are not structurally or temporally frozen but are provisionally filled by whoever fills them. In a democratic situation, according to Aristotle's stipulation, this "whoever" pertains to both domains (ruler and ruled) without qualification—hence being called to the responsibility of ruling by lot. In this respect, the mutual alterity between the positions of ruler and ruled does not disintegrate to mere opposition but, rather, remains involved in a mutual complicity where any primordial notion of *archē* as singular authority or singular origin of power is irreparably disrupted. This exposes the whole business of ruling as a veritably *an-archic* condition, in the sense that rule, although not abolished, is provisionally constituted on no other ground than the equal sharing of power among a people who occasionally perform the position of ruler and occasionally perform the position of ruled but are in essence always, *politically*, acting in both positions simultaneously. *In this very sense, anarchy is the* archē *of democracy*.

One may object that my quick reading of Aristotle's phrase is not very Aristotelian. Strictly speaking, this would be correct. By Aristotelian terms, it is a perverse reading—my conclusion at least, because the co-incidence of ruler and ruled is no doubt what the Aristotelian text pursues. My conclusion is perverse in the simple sense that anarchy, literally the nonbeing of rule (which isn't at all to say the lack of rule or unruliness), would be inconceivable to Aristotle as the core signification of democracy. Although not quite bearing Plato's vehemence—Plato explicitly identifies anarchy to be the internal and incurable illness of democracy—Aristotle would signify anarchy as the unraveling of democracy. However, the semantic multivalence of the Greek language enables a broader horizon of understanding the permutations of *archē*. This multivalence is not the mark of the genius of the Greek language (as the German Philhellenic tradition from Humboldt to Heidegger would have it) but the outcome of an explosive social-imaginary that, with extraordinary speed of formation and alteration, fashions new configurations of meaning while retaining the traces of the old in magmatic fashion, as Cornelius Castoriadis would say, so that what would seem to be semantic contradiction is in fact semantic co-incidence.[7]

Given our scant knowledge of the preclassical Greek world, the word *archē* first occurs as a philosophical principle in the famed Anaximander fragment, itself an interpolated text, possibly written around 570 BC and glossed by Theophrastus, Aristotle's premier student, around 350 BC. Theophrastus's commentary no longer exists, but reference to it is found in Simplicius, a Neoplatonist writing in 517 CE, who produces in turn a citation of the famed fragment of Anaximander, in effect, a whole thousand years later.[8] This initial philosophical use, by Anaximander, of a word (*archē*) already present in scant textual traces going back to Homer comes into conjunction with his introduction of a bona fide new concept: *apeiron* (infinity). The tenet of my argument should be obvious: the notion of *archē* (origin and rule) is first used philosophically in order to identify what has no origin and no end and over which there can be no rule. This is not at all a paradox. I quote the famous paragraph from Simplicius:

> Among those who say that the first principle [*archē*] is one and movable and infinite, is Anaximander of Miletus, son of Praxiades, pupil and successor of Thales. He said that the first principle [*archē*] and element of all things is infinite [*apeiron*], and he was the first to apply this word to the first principle; and he says that it is neither water nor any other one of the things called elements, but the infinite is something of a different nature, from which came all the heavens and the worlds in them; and from which things are generated in their substance and to which they return of necessity when they degenerate [*ex ōn de ē genesis esti tois ousi kai tēn phthoran eis tauta ginesthai kata to chreōn*]; for he says that they suffer retribution [*dikēn*] and give recourse [*tisin*] to one another for injustice [*adikian*] according to the order of time [*kata tou chronou taxin*], putting it rather poetically [*poiētikoterois outōs onomasin auta legōn*].

Two essential elements are established by this fragment, whose complexity is vastly disproportionate to its brevity:

1. *Archē* here is infinite. This does not preclude it from being a source (of all matter, of everything). Nor, however, does this mean that it is somehow ex-

ternal to this everything it enables because this everything decays, is finite, and thereby returns to become source again. Source, therefore, is not *Ursprung*, the one and only origin, the once and for all event of creation, but an infinite space of interminably enacted beginnings of an indefinite array of "things" that have one thing in common: they terminate. There is a crucial element in the meaning of *apeiron* we need to remember: whatever has no *peras* doesn't just mean whatever has no limit but also whatever cannot be completed. In this sense, the infinite is also incomplete. The paradoxical condition is that the incomplete/infinite enables the emergence of the complete/finite, an emergence that is, as such, a disturbance of the infinite. The finitude of existence is thus justified by its very violation of the infinite; it is this violation that inaugurates the question of justice (*dikē*).[9] In addition to signifying whatever is unlimited and incomplete, the infinite (*apeiron*), by virtue of the literal polysemy of the word, also means whatever exceeds experience (*peira*)—literally, something that cannot be empirically determined.[10] In this latter sense, insofar as it cannot be empirically known, the infinite (*apeiron*) is not just interminable (*atermon*), as it came to be understood in Aristotle's day, but indeterminable: something that in itself has no *telos*, no finality, no termination—which is another way of saying it lacks de-finition, de-limitation, de-termination.[11]

2. However, this disturbance of the infinite/indefinite/indeterminate by virtue of termination or finitude also means that the infinite source is not omnipotent, for it is thus crossed by time. Time is what makes things/beings decay and die and, in so doing, opens infinity to their re-admittance, to their return, which thus makes the infinite source, simultaneously, a sort of repository, a burial ground, of what has come into the world and has gone out of it. (Ground, here, is metaphorical, for *apeiron* rests on nothing—it is abyssal and only figuratively situated, precisely by this relation to finite things, for its spatial dimension is otherwise a void.) The condition of things/beings entering the world and necessarily having to go out of it constitutes, in itself and without any other qualification, an injustice (*adikia*). This is to say, with utter brutality, that time itself constitutes an injustice, which the infinite, though an *archē*, can neither overrule nor alleviate. The relation between infinity and time hangs in the cosmic balance that finite matter inevitably unsettles—for, on the one hand, matter is subject to time, thereby defying the infinite, and on the other hand, matter returns to the infinite, thereby defying time. This unsettling of balance, this injustice, is life itself—the tragic life, from which there is no redemption.

This impossibility of redemption ends any resemblance of this cosmological sense with views of humanity separated from the divine, fallen from grace by original sin, for example. The Greeks gesture toward a permanent cosmological condition that cannot be repaired in some messianic sense (Jewish or Christian), nor alleviated by some paradisal afterlife (Christian or Muslim). They gesture toward an injustice of which death (irreparable finitude) is both the mark and the cost of retribution, insofar as it restores the matricial integrity of the infinite. Imaginaries of original sin or the fall from grace celebrate an imposed-inherited limit of existence. This archaic Ionian imaginary, for which finitude itself constitutes an injustice, provides justice (*dikē*) precisely in determining that one makes one's own limits in the course of living, while submitting unredemptively to the ultimate limit of death. While living, one's life is potentially unlimited—one's imagination is infinitely capacious, partaking of the abyssal infinite, one might say—hence the danger of committing hubris and the demand thereby that one authorizes (I would say *poietizes*) one's own limits.

It is important to add—and about this matter alone a whole other essay would have to be written—that this astounding fragmentary thought, pertaining to the core of the cosmic and articulated in just a couple of sentences, is explicitly understood to be a way of speaking and thinking poetically. The force of *poiein*—what enables a society to create a world for itself and a mythic language (poetry) that makes this society fully accountable to the fact that *it and no other* has created this world—is essential to understanding the peculiar significance of both tragic life and democracy.[12]

In his stipulation of the substitutable nature of *archon* and *archomenos*, Aristotle reconfigures the stakes of Anaximander's cosmology in explicitly political terms; this cosmology echoes in his account of ruler and ruled, although I am not, of course, claiming that this account belongs to a pre-Socratic idiom. The temporal distance between Anaximander and Aristotle is a matter of historical interest, but this cannot be used to bar the fecund association I am invoking, first because if we know anything of Anaximander it is because of Aristotle and his students, and more important, because the power of the notion of *archē* in the Greek world does not wane in the least, nor does it undergo such transformation in the three hundred years that separate the two philosophers as to be altogether alien. As Jean-Pierre Vernant points out, what strikes Aristotle is the notion that infinity holds together a balance of contentious forces, so that "no individual element should be able to monopolize the *kratos* [power] and impose its domination over the world. The primacy [*archē*] that Anaximander grants to *apeiron* aims to guarantee the permanence of an egalitarian order in which opposing powers are balanced against one another in such a way that if one of them is dominant for a moment, it is then in its turn dominated, if any one of them advances and extends itself beyond its limits it then recedes as much as it has advanced, yielding to its opposite."[13]

In this respect, Vernant goes on to say (reading both Aristotle and Simplicius), infinity cannot be seen as one element among the many opposing elements of the cosmos, but precisely as the intermediary between the elements, what mediates them and is, by the same word (*meson*), in the middle of them: the mediating space of the elements—the *medium* of a limitless abyssal terrain—on which the limit and capacity for self-limitation in every element is tested (drawn and redrawn, broken and reconstituted).

The limitless is a mediatory field that enables limits to be self-instituted. The very constitution of the middle is itself a groundless condition of autonomy. According to Anaximander's vision, the earth exists in the midst of infinity, situated thus and sustained because of the equilibrium produced by interminably contending and opposing forces, an equilibrium that is never static but interminably dynamic, since if any one force achieves dominance, it must be immediately destroyed by an emergent opposing force, and so on. In this infinite dynamic, the earth is otherwise *ὑπό μηδενός κρατούμενη*, that is, literally "held by nothing" but also (equally literally) "beholden to no one," not dominated (*kratoumenē*) by anything, independent, autonomous.[14] That is, in the midst (*meson*) of the infinite universe, the *kratos* of the earth is self-authorized *dynamis*—there is no better evidence of the social imaginary of the democratic polis than the political hue of this language of cosmological physics. Indeed, Anaximander's physics marks the first instance of understanding the suspension of the earth in groundless space, by "spatial" equilibrium, a remarkable discovery given that his configuration of how the earth can hold itself suspended happens without a theory of gravity, or more precisely, without mathematizing the phenomenon of gravity.

Moreover, the significance of the middle—*meson*—is not only figurative, as mediating space, but geometric, as central space, in relation to which all elements, by virtue of the balance that they are thus pressed upon to sustain, are equidistant, or as Vernant (thinking in political terms) hastens to add, in a condition of *isonomia*: "It can thus be said of the centre, as of the *apeiron*, that it represents not so much a particular point in cosmic space, an *ἴδιον*, but the common mediator among all the points in space, a *κοινόν*, to which they all refer equally and from which they are all measured."[15]

Idion and *koinon* are related to each other by a mutual irreconcilable otherness—something that cannot possibly be conveyed by their plausible translation as "self-same" and "collective-common," respectively. This incapacity of translation encapsulates the profound difference between the Athenian democratic imaginary and the imaginary of today's so-called liberal democracies, in which any notion of collective is configured by some sort of phantasmatic multiplication of the individual.

Although in Anaximander's language *archē* and *dikē* pertain to cosmology, their political meaning is unquestionable. Not only because we know them to be explicitly political terms in subsequent phases of Greek society, but because the constitutive emergence of the polis as a specific mode of social organization takes place, before it even becomes democratic in Athens, within and through the same social imaginary that enables Anaximander's cosmology. There is a long discussion over the relation of pre-Socratic cosmologies and concurrent political structures, from Nietzsche and Heidegger to Werner Jaeger and beyond. Gregory Vlastos, whose philosophical reading of the fragment is celebrated, disputes that Anaximander's categories can be translated to political terms, even if they represent the first instance of a detheologizing process in philosophy. Vlastos's announced impetus is to correct Jaeger. However, his philosophical interpretation of the fragment ends up confirming Vernant's, for whom the political significance of Anaximander's cosmology is unquestionable.[16] In their seminal structuralist study of Cleisthenes's democratic reforms, Pierre Lévêque and Pierre Vidal-Naquet have stated the issue most succinctly: "The problem to discover is whether Cleisthenes' *isonomia* and the representation of the cosmos as it appears to the Miletians are two phenomena that, although parallel, do not have any common link or whether, on the contrary, the mental universe of Anaximander was of a kind to be understood by the founder of the new city."[17]

This is not some pedantic philosophical issue. We are talking of an archaic world whose cosmological understanding cannot be divorced from its political imaginary on grounds of some sort of epistemological or disciplinary difference. In such a world, it is not far-fetched to argue that a politics, and even an ethics, can in fact rise out of physics, which would not at all mean an argument on the basis of natural law. Anaximander's language articulates a field of observation of whatever exists around the observer, who is simultaneously the thinker and the poet—this is precisely the mark of its archaic epistemology. Whatever exists around the observer includes, of course, even the most distant things—the sea, the sky, the stars. The Anaximander fragment has been called the first instance of a naturalist way of thinking because it places whatever is based on observation and probable measurement at the center of philosophical/poetic speculation. But the very first level of observation is actually anthropological—Anaximander was in fact the first to speculate that all life, including human life, emerged from the sea—meaning specifically what happens to the human body: decay and then death. This is understood to be a natural condition. There is nothing peculiar about it; it is a brutal fact like any other fact, like water is a fact. So, from this standpoint, what would be called political or ethical rules, which pertain to how human beings interact and live together, are predicated on a brutal natural condition—yet, I repeat, not in a deterministic way, not as natural law. Nature (*physis*) is a necessary substratum; without it, humans—the world itself—would not exist. But the human organization of society (*nomos*) is the domain of working upon this substratum, ultimately exceeding it while never quite altering its bearing of a last instance; never abolishing it, yet also never allowing it to determine, to legislate, the institution of social law, what in *nomos* is *koinon*—*koinōnia*: society. The concept of natural law is just inconfigurable in the Greek imaginary, which is also to say that there can never be a *physis* of *nomos* that isn't already a societal *physis*.

So it is possible to say that because human-being is part of nature like any other, no better or worse, specific in its difference but like any other material specificity in the universe, human-being becomes an indication (not a model) of how everything works. In our time, we recognize the molecular association of everything in the universe, and yet we still dissociate the human from the nonhuman. But stars too are actually finite, like human-being; all matter decays. The infinite and the finite are the ways of the cosmos. And so the terms for justice or injustice are literally of existential cosmological significance. It is really unjust that we die. Even more so, it is really unjust that we live, for this means that we die. It is not death that signifies injustice, because this thought leads to the desire for an afterlife. It is life itself that signifies injustice because it interrupts the universal infinite fold. Finite creatures come into being and then this beautiful and perfect, even if incomplete, infinite is disrupted. Our death is retribution for the fact that we have come to be. No doubt only an archaic civilization could think that way. Nowadays, we would consider this thinking poetic. And it is—not only because the fragment ends on the phrase "putting it rather poetically," which could easily be a later interpolation, but because *poiēsis* means creation of forms and thus belongs to that same language of physics. In turn, this is the epitome of the creative/destructive capacity of the human animal: observation and measurement are already modes of transforming material elements into conditions of life.

There is enough evidence to argue for the institution of the polis, long before the Cleisthenes reforms in Athens, as a radical space of isonomy and *isēgoria* (equality of speech) actualized in the Ionian societies from which what we call pre-Socratic thinking emerged. A cosmology of groundless mediation and a geometry of equidistance from a central point are the essential registers that permeate all aspects of the city, from its architectural planning to the organization of its domestic space. Vernant specifically makes the argument that the centrality of the agora in Athens is not due to some economic principle in the modern sense (the centrality of the marketplace in the exchange of goods and ideas), but harkens back to the primitive circle of warriors (as described by Homer), in which the man who speaks takes a position at the center of the circle of equals and returns to the circle for the next man to step into the middle, and so on. Likewise, he argues that once the polis is instituted as a new mode of social organization, the hearth—the sacred space in every house that resides at the center and is implanted in the earth—is reconfigured as common hearth (*hestia koinē*) and placed in the center of the agora space, now identified explicitly as a *political* symbol devoted to no divinity and thereby desacralized.[18]

This geometrics of *meson*, of mediation and middle, which irrevocably alters any understanding of *archē* as the fixed point of origin and primary rule, operates in another often quoted instance in Aristotle: *πολίτης δ' ἁπλῶς οὐδενί τῶν ἄλλων ὁρίζεται μᾶλλον ἤ τῷ μετέχειν κρίσεως καί ἀρχῆς.*[19] This phrase demonstrates in the language itself not only how *archē* is indeed not constituted as a primordial whole—that it is, in fact, cleft, permeated by *différance* both as origin and as principle—but that it is also, by virtue of that permeability, a condition of mediation. The citizen does not possess or occupy (*katechei*) rule/origin (*archē*), but shares (*metechei*) in rule/origin. Considering the etymology, one could argue that *metechei* means also one "exists within it," or literally, one "permeates its possession" or, even more precisely, one "enters a medium of this possession." But it is not only this permeation/mediation that disrupts the illusion of a primordial and integral *archē*, or that it displaces its possession of the origin. It is also that, insofar as *archē* becomes a matter of share (*metochē*), it is simultaneously mediated and pluralized. Democratic *archē* can only be shared. If not shared, it does not exist. It sounds self-evident, but we better take seriously what it means for it not to exist. In addition—by virtue of the same language—democratic *archē* is also constitutively mediated by the transient community that shares in power. The very institutions of *isonomia* and *isēgoria* signify and *actualize* this mediation of *archē* achieved by the sharing of power. It's worth quoting Vernant here at length:

> *Archē* [in the *polis*] was no longer concentrated in a single figure at the apex of the social structure, but was distributed equally throughout the entire realm of public life, in that common space where the city had its center, its *meson*. Sovereignty passed from one group to another, from one individual to another, in a regular cycle, so that command and obedience, rather than being opposed to each other as two absolutes, became the two inseparable aspects of one reversible relationship. Under the law of *isonomia*, the social realm has the form of a centered and circular *cosmos*, in which each citizen, because he was like all the others, would have to cover the entire circuit as time went round, successively occupying and surrendering each of the symmetrical positions that made up civic space.[20]

Insofar as *one* (absolute singular) cannot occupy (*katechein*) this *archē*—which isn't to say that no one occupies this *archē*—one (generic impersonal and substitutable singular) traverses (*metechein*) this *archē*: the *archē* becomes a shared space of mediation that thereby disrupts the constitution or reconstitution of absolute singular (literally, monarchical) rule/origin.[21]

We thus reach the paradoxical situation, by modern logic, where what begins is already in the midst of what exists. A point of departure (and governing principle) is permeated by forces that can never be accounted for singularly, one by one, but together form the abyssal point of emergence, the opening in the infinite that creates this midst in what exists. But also, what exists is, as such (if this can even be said), indeterminable, impossible to subject to any singular origin, any singular reason for being, because it, too, exists within the infinite. The only thing that can be said about what exists is that it exists so as to cease existing; the only way to determine that something exists is because its existence is finite. Only insofar as it has a definite end (*telos*) can one understand that what exists has a beginning (*archē*)—finitude is the only rule (*archē*) of existence.

As a profound attempt to create meaning out of meaninglessness, while neither denying meaninglessness nor seeking to transcend it, this orientation may be called philosophical but is profoundly political, not only because it belongs to the social imaginary institution of the polis, but because it expresses an elemental struggle against heteronomous determination beyond the strictly physical realm. We can think of this another way. If, in the first instance, Anaximander's fragment entails a specific conceptualization of *physis*, in the last instance—as it becomes comprehensible within a social historical frame—it also conceptualizes a certain *nomos*. *Physis*, let us recall, is not a state of things; it is not nature as a given, in the way that modern thought (moral, religious, scientific) has configured it. It is literally a condition of emergence (the verb *phyein* means to sprout, to surge forth) out of an indeterminate abyssal infinite, which cannot quite be called source, at least not source as *Ursprung*. *Physis* is not a state of things as they are, but an interminable flux of generation and degeneration (*phthora*), literally a dynamic of living (and of course, dying) being. This dynamic sense of *physis* emerges out of the specific *nomothetic* imaginary of the Greeks, who now can stipulate that *physis* bears in itself a *nomos*—while the reverse is unacceptable, inconceivable—a mode in nature by which the cosmos is regulated and balanced, by which justice is achieved.[22] The ordinance of time (*kata tou chronou tixin*) expresses the necessity (*kata to chreōn*) of finitude, which thereby preserves the possibility of interminable generation (*archē*) from the matrix of the infinite.

The injustice does not reside in the struggle between the infinite and the finite, the indeterminate and the determined, as if they are two polarities as different universes. The struggle takes place within the infinite; what is determined to be (to live and die) emerges as determined within the interminable and indeterminable *to-be*, as Castoriadis would put it (*à-être*).[23] The paradoxical figure of the ontological injustice of death being at the same time a reconstitution of the order of the infinite, therefore a gesture of justice against the injustice of existence disrupting the infinite fold, suggests a social-imaginary that takes irrevocable death as ultimate limit of living being, the only untranscendable limit that thereby frees life from any other imposed limits. (Where "limits," we might also want to write "determinations.") It may seem, then, that heteronomy is removed from the realm of necessity in the course of one's life and relegated to one and only one place: death. But in death, there is no *nomos*, strictly speaking. *Nomos* occurs and has meaning only in the course of living. So the untranscendable limit of death is not the last instance of a naturalized heteronomy but the irrevocable limit point that denaturalizes heteronomy altogether. From this standpoint, limits or determinations in the course of one's life are open to becoming a matter of self-knowledge, self-determination, autonomy—in the strictest sense of determining the question of what *nomos* is within one's conditions of living. Both Sandywell and Castoriadis point out the co-incidence between Anaximander's fragment and the Aeschylian imagination in *Prometheus Bound*, specifically the notion of *physis* subject to (or crossed by) *nomos*, thereby opening the path for the creation of an autonomous life in a tragic universe.[24]

Later in the *Politics*, Aristotle reiterates his understanding of the undoing of *archē* as singularity and primacy by explicitly connecting democracy to the institution of existential liberty (*eleutheria*).[25] Against all inherited notions that the concept of individual liberty emerges in Enlightenment individualism and liberalism, one finds in Aristotle that the liberty of living as one likes (*τὸ ζῆν ὣς βούλεταί τις*)—for to live not as one likes is precisely the condition of being a slave—is an essential element of democratic *archē*. Living as one likes, as a condition of being, is expressed *politically* in the desire not to be ruled by anyone (*ἐντεῦθεν ἐλήλυθε τὸ μή ἄρχεσθαι, μάλιστα μέν ὑπό μηδενός*—"from there arises [the desire for] not being ruled, indeed by no one") or, if that's not possible, to rule and be ruled in turn (*εἰ δέ μή, κατά μέρος*). In other words, the necessity of sharing rule (of ruling as the practice of knowing how to be ruled) is predicated on the desire not to be ruled at all. However, it depends on the recognition that this desire is possible only as an existential desire—the prerequisite of an ontological freedom—since the coexistence of free citizens that makes up the polis makes some institution of rule necessary. We can also think of it in reverse: refusal to be ruled existentially can only be actualized *politically* in sharing rule (*μετέχειν τῆς ἀρχῆς*), in knowing how to be ruled. This only makes sense if we abolish our preconception that being ruled means having no power. In democracy, *being ruled means having power*—not as some sort of clientelist electorate or the alleged agency of public opinion, as happens routinely in contemporary liberal oligarchies, but precisely insofar as the decision to be ruled is made autonomously, in full cognizance of the fact that this is a decision made by the plurality of rulers, since rule (or more precisely, self-rule) is shared by all.

There is a curious configuration here where the self is radicalized as an autonomous entity and yet, simultaneously, pluralized and shared according to the isonomy of the polity. It would be erroneous to consider this along the lines of the divide between public and private, whereby one refuses to be governed in the private sphere and submits to government in the public sphere. This is a purely liberal formulation. Neither is it, however, akin to Kant's pious reversal—freedom of thought and speech in the public sphere, obedience to the (moral) law in the private sphere—because, though *oikos* and agora are distinct spaces, in the Athenian imaginary there is no stipulated separation between the ethical (private) and the political (public). One's existential condition of freedom is a matter of *physis*, while the political enactment of freedom is a matter of *nomos*. *Physis* and *nomos* are not contradictory; they are coextensive cosmological crossings permeating the entire ancient Greek imaginary.

Similarly, the relation between ruler and ruled is not simply dialectical; it belongs to the order of co-incidence. It is by this logic of co-incidence that I speak of anarchy, to return to my first thesis: *anarchy is the* archē *of democracy*. The term literally means the impossibility of fully constituted (or once-and-for-all instituted) *archē*, both as point of origin and as point of governance. It does not mean the refusal of governance or the refusal of principle—at least, not when it comes to politics in a democracy. In Herodotus, there is the famous episode of the three Persian princes, who are discussing the form of power that the Persian kingdom must have in the wake of the reign of Kambyses. As has been amply pointed out, Herodotus is here enacting an allegorical exercise to discuss different modes of politics. This is a theatrical exercise, and despite the fact that the actors are Persians, the dramaturgy is Greek. And so is the matter enacted. It is highly unlikely that three Persian princes would conduct a debate over which political mode would be the best to succeed the death of the king. Moreover, we know that Herodotus made a sojourn in Athens c. 447–443 BC (in Periclean times, as the Parthenon was being built), and we may just as well imagine that this specific scene could have been publically performed for the benefit and interrogation of the Athenians. The theatrical debate as to which mode of rule was preferable (democracy, oligarchy, monarchy) deserves a close reading, for it bears considerable rhetorical and political subtlety. Most striking, however, is the concluding phrase by Otanis (the advocate of democracy), who, upon facing the agreed-upon decision (by majority) that the preferable solution is monarchy, decides to withdraw his name from the process of succession to the throne by famously declaring: *οὔτε ἄρχειν οὔτε ἄρχεσθαι ἐθέλω* ("I want neither to rule nor to be ruled").[26]

This phrase in Herodotus is often identified as an expression of anarchist sentiment. This is absurd in any strictly political sense. I take it to be the mere expression of the desire to be exempted from the political, literally an option to withdraw into the private sphere. Otanis deliberately opts out of any participation in government and, in return, he and his family gain a sort of asylum, a freedom in a state of exception established by a certain rule—a rule of the game, a convention—but a rule of an Other nonetheless. For even if it is Otanis's own decision to opt out, the survival of the agreement he brokers is henceforth predicated on the goodwill of another, the one (the monarch) who will come to rule.

In the discussion that takes place before the agreement, Otanis defends the option of democratic politics, not using the name democracy, however, but *isonomia*, a notion that historically precedes democracy in name. Although it is generally accepted that democracy is first explicitly articulated in Aeschylus's

Suppliants in 464 BC (*δήμου κρατούσα χείρ*: "the people's hand of power"), the name itself does not appear until later, which is why Herodotus does not use it here. Lévêque and Vidal-Naquet call the word "democracy" "philologically anomalous" in relation to the various faces of *archē* (monarchy, oligarchy), which by itself signifies an entirely different order where there is no *archē* as reigning first principle, where *archē* is found in the midst (*meson*) of power (*kratos*) shared among equals.[27] Thus, they underline *isonomia* as the operative word for democratic rule, a quintessentially political notion that first appears specifically as the name of the regime that overtakes the institution of tyranny. Herodotus, again, is a reliable and revealing reference. In recounting the overthrow of the tyranny of Polykrates of Samos (c. 518 BC), he explicitly denotes *isonomia* as the setting of *archē* in the middle: *es meson tēn archēn titheis* ("you set the beginning in the middle").[28]

Otanis's critique of monarchy is precisely that it engages the law from a constitutive position of hubris—this is the word that Herodotus uses. By occupying the law absolutely, monarchy exceeds, violates, and thus annihilates the law. There is indeed a subtle but definitive shift in the language from *archē* to *nomos* (monarchy to isonomy), for democracy is qualitatively other to monarchy not merely by the fact that rule is exercised by the multitude (*plēthos*) as opposed to the rule of the one, but that rule (*archē*) is subject to law (*nomos*) according to the essential significance of the source verb *nemein*: divided, apportioned, allotted, mediated, shared. Though there can be rule of the one (*monarchia*), there can never be law of the one in any manner of speaking; the word *mononomia* does not exist in the Greek vocabulary. Otanis's final decision, however, is ultimately a rejection of the democratic politics he espouses, for no community, no polis and no *dēmos*, can be constituted on the basis of refusal to rule and be ruled. It is, moreover, a blatant violation of isonomy in that Otanis's decision pertains to himself only (his family is literally his property, proper to him). It is, if you will, an option for *idion* over *koinon*, thereby positing the exclusive privilege of just one: a monologic position that is, strictly speaking, monarchic, even if in name anarchic.

In other words, despite Otanis's overt naming of his decision, his position is actually not anarchic because anarchy, in the way I am defining it, can only exist *against* the provenance of the One (the singularity of *archē* as origin and rule). Moreover, as a political position, anarchy is not a matter of personal desire; it is an investment in a specific signification of *archē*, whereby the right to rule is a plural, shared, yet contentious affair. Anarchy can never be linked to some apolitical position, to the voiding of *archē*, whereby the right to rule is left to the others.[29] In that sense, too, anarchy is the *archē* of democracy.

NOTES

1. "There is a sort of rule pertaining to those similar in birth and free—this we call political rule—where the ruler learns by being ruled." Aristotle, *Politics*, book 3, 1277b; henceforth cited with my translation.

2. "*Archesthai* [being ruled] is not simple passive voice. Animals cannot be *archomena* [ruled], objects of an *archein* [rule]. *Archesthai* means to participate in a political community where one is, by necessity, also 'under authority'—as a subject of power in the double sense." Cornelius Castoriadis, *La cité et les lois—Ce qui fait la Grèce 2* (Paris: Seuil, 2008), 201n.

3. Aristotle, *Politics*, 1227b.

4. See Elizabeth Baughman, "The Scythian Archers: Policing Athens," in *Dēmos: Classical Athenian Democracy, The Stoa: A Consortium for Electronic Publication in the Humanities*, ed. C. Blackwell, n.d., http://www.stoa.org.

5. Two points are worth noting even when Aristotle considers the notion of *archē* in a purely philosophical sense, as in the *Metaphysics* when he discusses the matter of first principles and causes: (1) he always speaks in the plural (*archai kai aitiai*), as there can never be *one* first principle or cause in isolation and above all others; (2) nowhere does he place the philosopher—for philosophy is the mode in which first principles and causes are to be contemplated and understood—in the position of *archon* as such (see *Metaphysics*, 1.980–85.) But, insofar as the signifying range of *archē*—or rather, in the plural, *archai*—is limited to the temporal ("beginnings") and not to the political, Aristotle's thinking departs from the differential framework we see in *Politics* and attributes to this term a causal determination. However, even if naturalized, this determination retains a connection to the inaugural pre-Socratic signification of the inherent finitude (*telos*) made imperative by the *archē* of time.

6. See my essay "On Self-Alteration," *Parrhesia* 9 (2010): 1–17. Crucial to the argument in that essay, but not rehearsed here, is the epistemology of sexual difference.

7. Cornelius Castoriadis, *Thucydide, la force et le droit* (Paris: Seuil, 2011), 291–317.

8. For the most concise exposition of the many modern glosses of the Anaximander fragment, as well as their different registers and translations (from Nietzsche, Heidegger, and Jaeger to Vlastos, Vernant, and Castoriadis), see Vassilis Lambropoulos, "Stumbling over the 'Boundary Stone of Greek Philosophy,'" in *Justice in Particular: Festschrift in Honour of Professor P.J. Kozyris* (Athens: Sakkoulas, 2007), 193–210.

9. Note Barry Sandywell's succinct formulation: "Whatever exists is universally subject to justified destruction. Now the *kosmos* is perceived as a vast process of

coming-to-be and passing-out-of existence. Every existing thing is a site of expiation for its violation of the *apeiron*." Barry Sandywell, *Pre-Socratic Reflexivity: The Construction of Philosophical Discourse c. 600–450 BC* (London: Routledge, 1996), 141.

10. For this reason, as Castoriadis puts it, "a theory of the infinite is, in some ways, a literal contradiction" because there can never be an empirical (experimental and experiential) basis on which the infinite can be theorized. "Hence, only poets can touch the infinite." See Cornelius Castoriadis, *Philosophia kai Epistēmē* (Athens: Eurasia, 2003), 112. It is important to add that, although the Anaximander fragment is about physics, the thinking involved is not mathematical strictly speaking. In modern mathematics infinity is calculated, or rather, mathematized. It can be part of an equation that can be solved, even if infinity remains unknown as a specific number. In Anaximander, infinity is a non-mathematical entity. It does denote an order, but an order that cannot be determined, an order that is incomplete and intangible and therefore cannot be calculated.

11. See Castoriadis, *Ce qui fait la Grèce*, 175.

12. In his extensive reading of the Anaximander fragment, Castoriadis points out the peculiarity of this creation of the notion of the infinite precisely as an entirely noninstrumental and nondeterminant conceptualization, as thought itself—for him the *archē* (beginning) of philosophy. He would not disagree, I would argue, that this philosophical *archē* is indeed, contra Plato, poietic in essence. See Castoriadis, *Ce qui fait la Grèce*, 210–14.

13. Jean-Pierre Vernant, *Myth and Thought among the Greeks* (London: Routledge, 1983), 205.

14. Ibid., 186, 192.

15. Ibid., 206–7.

16. Gregory Vlastos, "Equality and Justice in Early Greek Cosmologies," in *Studies in Greek Philosophy*, vol. 1, *The Presocratics*, ed. Daniel W. Graham (Princeton, N.J.: Princeton University Press, 1995), 57–88. Next to Vernant, foremost in placing his commentary on Anaximander at the core of the social-imaginary institution of the polis itself is Castoriadis, *Ce qui fait la Grèce*, 185–224.

17. Pierre Lévêque and Pierre Vidal-Naquet, *Cleisthenes, the Athenian: An Essay on the Representation of Space and Time in Greek Political Thought from the End of the Sixth Century to the Death of Plato* (Amherst, Mass.: Prometheus Books, 1997), 53.

18. Vernant, *Myth and Thought*, 183–89. Vernant speaks of Hippodamus of Miletus, fellow citizen to Anaximander (but a century later) as the architect of the first polis based on an agora space at the center of a circular construction, adding that, although an architect, Hippodamus was indeed a political theorist (185). This geometrical imaginary of the polis can be said to be at work also in the ideal architecture of Vitrivius, according to which the city's center must be open to ventilation by a series of radial streets in a circle around it. But the speed with which the social-historical

field changes in less than a century between Cleisthenes and Hippodamus is remarkable. Lévêque and Vidal-Naquet point out that the urban geometry of Hippodamus already signals the way to a philosophical abstraction that becomes independent of the political, whose ultimate trajectory eventually leads to the Platonic architectural ideal that restores sacred space as the center of the polis (*Cleisthenes*, 73–97). In the end, for all the remarkable capacity of the Greek philosophical mind to mathematize the world, the most important legacy of the Greek democratic mind is that the political is indeed incalculable.

19. "A citizen is simply determined, above all other matters, in sharing/participating in judgment [*krisis*] and rule [*archē*]" (Aristotle, *Politics*, 3.1275a).

20. Jean-Pierre Vernant, *The Origins of Greek Thought* (Ithaca, N.Y.: Cornell University Press, 1984), 101.

21. See also Martin Ostwald's discussion of this significance of *metechein* in "Shares and Rights: 'Citizenship' Greek Style and American Style," in *Dēmokratia: A Conversation on Democracies, Ancient and Modern*, ed. Josiah Ober and Charles Hedrick, 49–61 (Princeton, N.J.: Princeton University Press, 1996). Notably, Ostwald reads Aristotle's phrase *exousian einai metechein* not in the sense that *exousia* means sovereignty or even power achieved by right but, rather, "something 'permissible,' 'allowable,' that is open to a person, not something to which a person is 'entitled'" (56).

22. By Anaximander's time, as opposed to Homer's or Hesiod's, the Greek world was marked by two crucial emergences/institutions: the collapse of the order of tribal kinship and the spread of alphabetic writing. *Nomos* gains by being written and displayed. Although carved in stone it is nonetheless *not written in stone*, according to the inherited biblical metaphor, because it is precisely its overt appearance—its coming out into the order of *phainesthai*—that enables it to be reviewed and revised, questioned and altered. On the contrary, as is famously claimed by Antigone, what remains "unwritten" tends to take the meaning of "written in stone"—that is, permanent and unalterable sacred custom (Sandywell, *Pre-Socratic Reflexivity*, 159). Much remains to be learned, in this regard, from studying the late work of Friedrich Kittler, who sees in pre-Socratic Greece a revolution in notational systems (alphabet, music, mathematics) that signifies an unprecedented social-imaginary (both as ontological and epistemological field), which has otherwise been eclipsed by the advent of Christianity and repercussions of globalatinization.

23. Note also the following: "The nondetermination of what is is not mere 'indetermination' in the privative and ultimately trivial sense. It is creation, namely, emergence of *other* determinations, new laws, new domains of lawfulness. . . . No state of being is such that it renders impossible the emergence of *other* determinations than those already existing." Cornelius Castoriadis, "The Logic of Magmas and the Question of Autonomy," in *The Castoriadis Reader*, ed. David Ames Curtis, 290–318 (Oxford: Blackwell, 1997), 308.

24. Sandywell, *Pre-Socratic Reflexivity*, 161; Castoriadis, *Ce qui fait la Grèce*, 113.

25. Aristotle, *Politics*, 6.1317b.

26. "I want neither to rule nor to be ruled" (Herodotus, *Histories*, 3.80–84).

27. Lévêque and Vidal-Naquet, *Cleisthenes*, 150.

28. Herodotus, *Histories*, 3.142. The essential meditation on the history and permutations of isonomy remains Gregory Vlastos's essay "*Isonomia,*" in *Studies in Greek Philosophy*, 1:89–111.

29. In his exemplary reading of this passage in Herodotus, Castoriadis argues that the essential articulation in Herodotus is the antithesis between freedom and despotism—which, incidentally, can never be reduced to the antithesis between Greeks and barbarians. In this respect, Otanis's phrase makes sense as the ultimate refusal of despotic logic. But, by the same token, it thus remains locked in this specific *existential* antithesis and can never become a springboard for the *political* freedom of autonomy. See *La cité et les lois*, 264–69.

2

BLOOD

Gil Anidjar

The inclusion of blood in a lexicon of political concepts would seem to require the removal of two quite formidable obstacles. First, blood is not a concept. And second, blood is not political.[1] I shall return to the first obstacle, but I should begin by deferring to understandable reservations with regard to the removal of the second. For who, after all, would want to claim blood *for* the political, to make blood political and tear down the wall, close the gap that separates blood from politics? Who would wish together to have and to hold in unholy matrimony blood and politics? Are not the worst perversions, the worst exceptions, of our global political history conjured easily enough by this ominous apposition? At the most basal, as the most basal, blood functions as a liminal marker, the potent sign of politics at its recalcitrant limits. Blood operates or, shall we say, circulates at the outer extremes of politics, there where the shedding of blood signifies the ultimate exercise of power (*ius gladii* and all that), as well as the undoing of the community that descends into violence. As Martin Luther limpidly put it, "Let no one think that the world can be ruled without blood; the sword of the ruler must be red and bloody; for the world will and must be evil, and the sword is God's rod and vengeance upon it."[2]

Accordingly, blood figures that which, from past to present, female to male, and status to contract, politics transcends, manages, or excludes; what it should, at any rate, exclude: the archaism of blood feuds, the threat of cruel and unusual punishment—or of menstruation—and the pertinacity of kinship, of tribalism, and finally of race. Like Diderot, we still "are filled with indignation at the cruelties, either civil or religious, of our ferocious ancestors, and we turn away our eyes from those ages of horror and blood."[3] In this broad perspective, the inclusion of blood in a lexicon of political concepts—the removal of the two obstacles I have mentioned—smacks of a strange revivalism, of fundamentalism even, minimally, an archaism of sorts. "To what extent have we escaped," Alain Brossat wonders with justifiable unease, "the archaic and obscure dramaturgy of blood, this political dramaturgy evoked by Foucault?"[4] The question should be answered thoughtfully, the inquiry conducted with care, for it requires the exertion of the same protective vigilance that has sought to keep the floodgates erect, which haltingly prevented blood from engulfing our political existence.

A distinct kind of exertion would perhaps be demanded by a simpler and antipodal acknowledgment, namely, that blood has played (and continues to play) a central role in, has been a constitutive factor or element of, whatever we conceive politics to be. Far from an exception, blood would be the rule. As I have mentioned, blood did not become a concept, was not reflectively elaborated as such, though Hegel—who else?—did propose, in *The Phenomenology of Spirit*, that the "universal notion, *der absolute Begriff*" may well be called "the universal blood," suggestively intimating that blood may be the very name of the concept.[5] But what of it? Blood never became a political concept, or one of the "foundations of modern political thought," yet its universality—its rule—is hardly diminished thereby.[6] It is merely of a different order, a different register. Indeed, as Hegel makes clear, what could be more universal than blood? The phrase "flesh and blood," which long defined the legal person (or its normative horizon) is everywhere.[7] But beyond and above it, who would deny the force of blood, the determining and general power of blood? Famously attending to a worm with a view, Spinoza opined that "all the bodies in Nature can and should be conceived in the same way as we have here conceived the blood."[8] Everything is as if, but for the realm of concepts, the realm of political concepts in particular, blood were ubiquitous and omnipresent, locally and even globally.

The emerging paradox, if it is one, should therefore be clear. Blood is at once very much present, universally so, and absent—or absented—from politics. Its presence is both exceptional (racism, Nazism) and normal, universal. Has the exception become, yet again, the rule? Whereas it might lead us to "question the rationality of the norm itself," of which blood is the center, a reigning universalism, one capable of finding political theologies at every corner of the globe, partakes of the sedimentation of this paradox, while claiming to resolve it.[9] It would have us accept that blood is everywhere and therefore that politics must be shielded from it. Rendered in a familiar declension: where blood was, there politics shall be.

What I want to argue, however, is that blood irrigates a particular conception of politics and defines a momentous political tradition that, unacknowledged as such—that is, in terms of its determined rapport to blood—may well claim universal status (with the means to prove and enforce it too) but has yet fully to achieve this status, at least reflectively and conceptually. In this tradition, which is of course not exhausted but is, rather, distinguished by this singular feature, blood is never a concept, but it exercises, across time, a peculiar and not inconstant dominion. Blood makes and marks difference, an allegedly universal difference inscribed between bloods. Considered in this manner, blood quietly traces the contours, the external and internal limits in fact, of a unique circulatory system, a system of different bloods. Law and science, race and economics, war and the culture of peace, along with the apparatuses of the so-called modern state, all deploy their "own" blood, while concealing blood's governing or defining role across these realms. But the argument may perhaps be phrased more clearly: "All significant concepts of the modern theory of the state are liquidated theological concepts not only because of their historical development, but also because of their systematic fluidity, the recognition of which is necessary for a sociological consideration of these concepts."[10]

Such is, at any rate, the formulation I would like to offer with this contribution. The phrasing is short and clearly plagiarized, recognizably memorable, therefore, and it should assist us as we attempt to take the measure of what connects us to, and distances us from, a concept of blood, from blood as a political concept. But allow me one preliminary remark before I embark on what can only be an abbreviated exposition toward a "sociological consideration" of our political concepts—concepts such as nation and emancipation, kinship and race, law and capital, sovereign and citizen, property, inheritance, and freedom, all of which are connected by blood. I will admit it is a rather futile engagement, meant merely to make the obvious manifest, this simple fact that, far from having "an invisible influence" as Daniel Defoe once surmised, blood rather ostensibly suffuses and unites the political life of the West.[11] In a manner that is at once unique and undeniable, blood distinguishes our political imagination—and the political institutions we insist on calling modern—and so perhaps to the precise extent that blood never comes to mind as an idea or concept. Not only has blood therefore not been evacuated from politics but also the ominous apposition with which I began is better understood as a simple equation. In the Christian West, blood is politics and politics is blood. Our political hematology.

A preliminary remark, then. When it comes to blood, to an understanding of blood, the distinction between literal and figurative must be suspended and rethought. For what we mean by blood has never been abstracted from what is said and done about, with, and to blood. More than that, the very distinction between literal and figurative blood—the difference between bloods—is part and parcel of the dominion of blood, enabling the dissemination of blood across seemingly distinct realms, which it covertly unifies. The absence of a concept of blood, at any rate, makes it impossible to assert with any assurance that the blood of kinship, for instance, is metaphorically derivative with regard to the presumed literal, allegedly primary, blood of physiology or medicine. The impossibility might be illustrated by way of a rich account, compellingly extensive, which brings together "the ancient belief that sperm is comprised of blood," the fact that "kinship ties were imagined as ties of shared blood," the transformation whereby the European nobility came to understand itself by way of "its genealogical records of the 'blood' ties of lineal kinship," and the sedimentation of "the rhetoric of blood" as "the means used to naturalize the role of reproduction and procreation."[12] While not inaccurate in the vectors it reveals, and most notably with regard to the connection between kinship and race (on which more later), this description implies that a primeval physiological conviction becomes the object of a "naturalization," which otherwise seems to have been universally given, firmly and originally in place beforehand. The argument, in other words, is that a bodily fluid is in fact a metaphor that continues, by mistake or by design, to be understood literally, which it incidentally always would have been. Truly, as Gail Paster rightly emphasizes, "blood's lexical unwieldiness should not distract us from noticing a significant correlation between the scientific account of blood," its juridical and political accounts, and the "hierarchies in which blood figures as a key signifier."[13] It is the singularity of blood's locations and its expansion, along with its persistence across realms and discourses that, prior to any received division into literal and figurative, will have to be confronted as a rhetorical, that is, political, problem.

All this, in brief, means that no community was ever a "community of blood"—to invoke the phrase famously deployed by Henry Lewis Morgan—that did not first deploy an insistent rhetoric of blood, that did not speak of blood as the substance of community, even if—especially if—to take its distance from it, as if metaphorizing it. How do we know this? The Old Testament for one never uses the phrase "flesh and blood," which I mentioned earlier, nor would it imagine blood as a site of distinction between creatures of any kind. Christian translators and exegetes, however, erroneously came to imagine humankind—and even then, only those admitted in it—as being "of one blood."[14] The universalization of blood, as well as its transformation into a marker of specificity, and of the latter's truth, was on its way (and recall that "to the mediaeval mind," at least, "the destiny and preordained end of Christendom was always identical with that of mankind at large").[15] Ludwig Feuerbach, to take but one instance, partly but effectively summarizes: "As the truth of personality is unity, and as the truth of unity is reality, so the truth of real personality is—blood."[16] Still, by what translation could the ancient Israelites, or other occupants of "the savage slot" as Michel-Rolph Trouillot calls it, ever be included in this anthropotheistic schema, understood, as they famously were by Ernest Renan and countless others, as a community of blood?[17] Like many aggregates of the hemophilic kind—I mean the term in its strictest technical, that is, etymological and nonmedical, sense—the translations of blood remain unremarked and unreflected. The postulated universality of blood grounds our political hematology, our political hemophilia. Our politics are drenched in blood, the love of blood.

"When several families are united," Aristotle famously said, "and the association aims at something more than the supply of daily needs, then comes into existence the village." Aristotle goes on to clarify the structure of the early political unit, the Greek city-state governed, he says, by kings. "Every family is ruled by the eldest, and therefore in the colonies of the family the kingly form of government prevailed because they were of the same blood."[18] From Aristotle to Henry James Sumner Maine, William Robertson Smith and beyond, blood—identical to, yet also narrower than, kinship—would have been the undisputed and primary ground, "the sole possible ground," of the political (incidentally, despotic) community.[19] In Maine's formulation, "the history of political ideas begins, in fact, with the assumption that kinship in blood is the sole possible ground of community in political functions."[20] Do we not believe it still? Do we not cling, as Alain Brossat does, to a model of political emancipation that at once affirms and denies blood? "I am sick to death of bonding through kinship and 'the family,'" writes Donna Haraway quite poignantly. Rather than retreating toward a less hematologically incorrect phrasing, however, she proceeds further to assert that "ties through blood—including blood recast in the coin of genes and information—have been bloody enough already."[21]

Of course, no conceptualization of blood as political can avoid the matter of race, which might otherwise be thought as the intensification of blood in the post-Reformation era. It is becoming increasingly evident, however, that there are deep and intricate connections between race and kinship—that other discourse of blood. Interestingly, what Alys Weinbaum refers to as "the race/reproduction bind"[22] constitutes in fact "a privileged, but still rather little-explored, way of grasping dimensions of race, ethnicity and nationality" together.[23] And indeed, few are those who have devoted their attention to the peculiarities of the "European cognatic kinship systems," and more precisely to that which, in them, "allows for a clearer understanding of certain dimensions of racist contexts."[24] As one scholar uncharacteristically puts it, "an important component of our identity is determined by the very act of generation, defined in terms of the consubstantiability contained in the blood, which at least from Christian times has been the major symbol of our kinship system." What should be underscored here is the contingency and the persistence, the unique rhetorical configuration, that has long equated blood and kinship, indeed, blood and community, in race thinking and, more importantly, before and beyond it.[25] In this perspective, at any rate, it is no accident that Émile Benveniste's justly celebrated compendium of our inherited lexicon deploys the language of blood without ever treating blood as a technical term, much less as a concept.[26]

To be sure, after Foucault and also against him, Ann Laura Stoler has already asked us to widen our hematological horizons. She alerts us to the limitations of Foucault's diagnostic and of his quite orthodox periodization, whereby history would have moved from one stage to the next, from "a symbolics of blood" to "an analytics of sexuality."[27] Stoler underscores that, after the Reformation, no blood was left behind. "The myth of blood that pervades nineteenth-century racism may be traced, as Foucault does, from an aristocratic preoccupation with legitimacy, pure blood, and descent, but not through it alone. It was equally dependent on an imperial politics of exclusion that was worked out earlier and reworked later on colonial ground."[28]

Stoler does more here than extend the historical and political frame whereby blood came increasingly to govern the political imagination in its social and national registers. From kinship to colonialism, by way of the state and the "global color line," she shows that the very notion of a community of blood not only persists beyond its so-called premodern origins but also, by far, exceeds the discourse and practices of race. Blood moves, rather, through the capillaries of power—an oft-repeated phrase that has not been sufficiently pondered, and least of all in its relation to the concept of circulation, the re-signification and dissemination of which we owe William Harvey, and upon which Foucault also insisted.[29] From the theorists of just war to the canon lawyers, from the doctrine of the sacraments to the philosophy of property and wealth ("inheritable blood," "corruption of the blood"), from the head of the sovereign to the sacred heart, the perdurance of blood, of the community of blood, marks and shapes a massive, albeit heterogenous, political tradition. It accounts for the laws that regulate kinship, citizenship, and ownership—and international law. Essential to the canonical figurations of the body politic, that "continually renewed dream, of community as a body united by some principle of life," which since John of Salisbury have strangely been devoid of it, blood covertly and overtly shapes and defines the channels and motions that carry the family, the class, and the race, the nation and the economy too.[30] "There is, indeed," as Adriana Cavarero points out, "a sort of embryology of the body politic."[31] Thus, following his mercantilist predecessors, and building on the work of Harvey, Hobbes writes of the "concoction" and the "sanguification of the commonwealth," the money and wealth that is the nourishment, the blood of the state (colonies, incidentally, were of a proximate metabolic order for Hobbes, that of reproduction).[32] Moses Hess well understood, and Marx also confirmed (both were redeploying an earlier claim made by Huldrych Zwingli), that the political and economic machine was feeding on the blood of the workers.[33] Not so distant from such exploitative hematologics, Hume suggested that "animals have little or no sense of virtue or vice; they quickly lose sight of the relations of blood; and are incapable of that of right and property."[34] A more recent formulation realizes the metaphor further still and thereby captures the matter in an exemplary way. After September 11, say Catherine Waldby and Robert Mitchell, "the excessive desire to give blood was perhaps driven by a sense that the body politic was itself wounded in the attacks."[35]

Thus filling a strange conceptual vacuum in the body politic, communities of blood have served and free-refilled, at different times supplemented, fashioned and preserved, the competing forms of our political hematology. Referring to one instance of this phenomenon, Foucault writes that "in these rituals in which blood flowed, society found new vigor and formed for a moment a single great body."[36] This accounts as well for the adoption of variants of *jus sanguinis* in the modern state, even if it conceals the fiction of its Roman filiation, and its essential relation to race and genealogical thinking.[37] At once widespread and historically contingent, blood defines a vision of politics that has yet to be recognized in its relative integrity. But contrary to the faulty translation I have cited above, its history does not go back to Aristotle, or to a proverbial Semitic bloodthirstiness. It does not hark back to Roman political notions, and even less to the otherwise obvious candidate, the concept of *consanguinitas* originally deployed in Roman law. As Gianna Pomata demonstrates, and Frank Roumy corroborates, the Latin notion of consanguinity only began to define the "community of blood" around the twelfth century, at the time when Aristotelian embryology was starting to compete with Galenic theories.[38] This extraordinary development—at once juridical and medical—involves a well-known redefinition of the family, and it has been more or less fully translated into the modern codes of law that have taken over the planet as if by miracle.[39] Claude Meillassoux uniquely argues, furthermore, that critiques and dismissals notwithstanding, blood continues to inform the anthropological study of kinship.[40]

The emergence of the community of blood mostly coincides—but this is no mere coincidence—with the first "disciplinary revolution,"[41] whereby each and every Christian was transformed into a vessel of Christ's blood; a blood the devout were given to drink en masse, if you'll forgive the interlingual pun, in a sacramental practice that was theologically sealed in 1215, and fully canonized in 1280. The community of blood, the *corpus mysticum* (an expression that "passed from the Eucharist to the Church," and came to designate the visible body of the Church, instead of the ritualized, and mysterious, action of the sacrament) was not only growing, it was hardening in a peculiar manner.[42] As theologians were reminding Christians of doctrinal subtleties—that "we eat God not so that he changes into us but so that we change into him," for instance,[43]—it was becoming clearer to many that Christian blood was not quite the same as other bloods. Interestingly, Ernst Kantorowicz describes in quite meticulous detail the historical (and physiological) transformation whereby a fundamental difference between bloods emerges, although he puzzled over its origins and strangely confined it to the sole body, that is, the sole two bodies, of the king. Having underscored the role of God (and not of blood, not explicitly) in royal birth, Kantorowicz goes on to highlight a process whereby ritual could ultimately be abandoned, as the essential difference it made had now become innate. "The Holy Spirit, which in former days was manifested by the voting of the electors, while his gifts were conferred by the anointment, now was seated in the royal blood itself, as it were, *natura et gratia*, by nature and by grace—indeed, 'by nature' as well; for the royal blood now appeared as a somewhat mysterious fluid."[44] What happened then was that "one began to combine the dynastic idea with philosophical doctrines implying a belief in certain royal qualities and potencies dwelling in the blood of kings and creating, so to speak, a royal species of man." We have just seen, of course, that there had been another ritual that could, and would, confer on a larger group of individuals a new kind of blood, "a somewhat mysterious fluid" indeed, and the status of a novel species of man.[45]

A peculiar history of Christian theophagy[46] and of sacrifice ensued; accusations of ritual murder, *limpieza de sangre*, projections of blood-thirst onto Jews, witches, and savages; and of course, mass murder, the long and short of it, all of which ensured further coagulation. In Roberto Esposito's terms, the *communitas* was being misunderstood. No longer an obligation and a subtraction, the giving of that which one does not own or have, blood became a property, a having and a being simultaneously, *res publica Christiana*.[47] One could have "Christian blood" or be of it. Christian blood, at any rate, would become completely distinct, completely good, and, more importantly, completely pure—if also vulnerable to all kinds of attacks and contaminations ("If thou dost shed/One drop of Christian blood " warns fair Portia Shylock).[48] One could then make peace, finally—in the year 1648, for example—in order to stop another "effusion of Christian blood" (as the Treatise of Westphalia describes it).[49] From there, at any rate, the community of blood moved rapidly ahead, toward the modern nation, with all due respect to Benedict Anderson's puzzling claim that "from the start the nation was conceived in language, not in blood, and that one could be 'invited into' the imagined community."[50] Contributing to what should remain a baffling development, Thomas Hobbes and James Harrington had incurred their debt to William Harvey, and "the revolution of blood" was pushing through the emergence of liberal—and illiberal—political thought.[51] Perhaps because his "early work with Boyle was on the human blood," Locke expressed doubts about the role blood played in succession and inheritance, or about the ability of power to purify blood.[52] He did think that "if language be capable of expressing any thing distinctly and clearly, that of kindred, and the several degrees of nearness of blood, is one."[53] The revolution of blood was easing other judgments, blood judgments, by way of reasonable doubt, and making its way to Rousseau's "ties of blood,"[54] to blood quantum, the "one drop rule," race science and eugenics,[55] and the "blood feuds" of the AIDS crisis.[56] Blood lies at the foundation of the modern state, and continues to irrigate it. As Edmund Burke aptly put it, "we have given to our frame of polity the image of a relation in blood."[57] And this "image" (Auden called it "a cement of blood" without which, he said, "no secular wall" would "safely stand") was fast moving forward still, toward what David Schneider described as "American Kinship."[58] One could argue (as I do elsewhere) that Richard Hofstadter might have expounded here on "the hematological style in American politics." But due considerations force me to acknowledge here that when it comes to blood (and to national anthems), the United States is hardly exceptional or paradigmatic. It is merely exemplary.[59]

Now, in a remarkable book, Kathleen Davis demonstrates the intricacies according to which periodization is among the most effective, and unacknowledged, technologies of rule.[60] Davis shows this by way of the concept of feudalism, which was essential to a double distancing that, always political, always juridico-political, separates the modern from the medieval, and the metropole from the colonial.[61] Medievalism is colonialism, Davis compellingly argues. And vice-versa. Key to her argument is the grounding of modern sovereignty—the legitimacy of the modern age—not only in time and space but more precisely in a radical rupture that leaves it as if suspended in "radical newness" (94). The medieval/modern periodization can thus serve "as a substitute for this absent foundation of sovereignty, and thereby installs certain characteristics of the 'modern' in the place of the sovereign. In this sense, periodization functions as sovereign decision" (80). Leaving aside the role and function of blood in sovereignty ("Do you not feel sovereignty coursing through your veins?" asked a French revolutionary),[62] it should be clear from what I have said so far that blood—the paradox of blood I laid out at the beginning of this essay—partakes of this very structure: where blood was, there shall politics be. By turning (as I shall shortly) to the so-called Middle Ages, I do not at all mean to produce another iteration of this periodizing narrative, another cutting decision to "sustain the 'cloak-and-dagger' drama of 'secularization'" (82). I wish, rather, to document a remarkable circularity in the way rupture—or shall we say, supersession—is articulated, the way in which blood operates as a site of decision and distinction, an index of sovereignty and community that is at once social, territorial, and temporal, ultimately legal as well. Stuttered otherwise, blood is through and through political, which is to say that Western politics, Christian politics, must be rethought in its hematological registers, and out of blood—the very concept.

BLOOD PARTS

"Traditionally," Tomaž Mastnak explains, "the Church had been averse to the shedding of blood. *Ecclesia abhorret a sanguine* was a principle ever present in patristic writings and conciliar legislation."[63] What this meant was that killing—shedding blood, in the inherited, biblical parlance—no matter whose and no matter the circumstances, was considered a sin. "Even killing a pagan was homicide," which means that this was an awfully serious rule. Indeed, "from the fourth century to the eleventh century, the Church as a rule imposed disciplinary measures on those who killed in war, or at least recommended that they do penance" (16). One pope had referred to bishops who did engage in warfare as "false priests" because "their hands were 'stained with human blood'"; another referred to "proponents of war (as) 'sons of the devil'" (14). What changed, then? The exception became the rule—and a different rule it was. Talk about a revolution. What happened is that the idea of warfare became licit; violence and the shedding of blood became permissible rather than something impossible to avoid or outright condemned. And Pope Gregory VII, all too easy to blame at this point, the same pope "after whom the Church reform has been called, is (also) held responsible for the profound changes in the Christian attitude toward bearing arms that this idea [of licit warfare] implied" (18). His followers, Alexander II and Urban II, did lend a helping hand. They were accessories to the perfect murder, as it were, and it was hardly a bloodless one. There were others, of course, who joined the efforts of the emerging *populus Christianus*, the Christian people. The most dramatic change occurred in 1054 (the year of the *filioque* controversy, which hardened the schism between the Eastern and Western churches) in the city of Narbonne.[64] Prior to this "peace council," there had been a rule, which, true to the church's abhorrence of blood, had "prohibited the shedding of human blood." Yet, and to make a long story short, "the councilors of Narbonne substituted, as it were, the word Christian for the world human" (37–38).[65] They also declared, for good reiterative measure, that "no Christian should kill another Christian, for whoever kills a Christian undoubtedly sheds the blood of Christ (*quia qui Christianum occidit, sine dubio Christi sanguinem fundit*)" (37, 37n215). This was a giant step indeed, if not necessarily for humankind, at least for God. For whereas it had earlier been recognized, as Alexander II wrote, that "God is not pleased by the spilling of blood, nor does he rejoice in the perdition of the evil one," and whereas "all laws, ecclesiastical as well as secular, forbid the shedding of human blood," it was now becoming possible to enact, practice, and enforce, for the love of God, a newfound distinction between bloods.[66] This great step was in need of only one additional, and very light, push. Urban II is the one who obliged. It was under his watch that it became "not only permissible but eminently salutary to use arms"—against whom? Against the infidel enemy, of course. War "against the enemies of God" quickly became "meritorious," it was "divinely ordered" (50). From there on, things took a rapid and increasingly bloody turn. Heads would soon begin to fall all the way to Jerusalem, where, as one medieval chronicle describes it, "men rode in blood up to their knees and the bridle reins." This is hardly a lone event in history, of course, which may be why the same writer goes on to add an important caption, commenting on its singular dimension, namely, "that it was a just and splendid judgment of God, that this place should be filled with the blood of unbelievers, since it had suffered so long from their blasphemies."[67] Thus it was that the peace of God ("no Christian should kill another Christian, for whoever kills a Christian undoubtedly sheds the blood of Christ") became the occasion for a new and novel notion of interventionism, a Christian interventionism, for the newfound and radical involvement of the church in a world of men newly divided. "*Intus Pax, foris terrores*" (95). Call it peace as the war on terror. More important, at least for our purposes, *Christianitas*, which had surely begun to take shape "among the various preconditions of the crusading movement," was now reaching an accomplished stage of its formation. It was establishing itself as "*populus Christianus*, the Christian people, united under the supreme authority of the pope . . . bound together as Christendom (in) a common worldly pursuit and a common army . . . fighting for the Christian *res publica*, the common weal" (92–93).

"Like his peacemaking predecessors," Urban II was filled with good intentions (incidentally, one reviewer criticized Mastnak, unfairly I think, for refusing to "accept that Westerners associated with the crusades"—but allow me to repeat this beautiful turn of phrase: "Westerners associated with the crusades"—"were ever well intentioned").[68] This pope too "condemned fratricidal wars in the West" (94). What was intolerable to him, indeed, unconscionable, was the spilling of Christian blood. Thus was the world divided. "Effunditur sanguis Christianus, Christi sanguine redemptus . . . Christian blood, redeemed by the blood of Christ, has been shed," he used to lament. And what he was thereby articulating, Mastnak says, was a new kind of "blood-brotherhood—the founding of Christian unity in blood" (94). This was, let me repeat this too, all well intended, all in the name of love, in other words, if not the love of blood (actually, it now depends on which blood, doesn't it?), which is why John of Salisbury wrote that he would refrain from calling those "whose normal occupation it is to shed human blood," those who "wage legitimate war 'men of blood,' since even (King) David was called a man of blood not because he engaged in wars which were legitimate but on account of Uriah, whose blood he criminally shed."[69] You could shed blood in the name of love, therefore, without becoming a man of blood. Or, shedding that blood which is not one (not true blood, that is, not one like Christian blood), you would thereby join in the brotherhood. You could become, you had become, a different man of blood, a man of different blood, since "the substance of that brotherhood was blood, consanguinity in faith. And once faith was filled with blood, it was just a short step to the letting of blood of the unfaithful. Or rather, if faith was in blood, with the shedding of unfaithful blood, unbelief was drained" (126). The church, which had long "considered bloodshed as a source of pollution now encouraged the shedding of blood—non-Christian blood—as a means to purification. When the reformed Church established its domination over Christendom, Christendom launched a military offensive to establish its domination over the world" (129).

Bernard of Clairvaux was yet another, among many others, who decided to join the Christian war effort and brought to it more novelty in the form of his propitious doctrine of *malicidium*, the killing of evil. "The soldier of Christ, Bernard was to repeat, is safe when he kills, even safer when he is killed. If he is killed, it is for his own good; if he kills, he does it for Christ."[70] Others, from Pierre Dubois to Catherine of Siena, would later support our troops and lend another helping hand. But we ain't seen nothin' yet. This was only the beginning, and the Eucharist, along with the doctrine of transubstantiation, had yet to come. Or the Reformation. It would take these and a few more additional steps for Christian blood to become fully distinct and distinguished, for it to become pure and "wonderful blood," as Caroline Walker Bynum describes it (though I should mention that Bynum writes about a later period and never refers to Mastnak's work). By then, one would of course come to wonder, with Catherine of Siena, "how anyone except Christ could save souls by shedding blood, especially the blood of others." In this too, I suppose, there "remained a mystery," one that had been "embedded in the context of the crusade, itself seen as a mystery."[71] One might further wonder how the shedding of blood could ever become the saving of souls—the blood and soul of others, too. But one could nonetheless be certain of one thing: when it came to Christian blood, every drop would count. As for the blood of others, it was on its way to start flowing in rivers and in floods. Alternatively, it was to be weighed and measured, sometimes drop by drop. By blood then. And this was not the first, or the last, time. What would no longer be in doubt by then was that there was a difference between bloods, that there was a blood that was—shall we say, essentially?—a different and purer blood. It had undergone a first and gigantic transformation toward an asymmetric universality, a generalized hematology, and the establishment of blood, not as a concept but as an indubitable foundation of Western, which is to say Christian, politics.

NOTES

1. By "blood is not a concept" I mean to say that blood does not appear to be a reflective notion upon which rulers, jurists, philosophers, or political theorists would have worked or, indeed, reflected; that they would have elaborated, instituted, or institutionalized in a manner comparable to the way they have worked and reflected on, institutionalized (or sought to institutionalize), say, sovereignty, or representation, justice, and democracy, or the body even. On the face of things, blood may or may not "properly" belong to medicine or to anthropology, but it does not belong, it does not seem to belong, nor should it perhaps belong, to politics and political philosophy.

2. Martin Luther, quoted in Sheldon S. Wolin, *Politics and Vision: Continuity and Innovation in Western Political Thought* (Princeton, N.J.: Princeton University Press, 2004), 142.

3. Denis Diderot, quoted in Sankar Muthu, *Enlightenment against Empire* (Princeton, N.J.: Princeton University Press, 2003), 109.

4. Alain Brossat, "Les dernières heures de la grande dramaturgie du sang?," *Drôle d'Époque* 19 (2006): 29; more assertive, Pheng Cheah, *Spectral Nationality: Passages of Freedom from Kant to Postcolonial Literatures of Liberation* (New York: Columbia University Press, 2003), declares that "the decolonizing nation is not an archaic throwback to traditional forms of community based on the blind ties of blood and kinship" (382).

5. G. W. F. Hegel, *The Phenomenology of Spirit*, trans. A. V. Miller (Oxford: Oxford University Press, 1977). The full passage in the section called "Consciousness" reads as follows: "This simple infinity, or the absolute Notion, may be called the simple essence of life, the soul of the world, the universal blood, whose omnipresence is neither disturbed nor interrupted by any difference, but rather is itself every difference, as also their supersession; it pulsates within itself but does not move, inwardly vibrates, yet is at rest. It is self-identical, for the differences are tautological; they are differences that are none" (100).

6. Blood never registered in Quentin Skinner's *Foundations of Modern Political Thought,* vols. 1–2 (Cambridge: Cambridge University Press, 1978), nor in *Rethinking the Foundations of Modern Political Thought*, ed. Annabel Brett et al. (Cambridge: Cambridge University Press, 2006).

7. Jean-Pierre Baud writes in "La nature juridique du sang," *Terrain—Revue d'Ethnologie de l'Europe* 56 (2011): 95–105, a unique, albeit brief, history of the juridical nature of blood, which he traces back to the Old Testament (Greece is not mentioned), by way of Roman law and the notion of person ("la plus remarquable création juridique de la civilisation romaine") and the tradition of blood donation that links Jesus Christ to military and civilian blood banks.

8. Benedict de Spinoza, "Correspondence," in *On the Improvement of the Understanding; The Ethics; Correspondence*, trans. R. H. M. Elwes (New York: Dover, 1955), 291. Letter XV [XXXII], dated November 20, 1665.

9. I quote from Norman O. Brown, "Filthy Lucre," in *Life against Death: The Psychoanalytic Meaning of History* (Middletown, Conn.: Wesleyan University Press, 1985), 234.

10. Carl Schmitt, *Political Theology: Four Chapters on the Concept of Sovereignty* (Chicago: University of Chicago Press, 2006).

11. Daniel Defoe, *The Complete English Gentleman*, quoted in J. C. D. Clark, *English Society, 1660–1832: Religion, Ideology and Politics during the Ancient Regime* (Cambridge: Cambridge University Press, 2000), 229.

12. I cite from Elise Lemire's important work on race in America, *"Miscegenation":*

Making Race in America (Philadelphia: University of Pennsylvania Press, 2002), 36–37, because it is exemplary in the conciseness, precision, and exhaustiveness of its account of "the rhetoric of blood."

13. Gail Kern Paster, *The Body Embarrassed: Drama and the Disciplines of Shame in Early Modern England* (Ithaca, N.Y.: Cornell University Press, 1993), 69.

14. *Acts of the Apostles*, 17:26; neither Greek nor Latin use the word "blood." For an account of the success of the phrase, see Paul Goodman, *Of One Blood: Abolitionism and the Origins of Racial Equality* (Berkeley: University of California Press, 1998). As Marvin Fox, *Interpreting Maimonides: Studies in Methodology, Metaphysics, and Moral Philosophy* (Chicago: University of Chicago Press, 1990), puts it in a proximate context, "all human beings are supposedly equally endowed with knowledge of the natural law, which is inscribed in their heart, but some are apparently more equal than others" (149). Marc Shell probably went the furthest in exploring the consequences of this equality of blood with regard to kinship in Christianity in *Children of the Earth: Literature, Politics, and Nationhood* (Oxford: Oxford University Press, 1993), while Uli Linke extends the argument to the entirety of Indo-European history in *Blood and Nation: The European Aesthetics of Race* (Philadelphia: University of Pennsylvania Press, 1999). I discuss this site of biblical translation in my "*Blutgewalt*," *Oxford Literary Review* 31, no. 2 (2009): 153–74.

15. Anton-Hermann Chroust, "The Corporate Idea and the Body Politic in the Middle Ages," *Review of Politics* 9, no. 4 (1947): 430.

16. Ludwig Feuerbach, *The Essence of Christianity*, trans. George Eliot (Amherst, Mass.: Prometheus Books, 1989), 146.

17. On the "savage slot," see M.-R. Trouillot, "Anthropology and the Savage Slot: The Poetics and Politics of Otherness," in *Recapturing Anthropology: Working in the Present*, ed. Richard G. Fox, 17–44 (Santa Fe, N.M.: School of American Research Press, 1991); on the concept of "anthropotheism," see Stefanos Geroulanos, *An Atheism That Is Not Humanist Emerges in French Thought* (Stanford, Calif.: Stanford University Press, 2010); on Renan in this context, see Benzion Netanyahu, "Américo Castro and His View of the Origins of the Pureza de Sangre," *Proceedings of the American Academy for Jewish Research* 46–47 (1979–1980): 397–457.

18. Aristotle, *Politics* at 1252b, trans. B. Jovett (Oxford: Clarendon Press, 1885), 3.

19. This argument is of course a mere footnote to Jacques Derrida's *The Politics of Friendship*, trans. George Collins (New York: Verso, 1997).

20. Henry James Sumner Maine, *Ancient Law: Its Connection to the History of Early Society* (Charleston, N.C.: BiblioBazaar, 2008), 99; clearly, as Karuna Mantena explains in her brilliant account of Maine, *Alibis of Empire: Henry Maine and the Ends of Liberal Imperialism* (Princeton, N.J.: Princeton University Press, 2010), 79, blood kinship is a fiction (Maine says "assumption"), but it is taken to be a universal fiction.

21. Donna J. Haraway, *Modest_Witness@Second_Millenium.FemaleMan©_Meets_OncoMouse™: Feminism and Technoscience* (New York: Routledge, 1997), 265.

22. Alys Eve Weinbaum, *Wayward Reproductions: Genealogies of Race and Nation in Transatlantic Modern Thought* (Durham, N.C.: Duke University Press, 2004), 5.

23. Peter Wade, ed., *Race, Ethnicity and Nation: Perspectives from Kinship and Genetics* (New York: Berghahn Books, 2009), 1.

24. Enric Porqueres i Gené, "Kinship Language and the Dynamics of Race," in ibid., 127; Christiane Klapisch-Zuber, *L'ombre des ancêtres: Essai sur l'imaginaire médiéval de la parenté* (Paris: Fayard, 2000), acknowledges and documents the particular "manière dont l'Occident s'est représenté la parenté et la filiation" (14), "les outils mentaux et graphiques dont l'Occident chrétien a disposé" (19), though she focuses on the arboreal rather than the hematological. The two are, of course, related (26–28, 97), although Klapisch-Zuber seems to suggest that the representations (such as the tree) are all figures of consanguinity (242, 249).

25. I elaborate on the overdetermined relation of blood and kinship in "We Have Never Been Jewish: An Essay in Asymmetric Hematology," in *Jewish Blood: Reality and Metaphor in History, Religion, and Culture*, ed. Mitchell Hart, 31–56 (London: Routledge, 2009).

26. Émile Benveniste, *Le vocabulaire des institutions indo-européennes* (Paris: Minuit, 1969), vol. 1 being the most relevant with regard to kinship (*parenté*).

27. Michel Foucault, *The History of Sexuality*, vol. 1, *An Introduction*, trans. Robert Hurley (New York: Pantheon, 1978), 148; earlier, and in a different register, Foucault had written of "the shift from a criminality of blood to a criminality of fraud" in *Discipline and Punish: The Birth of the Prison*, trans. Alan Sheridan (New York: Vintage, 1995), 77.

28. Ann Laura Stoler, *Race and the Education of Desire: Foucault's History of Sexuality and the Colonial Order of Things* (Durham, N.C.: Duke University Press, 1995), 51.

29. S. Todd Lowry, "The Archaeology of the Circulation Concept in Economic Theory," *Journal of the History of Ideas* 35, no. 3 (July–September 1974): 429–44; and see Michel Foucault, *Sécurité, territoire, population: Cours au Collège de France, 1977–1978* (Paris: Gallimard, 2004).

30. Jacques Rancière, *On the Shores of Politics*, trans. Liz Heron (London: Verso, 1995), 88.

31. Adriana Cavarero, *Stately Bodies: Literature, Philosophy, and the Question of Gender*, trans. Robert de Lucca and Deanna Shemek (Ann Arbor: University of Michigan Press, 2002), 113.

32. Jonathan Gil Harris, *Sick Economies: Drama, Mercantilism, and Disease in Shakespeare's England* (Philadelphia: University of Pennsylvania Press, 2004), 167; Thomas Hobbes, *Leviathan*, ed. Richard Tuck (Cambridge: Cambridge University Press, 1996), chapter 24, 174; on the absence of blood from the body politic, see my "Lines of Blood: Limpieza de Sangre as Political Theology," in *Blood in History*

and Blood Histories, ed. Mariacarla Gadebusch Bondio, 119–36 (Florence: Sismel—Edizioni del Galluzzo/Micrologus Library, 2005).

33. On Zwingli's "combination of money, blood, and the sale of bodies," see Valentin Groebner, *Liquid Assets, Dangerous Gifts: Presents and Politics at the End of the Middle Ages*, trans. Pamela E. Selwyn (Philadelphia: University of Pennsylvania Press, 2002), 105, 149.

34. David Hume, "Of Pride and Humility of Animals," in *Treatise of Human Nature*, vol. 2 (Edinburgh, 1826), bk. 2, sec. 12. "It is apparent," writes David Warren Sabean, "that dividing property among all the children regardless of sex, models the flow of property in a parallel manner to the way theologians modeled the flow of blood or substance." "From Clan to Kindred: Kinship and the Circulation of Property in Premodern and Modern Europe," in *Heredity Produced: At the Crossroads of Biology, Politics, and Culture, 1500–1870*, ed. Staffan Müller-Wille and Hans-Jörg Rheinberger (Cambridge, Mass.: MIT Press, 2007), 42.

35. Catherine Waldby and Robert Mitchell, *Tissue Economies: Blood, Organs, and Cell Lines in Late Capitalism* (Durham, N.C.: Duke University Press, 2006), 4.

36. Foucault, *Discipline and Punish*, 216.

37. As Paul Kahn writes in *Putting Liberalism in Its Place* (Princeton, N.J.: Princeton University Press, 2005), "the distinction between citizen and noncitizen is the fundamental inequality of political life. This inequality is defined both geographically and historically. The dual sources of this political inequality are represented explicitly in the dual sources of citizenship at birth: bloodline and geography, or ius sanguinis and ius soli. . . . Our political communities, even our liberal communities, are overwhelmingly founded on 'blood and soil'" (44–45). On *jus sanguinis* in modern Europe, see Rogers Brubaker, *Citizenship and Nationhood in France and Germany* (Cambridge, Mass.: Harvard University Press, 1992); and see Peter Sahlins, *Unnaturally French: Foreign Citizens in the Old Regime and After* (Ithaca, N.Y.: Cornell University Press, 2004); and see the following note.

38. Gianna Pomata, "Blood Ties and Semen Ties: Consanguinity and Agnation in Roman Law," in *Gender, Kinship, Power: A Comparative and Interdisciplinary History*, ed. Mary Jo Maynes et al. (New York: Routledge, 1996), 43–64; E. Champeaux, "*Jus sanguinis*: Trois façons de calculer la parenté au Moyen Âge," *Revue Historique de Droit Français et Étranger* (1933): 241–90; Anne Lefebvre-Teillard, "*Ius sanguinis*: L'émergence d'un principe (Éléments d'histoire de la nationalité française)," *Revue Critique de Droit International Privé* 82, no. 2 (1993): 223–50; Frank Roumy, "La naissance de la notion canonique de consanguinitas et sa réception dans le droit civil," in *L'hérédité entre Moyen Âge et époque moderne*, ed. Maaike van der Lugt and Charles de Miramon, 41–66 (Florence: Sismel—Edizioni del Galluzzo/Micrologus Library, 2008); on Aristotle and Galen, see Thomas Laqueur's account in his *Making Sex: Body and Gender from the Greeks to Freud* (Cambridge, Mass.: Harvard University Press, 1990).

39. Needless to say, blood ties were always fictive ties, as the practice of adoption would easily demonstrate; see, e.g., Kristin Elizabeth Gager, *Blood Ties and Fictive Ties: Adoption and Family Life in Early Modern France* (Princeton, N.J.: Princeton University Press, 1996), and see Zrinka Stahuljak, *Bloodless Genealogies of the French Middle Ages: Translation, Kinship, and Metaphor* (Gainesville: University Press of Florida, 2005).

40. Claude Meillassoux, *Mythes et limites de l'anthropologies: Le sang et les mots* (Lausanne, Switzerland: Editions Page Deux, 2001).

41. Philip S. Gorski, *The Disciplinary Revolution: Calvinism and the Rise of the State in Early Modern Europe* (Chicago: University of Chicago Press, 2003); note that Gorski entirely ignores Catholic precedents to his argument.

42. Henri de Lubac, *Corpus Mysticum: The Eucharist and the Church in the Middle Ages*, trans. Gemma Simmonds, Richard Price, and Christopher Stephens (Notre Dame, Ind.: University of Notre Dame Press, 2006), 250.

43. Quoted in Caroline Walker Bynum, *Wonderful Blood: Theology and Practice in Late Medieval Northern Germany and Beyond* (Philadelphia: University of Pennsylvania Press, 2007), 139.

44. Ernst H. Kantorowicz, *The King's Two Bodies: A Study in Mediaeval Political Theology* (Princeton, N.J.: Princeton University Press, 1997), 331; emphasis added.

45. Kantorowicz acknowledges the existence of "a race promoted by Christ from the very beginnings of the Christian faith, a most holy royal house to which God had granted a heavenly oil for the anointment of its kings," yet for him, such "a royal stock (was) endowed with miraculous gifts the like of which not even the Church could claim" (ibid., 333). He is, in other words, thinking about Christianity, but "the idea of a specially refined soul, 'subtle and noble,' and infused in the blood of princes" is neither Aristotelian, nor Stoic. It is "reminiscent rather of the Hermetic tenet concerning the creation of the souls of kings, but it seems doubtful that this doctrine was known at that time" (332).

46. Preserved Smith, *A Short History of Christian Theophagy* (Chicago: Open Court, 1922).

47. Roberto Esposito, *Communitas: The Origin and Destiny of Community*, trans. Timothy Campbell (Stanford, Calif.: Stanford University Press, 2010), 5–7.

48. William Shakespeare, *The Merchant of Venice*, ed. Jay L. Hallo (Oxford: Oxford University Press, 1994), 4.1.111–12.

49. Randall Lesaffer, "Peace Treaties from Lodi to Westphalia," in *Peace Treaties and International Law in European History from the Late Middle Ages to World War One*, ed. Randall Lesaffer, 9–44 (Cambridge: Cambridge University Press, 2004), 29.

50. Benedict Anderson, *Imagined Communities: Reflections on the Origin and Spread of Nationalism* (London: Verso, 1991), 145; see Shell's implicit answer to Anderson on the question "is there a nationalism without racism?" (*Children of the*

Earth, 179n). I would ask differently: could nationalism, as it is conceived in Christian Europe, exist without blood?

51. See Uday Mehta, "Kinship and Friendship: Two Conceptions of Political Action" (paper presented at Society for the Humanities, Cornell University, 2003); John Rogers, *The Matter of Revolution: Science, Poetry, and Politics in the Age of Milton* (Ithaca, N.Y.: Cornell University Press, 1996); and see Norman O. Brown's discussion of liberty and fraternity in *Love's Body* (Berkeley: University of California Press, 1966), as well as Shell, *Children of the Earth*. Michael Rogin explores the (blood) connections between liberalism and paternalism, primitive accumulation and Indian removal in *Fathers and Children: Andrew Jackson and the Subjugation of the American Indian* (New York: Vintage, 1976).

52. Ian Shapiro, "Introduction: Reading Locke Today," in John Locke, *"Two Treatises of Government" and "A Letter Concerning Toleration,"* ed. Ian Shapiro, ix–xv (New Haven, Conn.: Yale University Press, 2003), xii; Victor Nuovo mentions in *Christianity, Antiquity, and Enlightenment: Interpretations of Locke* (Dordrecht, Netherlands: Springer, 2010), that "the preface to Boyle's *Memoirs for the Natural History of Humane Blood* (1684) is addressed to Locke" (107n9).

53. Locke, *Two Treatises*, 67; for Locke's suspicion of the relevance of blood quantum in succession and inheritance, see 70; on power and blood, see 139.

54. James Q. Whitman, *The Origins of Reasonable Doubt: Theological Roots of the Criminal Trial* (New Haven, Conn.: Yale University Press, 2008); Jean-Jacques Rousseau, "Discourse on the Origin and the Foundations of Inequality among Men," in Rousseau, *The Discourses and Other Early Political Writings*, ed. Victor Gourevitch, 111–222 (Cambridge: Cambridge University Press, 1997), 118.

55. Daniel J. Kevles, *In the Name of Eugenics: Genetics and the Uses of Human Heredity* (Berkeley: University of California Press, 1985).

56. Eric A. Feldman and Ronald Bayer, eds., *Blood Feuds: AIDS, Blood, and the Politics of Medical Disaster* (New York: Oxford University Press, 1998).

57. Edmund Burke, *Reflections on the Revolution in France*, ed. Frank M. Turner (New Haven, Conn.: Yale University Press, 2003), 30.

58. David M. Schneider, *American Kinship: A Cultural Account* (Chicago: University of Chicago Press, 1980); and see also Schneider's *A Critique of the Study of Kinship* (Ann Arbor: University of Michigan Press, 1984). W. H. Auden, "Vespers," quoted in Brown, *Love's Body*, 27.

59. It is because "the United States of America and the Republic of France stand out uniquely in the modern world as states with . . . a conception of citizenship based on place of birth rather than on ethnic or 'blood' ties" that I would insist on the nonparadigmatic and unexceptional. Norman Ravitch, "Your People, My People; Your God, My God: French and American Troubles over Citizenship," *French Review* 70, no. 4 (March 1997): 515. This only appears paradoxical if one ignores the determining

role and function of blood in, say, kinship or property, nation and race, in the modern state at large.

60. Kathleen Davis, *Periodization and Sovereignty: How Ideas of Feudalism and Secularization Govern the Politics of Time* (Philadelphia: University of Pennsylvania Press, 2008); hereafter cited in the text.

61. A glance at Blackstone suffices to recognize that feudalism too is another bloody concept—that blood plays, in other words, an essential role in its elaboration. See Sir William Blackstone, "Rights of Things—Title by Descent," in *Commentaries on the Laws of England*, ed. Hardcastle Browne (St. Paul, Minn.: West Publishing, 1897), 275, 279, 285.

62. Cited in Charles Leslie Wayper, *Political Thought* (New York: Philosophical Library, 1954), ix.

63. Tomaž Mastnak, *Crusading Peace: Christendom, the Muslim World, and Western Political Order* (Berkeley: University of California Press, 2002), 16; hereafter cited in the text.

64. On the *filioque* controversy, see Harold J. Berman, *Law and Revolution: The Formation of the Western Legal Tradition* (Cambridge, Mass.: Harvard University Press, 1983), 105n178, 581n26.

65. Earlier, "around 861, Pope Nicholas I had declared that soldiers of this world (*milites seculi*) were distinct from the soldiers of the Church (*milites ecclesiae*), so it was not becoming to the soldiers of the Church to fight worldly battles (*saeculo militare*) in which blood would necessarily be shed" (Mastnak, *Crusading Peace*, 22–23).

66. Alexander II, quoted in ibid., 21.

67. Raymond of Aguilers, quoted in ibid., 60–61.

68. Bernard Hamilton, review of Tomaž Mastnak, *Crusading Peace: Christendom, the Muslim World, and Western Political Order*, *American Historical Review* 108, no. 4 (2003): 1204.

69. John of Salisbury, *Policraticus*, ed. Cary J. Nederman (Cambridge: Cambridge University Press, 1990), 173; and see Mastnak, *Crusading Peace*, 154.

70. Bernard of Clairvaux, quoted in Mastnak, *Crusading Peace*, 169.

71. Mastnak, *Crusading Peace*, 345.

3

COLONY

Ann Laura Stoler

Political concepts work upon us for very different reasons and entreat our attention in very different ways. Some impose their authority over our thinking and actions because they saturate our environment, incanted strategically, or wondrously shorn of reflection on the public stage. We might seize on them for scrutiny because they seem to offer the possibility of disrupting the dulling familiarity of common nouns, or allow us to cut through to the interpretive dissonance of contemporary political predicaments. Not least, we seek those that can render more legible, if not more reasoned, what buttresses the predisposed disregard or unfounded passions that move us in our everyday lives.

Some announce their force by their ubiquitous historical presence. Some command our attention by association with the formidable list of thinkers who have long signaled their import, who have wrested them from the obscurity of an innocuous noun by drawing them into the conceptual orbit of their ethical frames. Other concepts (think "liberalism," "freedom," "democracy") are so infused with the vacuous rhetoric of the contemporary political sphere that they seem to dull the senses, slipping by unnoticed as if protected by the numb of iteration.

Some of the most favored concepts of political theory acquire their critical force precisely because they are not considered political concepts at all, or because they have so long been considered benign and removed from the domain of contemporary politics. We can make their presence felt retroactively because of what we do with them: lifting them from the sludge of murkey noun by setting out their subliminal force, gleaning their potency from the veiled fashion in which they craft subjects, requisition objects, and couch their command. Those that tend to grab us—those that assert themselves as political, or that we assert as squarely political for them—do so because they offer to help us think otherwise about what is assigned as common sense. They invite exit from our own casts of mind, challenge our commitments, counter the silence of political decorum or the distracting din of analytic convention.

"Colony" inhabits an ambiguous sort of space in its oscillation between the still neutrality of a common noun and a political concept in waiting, poised to discharge its potentiality. Philosophers bypass it. As a common noun with no conceptual cachet its referents fall too easily into an unproblematic and manifest place. For political theorists who prefer to grapple with the more compelling "isms" from which the "colony" arises, or is given rise to, the term is of little interest. Specialists instead vie for definitional authority over what colonialism is or is not, a contest perceived to have higher political stakes. Today, "What is a colony?" barely merits an analytic pause; it remains undisturbed, a quiescent nonquestion.

For students of social formations as well, "a colony" warrants little intellectual work. Tracking homonyms is a trivial pursuit. Sociologists and anthropologists who favor delineated contexts and concrete moments offer descriptive profiles of a particular colony, or comparison with those that meet their prior requirements for inclusion, entities whose preassigned attributes bear out that name. Among those of us who work in this mode, *a colony* tends to be treated as transparent. It describes a physical and social location of a specified aggregated population, a place, a specified distribution of colonizer and colonized, distinctions productive of and dependent on a set of trained dispositions, on unequal entitlements to resources and rights, on conquest as dispossession, on dispossession as progress, and not least, on a requisite set of embodied and durable racialized relations.[1]

But this is only one version of its manifestation and its temporally capacious political career. None of these points of entry broach the changing force fields in which the term "colony" has operated, nor the geopolitical and historical breadth of the political visions embedded within it. Each assumes an essence rather than tracks its coordinates, ascribes rather than poses what a colony is, and what generates and makes up its multiple logics. Such starting points are poorly positioned to address a colony's range of mutation. Not least, a foundational if shadowed feature is lost: namely, that *the colony* (the penal colony, the military colony, the settler colony, the nineteenth-century agricultural colonies in France) is marked by the instability of both its morphology and the political mandates to which its architects and agents subscribe. Such vantage points are ill poised to address what Hannah Arendt calls the "wild confusion of historical terminology" to which imperial formations give rise.[2] Few (Arendt included) have asked whether this "wild confusion" is not significant in itself. Already knowing what a colony is precludes asking whether ambiguous nomenclatures, competing visions, repeated failures, and reversals of course (and the violence, alleged permanence, and fortressed settledness they engender) prefigure *the colony* not as a site of settlement but as always unstable and precarious, plagued by the expectant promise and fear of its becoming another sort of entity. For some who inhabit it, *a colony* is both a promise and the anticipation of a future. For others, it is the suspension of time, the ordinary is reordered in a cordoned-off, designated space—in a holding pen that constricts sociality, nourishes suspicion, and further confines the recalcitrant. *The colony* does more than criminalize dissidence. It produces enemies within and without and anxiously awaits their moments of capture. Its agents are emboldened by the fervent search for those who elude its strictures by disguise and feigned acquiescence. Those most favored, disdained, and held in contempt are those whose speech and comportment allow them to "pass."

If the concept of security, as Foucault argues, is one that works on "possible events" as much as on those that are current and operative, then *the colony* as a political concept is in part defined by its potentiality in this conditional mode.[3] The problematization of security may be muted or manifest, confronted or quelled with different degrees of intensity. But the incitement to, and leveraging of, security—of that which must be potentially defended against—is at its heart. Security may have become, as Agamben insists, "a veritable paradigm of government" today, but it has been paradigmatic and elemental for the practices of imperial governance far longer than his assertion suggests.[4] It raises an issue that eluded both Foucault's treatment of "the carceral archipelago" (from which he excluded the penal colony as too early and the camp as too extreme), as well as Agamben's own treatment of the (refugee) camp as the first in a series of exceptions that has become at once "the nomos of the modern" and the norm: the colony and camp are both containments, enclosures, and unsettled encampments that are more closely allied than we may have imagined. One might describe them as distinct but dependent and not apart. Or, perhaps more apt, they share a "family resemblance" (in Wittgenstein's sense), not any one essential core feature so much as an "overlapping, crisscrossing" set in "a complicated network of similarities."[5] Colony and camp make up a conjoined conceptual matrix, twin formations and formulations of how imperial, rather than national, logics of security operate. They borrow and blend features of their protective architecture and anticipatory fear. They are in a deadly embrace from the start.

The conceptual work marshaled to maintain the colony as a political principle is protean, transitory, and contingent in its inception and instantiations. As a political entity, a colony stands apart and is part of something else. Ontologically, it exists in virtue of its dependent status as a subset of another commanding polity. Those who inhabit a colony stand in a skewed relationship to a broader biopolitical and legal norm. Conceptually, the colony is a tenuous, illegitimate, provisional political formation that can only sustain itself by turning people into other social kinds and its political subordination into something else.

Rather than assume unity of what is called a colony, I begin elsewhere: not with an etymological exercise—not with the word's firm founding in the Latin *colonus*, farmer, and the verb *colere*, to till—but with what Ian Hacking (building on Foucault) would call its historical ontologies.[6] This tack is at once tightly bound to the historical coordinates of the conceptual and concrete landscape a colony inhabits. It favors the sometimes peculiar associations a colony calls forth, the disparate and convergent uses to which the term and the site it named were put. One pursuit would be to follow the divergent trajectories of the term itself. Alternately, one might track that which it has elicited: that is, the comparisons that were made by its social technicians (as Paul Rabinow has called them) between arrangements of people in space that were not named colonies but that their conceptual architectonics called to mind. Such a tack follows the contour of the colony by the range of commensurabilities it called forth and upon. Modular, modified, and minute variations are not to be distilled or discarded but retained, as Gilles Deleuze and Felix Guattari remind us, near at hand.[7] Such a treatment might render historical labor not as the enumeration of "cases"—reduced to the empirical groundwork of concept formation—but, I would argue, a privileged, generative site where concepts come into creation, a venture for which I borrow John Austin's term (and use differently than would Pierre Bourdieu and later Paul Rabinow) that may grant history its distinctive status as a rich ethnographic site for "fieldwork in philosophy."[8]

A PROTEAN ARCHIVE

If concepts, as Deleuze and Guattari insist, are condensed "centers of vibration," nowhere is that resonance more palpable for the political concept of the colony than in the pulse of the archive that it produced, in the paper trails that track the obvious and oblique connectivities to other entities that might share its proclivities, and to other concepts congealed around it. Let me be clear.[9] My starting point is not a colonial archive as we have come to understand that thing and that term. It is not a prior, bounded collection of colonial documents, with policed categories and borders, with inclusions and excisions shaped by the exigencies of imperial governance and the acquisitive bureaucracies that it sustained. Rather, it is a virtual archive, a nodal network, more like a *dispositif*, "gradated," "compact and diffused," and as such freed of the "house arrest" that Derrida imagined keeps archives sequestered, coveted, out of reach, and in place.[10] Just as important, it is a protean archive borne out of the imagined, real, blueprinted, studied, dismissed, and cross-referenced articulations that have emerged from its own filiations. It is an archive that follows the morphology not only of what a colony was, but also the contours outlined by the imagination of what it could be, should be, and might become. Strategies to secure control over a people and place, or to monitor inchoate refusals to succumb to the colony's command are generative of anticipated enemies and anticipatory fears. Documentation of what was imagined to be in the making—and scrupulous projections of what might be—produces an archive of accelerating accumulations that exceeds the colonial archive proper, and which thrives on preemptive (un)reason and the future conditional tense.[11]

It is a protean archive in another sense: one constituted by scripted documents of island and landlocked colonies that stretched across the coercive and curative carceral and humanitarian globe. Its archival web sprawls across the hundreds of agricultural colonies for delinquent youth established throughout France and the Netherlands in the 1840s and 1850s; the pioneer colonies on the Russian steppe; the penal colonies of the French Antilles and British Guiana plotted across the Caribbean, always proximate to the white settler sugar colonies that could be seen from their shores; the leper colonies of Trinidad, Tobago, and Hawaii; the Algerian prison colonies where French dissidents were deposited after the 1848 revolution; the agricultural colonies in the same Algerian countryside designed to remove from Europe and resettle its increasing numbers caught in the intemperate economic zones assigned to the urban poor. Not least, it is an archive that encompasses and moves across different scales. It includes prison penal colonies within settler colonies (as Mauritius served for the British in Bengal in the 1820s), as well as enclave colonies of containment like those planned for poor Indo-European mixed bloods in the highlands of the Netherlands Indies—in the outreaches of New Guinea (in the 1930s) and in the heartland of nineteenth-century Java.[12] Only one rule commands our treatment of this virtual archive: the connections and linkages emerge from the shadows of political imaginaries within the documents; they are not ours to make.

Thus we might do well to begin with the actual filiations that were drawn between these different sorts of colony, and with a documentary trace that made precisely those connections. It is an essay of five hundred pages, in four volumes, written by a certain Count de Tourdonnet in Paris, published in 1863 under the title "An Essay on the Education of Poor Children: The Agricultural Colonies," of which the French agricultural colony of Mettray was hailed as a template for the sixty that were created in the following decade.[13] It was internationally known. Its fame was not accidental. Its founder, the former magistrate Frederic-Auguste Demetz, had traveled far and wide in search of models on which to draw. He welcomed dignitaries from Britain, Belgium, Germany, the Netherlands, and the United States and built a "Hotel de Colonie" just outside the guarded grounds to publicize his experiment in cure and reform.

If these children's agricultural colonies designed as "seedbeds" to raise honest citizens with limited aspirations had iconic status in the nineteenth century, Foucault's *Discipline and Punish* was to endow the exemplary one of Mettray with more. For Foucault, Mettray's opening in 1840 marked at once "the completion of the carceral archipelago," the dawn of "a new era" in the "art of power relations." It was here that he located "the art of punishing that is still more or less our own."[14] Foucault's analytic sweep and dramatic prose are compelling, but they belie a truncated history, partial, schematic, and skewed in time and place. Mettray was a node in a network, many of whose linkages Foucault bypassed, knew little of, or had not sought to name. For one who has compelled us to rethink an event as a "breach of self-evidence," Mettray's opening falls short on too many counts. It was neither an epistemic breach nor an assault on political common sense. It was, rather, a predictable extension of decades of recalibrations of what constituted the most effective balance and gradations of punitive and curative arrangements across the colonies and imperial globe.[15] Foucault's carceral archipelago was bound by Europe and it alone, with penal colonies relegated to vestiges of another moment. But, as Peter Redfield notes, they were not "marginal spaces on the edge of the nation" as Foucault saw them.[16] They were part of a constellation of templates that produced the barricaded security regimes of empire, and count among the refurbished and central geopolitical technologies that endure in the distribution of protected spaces and sites of containment today.

De Tourdonnet was not alone in the mid-nineteenth century in seeing the filiations among different sorts of colonies. His map is far more vast than Foucault's and spreads across the imperial map. His extended essay begins not with the children's *colonies agricoles* in northern France but with Catherine II's mid-eighteenth-century projects to establish colonies on Russia's borders, rural colonies to house abandoned children on St. Petersburg's outskirts, and the "remarkable Russian colonies in the Volga basin." The penal colonies in Guiana and New Caledonia, Siberian colonies and the Algerian *colonie agricole* at Lambèse, reserved for France's political dissidents, figure squarely within de Tourdonnet's purview as well. Colonies of forced resettlement, confinement, cure, and cultivation were all subject to consideration. Connections that escaped Foucault's carceral archipelago are placed full front on de Tourdonnet's conceptual, visionary political map.

Mettray tells us of other connections: images of its central courtyard are marked with a punctum, that "prick," that unexpected detail that Roland Barthes would have relished, the replica of a sailing ship on dry land (an item rarely mentioned in the historiographies of *colonies agricoles*).[17] But the ship was not really out of place. It marked the nexus of multiple kinds of colonies and their overlapping projects. These were colonies designed to prepare their urban inmates, the *colons* (colonists), for their voyage to Algeria, and others for naval jobs on the higher seas. This was the means by which de Tourdonnet and many others saw to alleviate metropolitan Europe of its déclassé underclass, and create out of Algeria a "second continental France."[18]

But the linkages stretch further around the imperial globe. Mettray's founder, Demetz, drew his inspiration from other sites: from one established by one of the most prominent Dutch colonial governors and reformists, Johannes van den Bosch, who established the first agricultural colonies for the criminalized poor in the Netherlands in 1817 and a forced cultivation system for Javanese farmers in the following thirty years, making Java, as one historian has called it, a "para-penal colony."[19] And it was Alexis de Tocqueville who both lauded Mettray, and so praised Demetz, and who after visiting Philadelphia's new penitentiary cast the carceral net back through the conquest of Algeria.[20] This truncated account only gestures to the conceptual lines that were drawn between what today we take to be such fundamentally different experiments, governing projects, and incommensurate colonies. But even a glimpse of these connectivities should slow our steps and humble our assessments of what we know about the enclosed, cordoned off, carceral arrangements spread across the imperial globe. Conceived concurrently, often in collaboration, they drew on and amplified political logics of security, reform, and managed mobilities that remain submerged within our own.

This is not an archive in which a colony is secured as a political concept once and for all. It is, rather, a site where the distinction between its staid life as a common noun and its vibrant life as a political concept is messy, elusive, and besmudged. Nor is this the virtual archive of what might be immediately recognized as a governing concept that organizes the bounty of a dense conceptual constellation. We might think of it more as a subjacent political concept, a muted one that exerts surreptitious command. It resonates but does not cohere. It invites us to follow its "movable bridges" and the rugged passages and detours through which it unfolds.[21] Its discernability must be traced on the outer ridges of its concrete achievements and its conceptual "success": in the short lived projects, borrowed technologies, blueprints realized and scrapped, revised projections, failed attempts, and aborted plans.

A colony does not announce itself as a political concept but exerts its force nonetheless. It organizes visions, imaginaries, and futures. It neither stands alone nor exists complete, unto itself. It is a potential concept, completed only by what attaches to it, what is excluded from it, and what it attaches to. It is always relational, measured against and distinct from a broader and more stable normative physical, political, and social space: distinct from the normative conventions of "free" settlement, and from a normal population (of those not exiled, excommunicated, diseased, politically contagious, socially unfit, vagrant or otherwise dis-abled). A colony as a common noun is a place where people are moved in and out, a place of livid, hopeful, desperate, and violent—willed and unwilled—circulation. It is marked by unsettledness and regulated, policed migration. A colony as a political concept is not a place but a principle of managed mobilities, mobilizing and immobilizing populations, dislocating and relocating peoples according to a set of changing rules and hierarchies that orders social kinds: those eligible for recruitment, for subsidized or forced resettlement, for extreme deprivation or privilege, prioritized residence or confinement. This does not occur in a given, fixed, designated space (though claims to rightful sovereignty over a particular place as in the case of colonial conquest over new and otherwise "unproductive" territories and alleged "wasteland" would suggest otherwise). That space is not demarcated once and for all. Its borders shift as do the means to secure them. Some were holding pens and returned to that function in later times; some took as their goal the making of new social kinds sculpted from those cajoled, seduced, chosen, or forced to be there.

A colony as a political concept assesses the value of human kinds. It organizes activities of labor and leisure and decides who is deserving of them. It defines transgressions and metes out punishments by the goals it has set for itself. Many die there in pursuit of a better life for themselves; many die or starve there crushed by the same quest but subject to the degraded labor conditions that produce and allow a better life for others. A colony not only serves both purposes but these two senses of possibility are tightly bound and depend on each other as well.

As such, a colony as a political concept not only identifies recurrent problematizations; it is also the crystalization of one problematization that always gives way to many more. These problems may be framed as "the mixed-blood question," the "poor white question," "the security issue," or "the problem of immoral conduct," among others. Such problems are insistently and incessantly re-posed, reformulated, reworked, and strategically reanimated: who should be there, how many, who will work with their hands, who will be exempt from certain kinds of labor, who will be charged with letting some out and others enter—all pragmatic problems of the everyday but also feats of social engineering designed to monitor how much pressure to apply and where to apply it: on the social body or on strategic points of a person's flesh. Concepts of security, fear, preparedness, expendability, risk, and reform make up the shared vocabulary of those charged with its quotidian and conceptual management and care.

The filiations that are drawn in this virtual archive of the colony or camp are not unreasoned fabulations between an agricultural colony for wayward boys and a prison in the fields, or between a military camp in 1845 Algeria later turned into an agricultural settlement. The very substitutability and morphed exchangeability between these forms suggest lineages and kinships that are uncontained by the distinctions between metropole and colony, and badly served if the starting point is assumed knowledge of what distinguishes the arts of governance as nation-bound political logics from those of imperial formations.

In our virtual archive of the colony that joins penal colonies, settler colonies, and agricultural colonies of delinquent youth, one is struck by several things: one, that virtually all colonies, no matter their intent, their location, or their designated population, are artefacts of deliberate and concerted design. Design is key for it announces how much the colony as a political concept commands the preemptive, calculates malintent, assesses future transgressions and potential breaches of security. Design works in the subjunctive mood and gravitates to the possible. The colony as common noun and as a political concept, as a place and a potentiality, is imagined, implemented, and lived in its conditional, future tense.

If the concept is, as Deleuze and Guattari argue, "the contour, the configuration, the constellation of an event to come," the colony anticipates that event in its very making.[22] The colony is a provisional configuration that promises something else: the recalcitrant, impoverished poor white *colon* who will be reformed, domesticated through rigorous agricultural labor and love of the land. As de Tourdonnet saw it, young thieves roaming Europe's plush avenues and slums would be quarantined in Rousillon or Provence until they were "made ready" to reinhabit France's depopulated countryside or adapted to work in a hotter clime, to work the land, settle the colony, and defend the empire. Thus the colony assesses social kinds but also inscribes their factuality in its everyday implementation and design: in who gets how much cloth or meat and what quality, who is allocated what shelter, services, privileges, water, and land. This meticulous partitioning, however, does not secure the success of the colony. Even indelible inscriptions on the body, as Kafka so vividly described, provide no guarantee that the planning works.[23] On the contrary, they register the repeated efforts of the colony's purveyors to affirm acquiescence of body and soul. The concept of the colony is not foretelling a future colony held in place by design but, rather, the unstable morphology of its provisional making and remaking again and again.

Second, despite that deliberate design, there is no one commanding logic that can account for a colony's content or form. Dissension, refusal, and conflict animate their beginnings and permutate into what might go by another name. This then is not only the archive of a different history from those of penal histories, colonial histories, and histories of social reform that have stood apart for so long. The archive of the colony condenses what Foucault identified as the prime subject of genealogy. It is not the entry point to a different history but to a differential one that recuperates the lines of force, relational histories, and, as he put it, "the dissension of other things."[24] As a political concept, a colony is the sifted remainder of disparities and of the contradictions that made it up. As an always already unfinished project that can never be settled or finished once and for all, the contests over degrees of sovereignty and gradations of unfreedom produce recurrent forays and standoffs in a thickly embattled space in which no one is really safe. Imperial formations thrive on the tangible and intangible opacities of privilege and privation that reinvent what constitutes the law.[25]

Rather than imagining a typology of colonies that emerged clean out of whole cloth—a settler colony, a penal colony, an entrepôt with few colonists at all—we see the tangled projects and investments that defined their distinctions as well as the convergences among them. Consensus on how they should be managed and who should be in them were always provisional at best. More meticulous order was symptomatic of the fear of less. Settlements of abandoned children, unemployed Parisian families in the Algerian bled (or interior), North African Jews sent to the borderlands of Israel's declared borders or deposited squarely on Palestinian land in active cultivation, Spanish reconcentration settlements for Cuba's volatile and recalcitrant urban poor cannot be charted on a linear or developmental scale as they would in an originary tale.

What is more striking is how many of these disparate settlements were conceived as political projects with interchangeable parts and substitutable populations. Penal colonies of the late nineteenth century were not vestiges of another earlier form of disciplinary control, as Foucault would have it. In the virtual archive of the colony there is no clear line to be drawn. Tasmania's Port Arthur penal settlement established in 1830 may have belonged to the old regimes of spectacular punishment written on the body, but as John Frow argues, it was also part of the new humane regimes of moral inculcation operating on the soul.[26] These are recursive elements and enduring properties.

As a political concept designed to distribute power, a colony is doomed to fail. Inside and outside are mobile locations that cannot be maintained as viable borders. Interior frontiers stretch obliquely across and within their guarded space. Enclosure, gated enclaves, barb wired encampments, and sequestered populations produce imagined threats: transgressions of the private, intrusions on the safe, a storming of the gates. They take the form of enclosure, but what and who must be kept out, and what and who must stay in are neither fixed nor easy to assess. Internal enemies are ever-present potentialities: signs of their emergence may appear, and be conjured, anywhere. To protect those within or contain them, or protect those without who might be disturbed, at risk, or endangered by exposure to them, is no easy task. These are not mutually exclusive projects. They are certainly not opposing ones. Being "at risk" and "a risk" is a thin political line that colonial histories rarely seek to address. Being protected is not designated only by who is within the colony and who is not. This quality of boundedness within and without produces anxious movement, escapes, desertion, capture, captivity, predator and prey, and more surveillance.[27] From inside and out, a colony mobilizes fear, insecurity, and force. Colonies, designed as safety nets and havens, are never safe. Such settlements called "colonies" are nodes of anxious, uneasy circulations, settlements that are not settled at all.

Foucault's "carceral archipelago" could never work as one bound by Europe, and its practitioners knew it well. The carceral archipelago was a metaphor with generative conceptual weight. These networks were literal archipelagos but also figurative in more legal senses than Foucault might have envisioned. These were zones of semi-extraterritorial status, part of, but removed from, certain legal restrictions, inside and outside the nation proper. Like the detention and refugee camps in Europe today, which Didier Fassin describes as removed from the polis proper, they were clusterings of types of persons, both of and at biopolitical risk, relegated to the edges of legality, to the outskirts of the nation and on the edges of empire, but not outside their networks of security, surveillance, and intelligence, or their visionary bounds.[28] Michel Agier goes further, arguing that exile is always "interior, with no outside, and depends on the creation of artifacts [and fictions] of extraterritoriality."[29]

Foucault was right that many of the projects to use the children housed in France's agricultural colonies for conquest and protection never got off the ground. However faint their imprint might remain, they are indelible watermarks of empire that trace the lineaments of how broadly security regimes were conceived. There are no straight historical lines that lead from *les colonies agricoles* to Guantanamo. Nor do the late nineteenth-century reconcentration centers in Cuba or the German camps for the Herero provide a direct link to Nazi concentration camps or humanitarian refugee camps, as some German historians are wont to claim.[30] Re-orienting our historical and conceptual maps has to do more than reverse directionality, revise chronologies, and the spatial scope of European history. At issue are our questions that direct new comparisons and convergences about the shared spaces, factualities, instruments, and persons created and driven in and out of circulation. Such a historical analytics adheres to and demands the empirical to question changing conceptual architectures and the political principles lodged within them.

A colony is a ravaged home. Memmi held that there is no going home from a colony. One is never again the same. But that is not really the case. It is rendered unhomely for those on whom it is imposed, as well as for those to whom it is offered as a stolen gift. There is no being "at home," only unsettled waiting for something else, for release from those unfulfilled promises and that anxious unfilled labor.

NOTES

I thank J. M. Bernstein, Val Daniel, Adi Ophir, Lawrence Hirschfeld, and members of the Workshop on Political Concepts held at The New School for Social Research, December 2010, for their comments, queries, and incitements to clarification. A more comprehensive treatment of the relationship between camp and colony, and with more extensive citations, appears as chapter 3, "A Deadly Embrace: Of Colony and

Camp," in Ann Laura Stoler, *Duress: Imperial Durabilities in Our Times* (Durham, N.C.: Duke University Press, 2016), 68–121.

1. In this treatment of colony as a political concept, my discussion is framed around and limited to the modern colony. It excludes colonies in the ancient world and makes no attempt to create or contest continuity between the ancient and the modern concept.

2. Hannah Arendt, *The Origins of Totalitarianism* (New York: Harcourt, Brace, 1979), 131.

3. Michel Foucault, *Sécurité, territoire, population: Cours au Collège de France, 1977–1978* (Paris: Gallimard, 2004), 22. See also Ann Laura Stoler, *Along the Archival Grain: Epistemic Anxieties and Colonial Common Sense* (Princeton, N.J.: Princeton University Press, 2009).

4. Giorgio Agamben, "Le gouvernment de l'insecurité: Entretien avec Giorgio Agamben," *La Revue Internationale des Livres et des Idées* 4 (March/April 2008): 18–20. Also see Giorgio Agamben, "The Camp as the 'Nomos' of the Modern," in *Homo Sacer: Sovereign Power and Bare Life* (Stanford, Calif.: Stanford University Press, 1998), 166–80.

5. Ludwig Wittgenstein, *Philosophical Investigations*, trans. G. Anscombe (New York: Macmillan, 1958), 32.

6. Ian Hacking, *Historical Ontology* (Cambridge, Mass.: Harvard University Press, 2006), 26.

7. Gilles Deleuze and Felix Guattari, *What Is Philosophy?* (New York: Columbia University Press, 1994), 20.

8. See John Austin, "A Plea for Excuses," *Proceedings of the Aristotelian Society*, n.s. 57 (1956–57): 1–30, accessed October 28, 2016, https://sites.ualberta.ca/~francisp/NewPhil448/AustinPlea56.pdf; Pierre Bourdieu, "Fieldwork in Philosophy," in *Choses dites* (Paris: Minuit, 1987); Paul Rabinow, *French Modern* (Cambridge, Mass.: MIT Press, 1989), 16.

9. Deleuze and Guattari, *What Is Philosophy?*, 23.

10. Jacques Derrida, *Archive Fever* (Chicago: University of Chicago Press, 1996), 2.

11. For more on these visions, see chapter 4, "Developing Historical Negatives," in Stoler, *Along the Archival Grain*, 105–40.

12. Claire Anderson, "The Genealogy of the Modern Subject: Indian Convicts in Mauritius, l814–l853," in *Representing Convicts: New Perspectives on Convict Forced Labor Migration*, ed. Ian Duffield and James Bradley, 164–82 (London: Leicester University Press, 1997).

13. See Jeroen Dekker, "Transforming the Nation and the Child: Philanthropy in the Netherlands, Belgium, France and England," in *Charity, Philanthropy and Reform: From the 1690s to l850,* ed. H. Cunningham and J. Innes, 130–47 (New York: St. Martin's, 1998); and Ceri Crossley, "Using and Transforming the French Countryside: The 'Colonies Agricoles,' 1820–1850," *French Studies* 44, no. 1 (1991): 36–54.

14. Foucault, *Discipline and Punish*, 296.

15. Michel Foucault, "Table ronde du 20 mai 1978," in *Dits et écrits, tome IV* (Paris: Gallimard, 1994), 27.

16. Peter Redfield, *Space in the Tropics: From Convicts to Rockets in French Guiana* (Berkeley: University of California Press, 2000), 64.

17. See the cover image that adorns *Eduquer et punir: La colonie agricole et pénitentiaire de Mettray (1839–1937)*, ed. Luc Forlivesi, Georges-François Pottier, and Sopie Chassat (Rennes, France: Presses Universitaires de Rennes, 2005).

18. Le Comte A. De Tourdonnet, *Essais sur l'éducation des enfants pauvrès des colonies agricoles d'éducation,* vol. 2 (Paris: P. Brunet, 1862), 162–64.

19. Albert Schauwers, "The 'Benevolent' Colonies of Johannes van den Bosch: Continuities in the Administration of Poverty in the Netherlands and Indonesia," *Comparative Studies in Society and History* 43, no. 2 (2001): 298–328.

20. See Stoler, "A Deadly Embrace," 68–121.

21. Deleuze and Guattari, *What Is Philosophy?*, 23.

22. Ibid., 32–33.

23. Franz Kafka, *The Penal Colony* (New York: Schocken, 1948), 191–227. For a brilliant analysis of Kafka's penal colony and the concept of the *colonie* (which I first learned about after this essay was completed), see Seloua Luste Boulbina, *Le singe de Kafka* (Lyon: Sens Public, 2008).

24. Michel Foucault, "Nietzsche, Genealogy, History," in *Language, Counter-Memory, Practice* (Ithaca, N.Y.: Cornell University Press, 1977), 142.

25. Ann Laura Stoler, "On Degrees of Imperial Sovereignty," *Public Culture* 18, no. 1 (2006): 125–46.

26. John Frow, "In the Penal Colony," *Journal of Australian Studies* (2000): 6.

27. On the interchangeability between predator and prey, and the manhunt as an enduring nexus of political philosophy, see Gregoire Chamayou, *Les chasses à l'homme* (Paris: La Fabrique, 2010).

28. Didier Fassin, "Compassion and Repression: The Moral Economy of Immigration Policies in France," *Cultural Anthropology* 20, no. 3 (2005): 381.

29. Michel Agier, *Le couloir des exilés: Être étranger dans un monde commun* (Paris: Editions du Croquant, 2011), 23.

30. There is now extensive literature and intensive debate on this subject. See, for example, Benjamin Madley, "From Africa to Auschwitz: How German South West Africa Incubated Ideas and Methods Adopted and Developed by the Nazis in Germany," *European History Quarterly* 35, no. 3 (2005): 429–64; Jürgen Zimmerer, Joachim Zeller, Edward Neather, eds., *Genocide in German South-West Africa: The Colonial War (1904–1908)* (Monmouth, Wales: Merlin Press, 2007).

4

CONCEPT

Adi Ophir

1

Of the many thinkers engaged in conceptual work, only few stop and ask, "What is a concept?" This is the question I wish to explore here. Its form is Socratic, and it first appears in Socrates's inquiries.

"Philosophers have not been sufficiently concerned with the nature of the concept as philosophical reality," argue Deleuze and Guattari. "They have preferred to think of it as a given knowledge or representation that can be explained by the [mental] faculties able to form it (abstraction or generalization) or employ it (judgment)." The two then add, "But the concept is not given, it is created; it is to be created."[1] They thereby assume that a concept can be conceived as either given or created. The idea of the concept presented here opts for a third alternative. A concept is neither given nor created but, rather, performed or played in the act of conceptualization. This play both invents and discovers the concept, both lets it appear and gives it existence, and in doing this it also blurs the distinction between what is given and revealed, and what is invented and created.

Socrates was the first master of this kind of performance. After some greetings and small talk, the typical Socratic inquiry usually begins by posing a simple question about some abstract noun x. "What is x?," asks Socrates. The answers that are examined and ruled out one after the other are given in the form of definitions: "x is p." Thus, p is a description of x that should, according to Socrates, provide the necessary and sufficient conditions for identifying something as x. The Socratic inquiry reveals that the conditions contained in the definition are either unnecessary, insufficient, or both. Sometimes they turn out to contradict each other or some other widely held opinion. But the aim of the Socratic inquiry, as Plato presents it starting with the middle dialogues, is not to arrive at a contradiction-free definition but, rather, at a pure form of x that can be immediately perceived by the mind's eye. The Socratic inquiry is meant to lead the soul beyond language toward that pure form, which cannot be captured by a definition and is not a linguistic or mental entity. The attempt to define is part of the nature of conceptual inquiry, and the pure form that the inquirer is supposed to perceive in the mind's eye is its goal.

The difference between the philosophical discourse's *form of inquiry* and its goal is manifest in Plato's dialogues without being explicitly articulated: it is the difference between the dialogue as performance, show, and event, and the object of inquiry that is at the center of the Socratic language game. This difference disappears somewhere in the history of the definitional view of concepts. In their broad comparative study, Stephen Laurence and Eric Margolis argue that what is common to most contemporary approaches to the study of concepts, in the modern Anglo-Saxon versions of epistemology, philosophy of mind, and related cognitive studies, is their rejection of the definitional view of concepts.[2] What they reject is not the attempt to define concepts but the view of the mental apparatus of cognition as consisting of definitional patterns, which are regarded as necessary for conceptual cognition. For the majority of those working in these fields, a concept is a unit of mental representation, a linguistic-perceptual capacity or, following Gottlob Frege, an objective sense.[3] And in all these versions, concepts don't function like definitions.

A definition is a specific kind of speech act that is part of a particular language game. With the rejection of the classic definitional view of concepts, this aspect of the concept has been ignored and the concept has become an achievement, a cognitive tool (a unit of mental representation), or an object that directs our cognitive effort (a sense, an idea). This goes back far earlier than the cognitive turn in epistemology in general and in the study of concepts in particular. It appears already in Aristotle's discussion of definitions in the *Organon*, where he narrows concepts down to definitional, linguistic formulas that tell us "what it is for x to be" (*to ti ên einai*).[4] This neglect assumed a series of new forms in modern philosophy, with the empiricists, rationalists, and, above all, with Kant. All of them regard concepts as elements of our cognitive apparatus: patterns that organize sense data and allow us to identify objects and to grasp the relations between them. For Kant, a concept is a pattern that allows us to recognize what appears before us as-what-it-is when it appears. Kant's concepts (or Husserl's ideas, for that matter) populate the mind and have nothing in particular to do with the language through which they are acquired, and which only—thanks to its mediation—can attain their full meaning.

The "linguistic turn" has brought back the hitherto neglected linguistic dimension of concepts, usually at the expense of giving up their special cognitive and ontological status. For Wittgenstein, not much is left of concepts except for the meaning of words, determined by their use in specific language games. But the use of the same word in different language games may indicate something these uses have in common, which is more than a family resemblance; something the explication of which calls for yet another language game. In this other game, it is not enough to answer the question "what is x?" by demonstrating the use of the word in a particular language game. Instead one is looking for an explication of the very possibility of using the word differently in different language games, while easily moving between these games without much translation effort, based on the realization that it is not a mere coincidence that one uses this same word in different games. By asking "what is x?" across several language games in which "x" is used quite distinctly, one is looking for a possible "conceptual definition" that somehow encompasses a variety of uses, and yet is not reducible to any one of them. A conceptual definition is a special case of what Wittgenstein called "verbal definition" precisely because conceptualization is a distinct language game. However, concepts for Wittgenstein were discrete meaning-units, and he ignored the differences between kinds of meaning and ways to understand them and did not study the specific language game in which concepts appear.

We may start, then, by asking where concepts appear—literally, to the senses—as concepts. Clearly, they appear when people speak, write, or use general nouns. But many nouns are often used without being conceptualized at all, without the addressor or the addressee grasping them as concepts. Concepts, I suggest, appear as such only within a discourse that connects the conceptual language game and the question that summons it. They do not appear when a child, a layperson, or a philosopher expresses some capacity for generalization and uses general nouns properly, or when a scholar uses preconceived technical terms. In such cases, concepts are at most hinted at or implied, leaving certain traces in the speaker's performance. Concepts properly appear *when one tries to explain, to present, and to express the essence of what the concept refers to.* This description holds regardless of how true the concept is to the essence of the thing in question, or whether that thing has an essence or even an existence.

A concept is linguistic performance oriented to the essence of something in question. As a discursive entity, the concept does not depend upon the relation between that essence and its description, or upon the validity or reliability of that description, but only upon the *orientation toward* such essence. Concepts are not propositions, which can be either valid or not, true or false. They can only be more or less faithful to the essence in question. An unfaithful concept is still a concept, just as a false proposition is still a proposition.

Concepts appear when terms are conceptualized. There are no concepts without conceptualization. This holds just as much for someone who does not yet have a clear concept of the general noun he or she is using, as for someone who uses a general noun as if its concept were altogether clear. A concept appears only when "I have no idea what this is" becomes a problem for which the concept would be a solution. S. H. Bergmann writes that "a concept turns distinct through its definition,"[5] but the truth is that it *becomes* a concept in the first place through the *effort* to define (and clarify and explicate) it. When speakers of some natural language make use of unclear or indistinct concepts, they actually "have no idea what they are talking about,"[6] that is, they are unable to present the concepts they imply or that may be ascribed to them. They know how to use nouns or terms so as to let communication flow, speakers function and acts to be carried out. But this does not mean that they grasp these terms as concepts. To find out whether or not they do, speakers should postpone the flow of communication for the sake of explication and presentation. This flow cannot be postponed without invoking some authority, using some force and power, as the case may be. Hence this postponement—a crucial moment in the life of concepts—is responsible for the fact that the concepts are always already political.

A term becomes a concept only when we take the time to disengage it from its daily use in order to put it on display, wonder about its meaning, explicate it, and render public its discursive being. When philosophers, scientists, jurists, or artists, working within a certain discursive community, use terms they don't bother to explain, they are using them as "subjects supposed to know" [*sujets supposés savoir*], and address their addressees as subjects who are supposed to know as well. They use these terms as if they had already been conceptualized and clarified, and as if among the interlocutors there is a substantial enough consensus about their meaning, the essence of what they refer to. But every time we cast doubt on these presuppositions, we might be surprised about the extent of disagreement among interlocutors, even when it comes to common terms. Terms and intimate communities are "black boxes" of meaning that people know how to put to use in order for communication to flow, arguments to be understood, and actions to be successful. Concepts are what happens when people open these black boxes and ask, "what is this, anyway?"

Often enough, it's precisely those terms that are most commonly used—that have already become common currency, and we can swear by and keep coming back to—that people don't bother to explain, and that are used as if they were familiar and well known, albeit in varying and sometimes contradictory ways. Such terms function as "placeholders," and they appear in dense semantic intersections that connect them with many other terms. Think about "amazing," "critical," "love," "security," or "Jewish-Democratic state." The power of such terms derives from their relative emptiness (which allows them to assume different meanings and to relate to many other, different, and conflicting terms), but also—and this is the flipside of the same coin—from the semantic density of the intersections in which they appear. Because of their privileged status, any attempt to determine their semantic content (for instance, through a successful explication or a novel use) will affect their interrelated constellation, but also narrow down their possible spaces of denotation and connotation.[7]

Often, such placeholders have the status of "discursive celebrities." It pays to rely on them: to keep saying "security," "democracy," "change," or "crisis." When people use them, they often suggest that they know what they are talking about. They speak as if they already understand it, using the name of the concept as an index that points to a complex theory operating in the background, which they can always retrieve if there's a need. In a functioning discourse, placeholder terms are far more important than concepts, and the insistence on conceptualization is regarded as a disturbance to this functioning.

The investigation of concepts suggested here begins with the appearance of concepts, rather than with the mental capacity to conceptualize, which we tend to attribute to people based on their ability to identify, recognize, or correctly use a certain term. It is an investigation that asks how concepts appear, and tries to learn about their essence from their appearance. To proceed otherwise means to presuppose a clear concept of the concept, together with the ability to recognize concepts even when they are not stated as such or not stated at all. Observers of cognitive behavior often attribute to their subjects a degree of understanding that is more comprehensive than what is expressed by their performance, by their reactions that indicate recognition of the concept, or by their recurrent use of a certain word. The concept attributed to the subject contains, in principle, some excess over what is being perceived by the observer—at minimum, the attributed capacity to repeatedly recognize the concept embodied in some object, or an object as a concept's embodiment. Although the observer attributes to the subject a capacity for repetition (re-cognition, re-iteration), what repeats is not part of the repetition itself but, rather, needs to be complemented: the observer has to complete what is missing from the speaker's "conceptual picture."

Thus the child's capacity to recognize something, or the speaker's repeated use of a word, must already be conceptualized in the discourse of the linguist, philosopher, or cognitive scientist in order to appear as a concept. In order to identify a baby sucking on a pacifier and to attribute to it the concept "pacifier," one needs a richer (more complex or adequate) concept of pacifier than that of the baby. One assumes, either explicitly or implicitly, that one has such a concept when one points to the baby's actions as expressing the baby's having the mental representation or cognitive unit "pacifier." More generally, the ability to pick out and recognize such a cognitive, logical, or semantic unit presupposes the discursive act of conceptualization and suggests the existence of a discursive concept that one can always go back to in order to validate this recognition. *I assume therefore that prior to being a mental, semantic, or logical unit, a concept is a principle of discursive activity*, which gives shape to a certain kind of discursive practice, and this practice cannot be possessed but only performed with others. In order to recognize it, one has to correctly characterize this practice.

The discursive view of concepts presented here is based on Foucault's principles of discursive analysis in *The Archaeology of Knowledge*.[8] Discourse, according to Foucault, is a more or less regularized linguistic activity that regulates the production and reproduction of statements, through somewhat regular reiterations of the relations between words and things, the "expressible" (in speech or writing) and the visible, between speaking subjects and subject matters (and later we will add: addressors and addressees), between different groups of statements, and between a statement and its material medium. A discursive formation, according to Foucault, consists of a regularity or stabilization of four dimensions of the "enunciative function," or of the statement (*énoncé*) as a function of relations: the regularity of the appearance of objects in a certain space of appearance and denotation; the stabilization of subject positions with certain spaces of authority (the authority to speak, to interpret, cite, denote, show, conclude, etc.); specific groupings of different statements that have different practical effects (telling a story, making an argument, etc.); and the existence of established material ways for reproducing statements.[9] For Foucault, the existence of a conceptual function or a conceptual moment (unlike a subject position or a space of denotation) is not a necessary condition for the production of statements in discourse. Indeed, some discursive regimes do not require concepts or allow for their production in the first place.[10] Concepts are required only for certain kinds of discourses, and only in very few of these, like philosophy or theology, do they become what is at stake in the discursive activity.

Foucault did not discuss the individual concept as having a distinct discursive status, since he did not regard it as one of the four dimensions of the enunciative function that make discourse possible. In the same way he promoted a shift of focus from meaning to discursive patterns, he promoted a shift from individual concepts to what he called the "pre-conceptual" level, where he looked for more or less regular patterns of relations between statements that operate concepts grouped together by the discourse. He regarded this relative regulation as a condition for the use of concepts in discourse and for the temporary stabilization of their meaning.[11] We can accept this claim (just as we can accept Wittgenstein's view, according to which the meaning of a word—including, for that matter, the meaning of the signifier of a concept—is nothing but the way it is used in a certain language game) without thereby dismissing the question, "what, after all, is a concept?" The kind of discursive analysis suggested here is thus meant to fill the lacuna with respect to concepts left unattended by Foucault, as well as other figures who brought about the linguistic turn in philosophy.

I propose to fill this lacuna mainly by Foucauldian means. A second influence on the analysis presented here, besides Foucault, is Deleuze and Guattari's idea of the concept in *What Is Philosophy?* In what follows, I shall adopt some of their observations without committing to their complex ontology and while explicitly rejecting two of their fundamental presuppositions: (1) "The concept is not discursive, and philosophy is not a discursive formation";[12] (2) only philosophy, and not science or art, invents concepts and thinks through concepts; science and art have other means for creative thinking, and what they believe to be concepts are not really that.[13] The first presupposition is in line with Foucault's treatment of concepts,[14] expressing the same kind of waiver or disregard typical of the philosophers of the linguistic turn: giving up on understanding the act of conceptualization as a unique discursive gesture or act that is responsible for the creation, appearance, and existence of concepts. This essay presupposes that concepts are indeed discursive, that their existence cannot be detached from the event of their discursive conceptualization, and that their nature changes between different kinds of discourse. There are different ways of conceptualization according to the different discursive regimes that allow conceptualization, and unlike what Deleuze and Guatarri thought, concepts are not just a matter for philosophy, even if they are a matter of the kind of thinking that can always be called philosophical.

2

What kind of discursive entity is the concept if it is not one of the functions that define a statement? If discourse, according to Foucault, is a more or less regularized linguistic activity, which regulates the production and reproduction of statements through the regularity of the relations between things, words, speakers, and addressees, then a concept is a special form for realizing these relations. In other words, a concept is a particular kind of statement. Unlike a term, such as "energy" or "justice," which can be identified with a noun based on its grammatical function and while ignoring its meaning, a concept is a complete statement that can always be regarded as "polysemous." Let us try and find out what kind of statement the concept is, according to Foucault's four enunciative functions.

First, as a statement, *a concept is defined according to its relation to a space of the appearance of objects*. Every conceptual statement marks some space in which the objects that embody the concept appear (or may appear). The object's referents are either real or possible objects that may have existed, currently exist, or might exist in some plane of reference, in a real, possible, or fictional space. There can be concepts of objects and properties that never existed: fictiveness then becomes part of those concepts (e.g., an atheistic concept of epiphany), and their space of appearance is then limited to texts that describe some fictive world. A statement is a function of the relation between the spoken and the visible or the sensible, between what can be said and what can be seen. Hence the concept's conditions of intelligibility (its distribution in a semantic space, its distinction from other concepts, and its relations to them) are not enough: to these we must add the conditions under which the objects embodying the concept become visible and presentable (including the conditions of what is invisible and nonpresentable). For example, the concept of the state includes a reference to the space or spaces in which the state, its elements, or its representative entities can appear. This concept is altered when we realize that the state also appears in the market and in the household, and that in fact there is no social space in which the state is prevented from making an appearance. This omnipresence of the state can be countered by an "ontological anarchism" that attributes to the state all that the regime attributes to it, except for the reality of its appearance.

According to this anarchist, the state can appear only in those texts that pretend to represent it.

Second, as a statement, *a concept is defined according to its relation to subjects—to a speaker and to an addressee*. There are concepts that everyone can acquire but only authorized speakers can produce, redefine, interpret, or deliver to others. There are concepts whose definition bears the signature of the subject who authored them (Plato's concept of the Idea, for example, which is different from Kant's or Hegel's), and this signature hangs over uses of the concept by others who are inspired by, interpreting, or criticizing the relevant writings of the signed authors. Similarly, there are concepts that only subjects with a privileged status can present (e.g., the concept of God, reserved for prophets who experienced revelation), and only addressees with a certain status can attain (those who went through the proper qualification, who know enough, whose faith is strong, and whose heart is willing to understand). The addressees and speakers don't have to be real or exist. Hence it is possible to discuss concept x according to some ancient author whose addressees were part of a bygone discursive community, and to write histories of concepts and conceptualizations (which is not the same as a history of some discourse that includes those concepts). Hence, it's also possible to reconstruct a concept without committing to its content.

Third, as a statement, *a concept is defined according to its relation to a cloud of adjacent conceptual statements*. This cloud doesn't necessarily have a well-defined structure or field. Its nature changes from one discourse to another, and it is one of the variables that distinguishes a discourse. The concept of the state, for example, appears alongside statements that define concepts such as sovereignty, territory, border, government, law, democracy, fascism, globalization, and so on. Some (but not all) of these statements aren't just adjacent to the concept but also essential components of it. Other statements define the concept from the outside (e.g., statements about political associations that preceded the state or exist outside it). However, they may indicate that what is excluded from the concept in fact belongs to it by way of negation (a subject is a nonobject, a Jew is a non-Gentile, etc.). The environment that the conceptual statement relates to may be relatively thin (as in the case of concepts that were coined but not well received) or dense (the concept "state," for example), highly structured (mathematical concepts) or relatively amorphous (e.g., "sadness" or "happiness").

Fourth, as a statement, *a concept is also defined in relation to a material medium that allows it to appear and to be reproduced*. This relation might appear as a fairly weak requirement, one that we tend to take for granted: concepts appear when they are conceptualized, either in written or spoken language. But this difference between the spoken and the written has been the source of much debate from Plato to Derrida. Furthermore, the entire history of the theory of the concept as a mental unit can be understood as being based on a different way of constraining the medium for the appearance and reproduction of concepts. For the cognitive sciences and the entire philosophical tradition (at least since modern empiricism) that converges into them, this medium is the knowing mind. Conversely, in the theory of the concept proposed here, the conceptual statement's medium of reproduction is a space of discursive practices. For the cognitivists, a concept is not reproduced by reappearing in the knowing mind but only by the slow process of its learning, that is, its transmission from one mind to another. From the Foucauldian perspective I am offering here, this learning process is replaced by discursive event, where a kind of performance that can never be reduced to or described by what goes on in the knowing mind is taking place. In what follows I will examine the four functions of the conceptual statement.

The Plane of Appearance

Whether conceived as a mental unit or an ideal sense, a concept has long been recognized as unifying a multiplicity of appearances in a single scheme, and this scheme does not itself appear. It can only be signified or described, its existence presupposed or concluded, but one cannot point to it. The concept as the unity of a multiplicity or as the multiplicity of a unity does not belong to the space in which the things that incorporate it appear. For example, the concept of speed is embodied in moving bodies, but as a unifying scheme it appears only in that space in which it is signified, for example, via the formula $v = s/t$. That is to say, in order for a concept to *appear*, it is not enough that something that embodies it or a signifier that signifies it would appear; nor is it enough that a conjoining of its multiple instances will take place. *This conjoining itself must appear*. The aim of a conceptual statement is not to explain, to justify, to request, or to tell a story. It is to present the multiplicity-unifying scheme in a space of appearance—to show the multiplicity in its unity. In this sense, the conceptual statement aims to function in the same manner as a diagram, table, conjugation list, or map—all of which present a multiplicity of detail, merge it in a single scheme, and allow grasping that multiplicity at one glance.

A concept, then, is a statement that presents a unifying scheme. This presentation usually takes place through a description marked by a double movement: a movement of individuation from the unifying scheme to the moments[15] comprising the concept, and a movement of generalization from the moments back to the structural skeleton of the scheme. The scheme can't be presented without presenting what it brings together, the conjoining can't be presented without re-presenting the scheme, and this re-presentation can't take place without verbal description. The concept's plane of appearance is thus the discursive plane in which its description takes place.

Obviously a description requires more than repeating the concept's name. More important, in order to capture the multiplicity of instances that embody the concept in a given space of appearance, a denoting won't suffice either. Denoting is the zero point of conceptualization, but when a denotation serves as an answer to a "what is x?" question, it is usually a means for clarification or identification. The act of denoting creates the impression of a direct relation between the word and its referent, where conceptualization is superfluous. This is the case not only in the context of identifying a person or a color, for example, or a certain device or instrument but also in the context of using a term, a linguistic instrument: "this is the USB port," "here is a Siamese cat," "this is happiness." The word or phrase only appears as a concept when someone places this direct relation under question. At that moment, when the seemingly automatic movement from signifier to signified fails, it becomes clear to the interlocutors that in order to clarify the term one has to reconstruct the way it is interconnected in a semantic network; that is, to manifest its being a linguistic entity that exists thanks to its place and function in a discourse, and not only as an allegedly transparent signifier of a thing in the world. This is the beginning of conceptualization, the moment in which a concept first emerges.

Conceptualization ends when the concept disappears. Does the concept still exist outside the act of conceptualization? Like the toddler who early on learns how to distinguish the doll's disappearance from its complete loss, the one who conceptualizes also knows how to distinguish disappearance from nonexistence. She knows she can reconceptualize when asked because she has grasped the concept. The concept exists then as a potentiality to perform conceptualization. For the others, however, this potentiality can only be known through the actual performance.

From disappearance to loss or nonexistence is a slippery slope. What is true for the toddler's doll is true of any concept. It makes sense to question the existence of a concept when the traces of the conceptual performance, namely, the event during which the concept appeared, no longer suffice to recall or recreate it. There is a continuum between the appearing concept and the concept that has been black-boxed and turned a term ready-to-hand. Whoever moves freely between the black-boxed term and the performed concept is like a child who knows how to keep rediscovering the doll that disappeared. But sometimes people act as if they know how to find what is lost while denying that it has in fact been lost; likewise, they use terms and pretend they know how to reconstruct their lost concepts. Their vain pretension may be exposed by the simple question "what do you mean by x?" (or "what is x for you?"). This question is also the moment when the particular relation of the concept to a speaking subject and to an addressed subject appears.

The Relation to Speaker and Addressee

Prior and in addition to the authority of the speaker and the qualification of the addressee, there is their special interest in the concept, which is a precondition for a term to appear as a concept. The speaker or addressee of a conceptual statement must have an interest in the essence of the thing being conceptualized. This interest depends not upon a subjective intention but upon an objective position: the speaker and addressee of the conceptual statement (the latter more than the former) must occupy the speaker's position of a previous "what is x?" question. The special status of the concept-indicating word is derived first and foremost from the way it is positioned as the focus of a question about the essence of something. A concept appears whenever a term (word or phrase) is placed at the center of a discussion in which the definition, explication, or reconstruction of its sense—either in a general manner or in some specific historical context—is at stake. To be more precise, a concept is a term placed in the empty position of the question form "what is x?," which cannot be answered by denoting or providing instructions for use. The subject of a conceptual statement is someone who asks "what is x?" and is unwilling to settle for a denotation or instructions for use. Rather, it is a subject who is supposed *not* to know, or at least one who pretends he does not know and therefore asks. The *request* to explicate a term, to explain "what is x?" (and not merely point to it or show how it's used) is responsible for its appearing as a concept.

The querying subject is never alone. In order for a conceptual statement to take place, the addressee must be someone who is in no hurry to provide a ready-made answer, an answer that fulfills the function of denotation and immediately closes the door to conceptual movement. A conceptual statement requires a community of discourse, small as it may be, whether real or imaginary, whose members share a similar conceptual interest. This interest sets a conceptual deliberation in motion, and it is only with respect to this interest that the concept appears as such. This interest is responsible for the concept being an event and a kind of performance: an investigation triggered by a particular kind of question and shared by an entire discourse community. The existence of this community is the condition for the political existence of concepts, for concepts as political events.

Sometimes a question is all it takes to grant special status to the word that indicates x and that would become the concept name. Unlike a term that is ready to use, the haloed concept name bears an injunction to avoid using it, at least insofar as what has to be clarified about x has not yet been clarified. This injunction to avoid use is not yet conceptualization. The haloed name signals there is still work to be done, that one has to be responsible, wary of irresponsible uses, and suspect those who pretend to understand where there is yet no understanding. It might also signal that there is someone to direct the question to, an authority who can answer it, a subject whom one is supposed to know, and a community of discourse that cherishes the concept's name.

Yet it's not the subject who is supposed to know who sustains the concept, but instead those who wish to understand,[16] and the community itself could be imaginary, implicit in the questioning gesture, or actual but unaware of the new question that has emerged. The querying subject assumes the responsibility of awakening others to her question, and it is the question that should be shared with others and not necessarily the answers. No agreement regarding those is required. Consensus might bring conceptualization to an end and let concepts die. Hence a dictionary does not contain a list of concepts but at most a list of potential concepts and faded traces of past conceptualizations. The dictionary's definitional propositions do not necessarily exist in relation to a querying subject. There might very well be a way to silence and discipline them by stipulations designed to remove ambiguities, standardize measurements, titles, or forms of usage. But when I *consult* the dictionary, its definitions may become a starting point for a new series of questions for which I am responsible; the concept is now under my responsibility (in the context of a shared language and of a shared interest in both the questions and the answers). My questions guide the work of conceptualization, which has an irreducible performative dimension: presenting a question, sharing it with others, looking for an answer. A concept exists only as long as it maintains an element that has *not* been conceived yet, which is still unattained and is perhaps unattainable,[17] which is summoned by a question and which itself summons new questions.

This is a weaker, though perhaps more precise claim than that of Deleuze and Guattari, according to which a concept always appears in relation to a problem as its solution. The concept presupposes the problem's "plane of immanence"—the space within which the problem has sense as well as possible solutions—and it brings together those possible solutions.[18] For Deleuze and Guattari, a problem is independent of an inquiring subject. It has an objective sense, as does the concept that offers to solve it, and this sense is different in science and in philosophy. Hence Deleuze and Guattari's attempt to limit concepts to problems, parallels (or constitutes part of) their attempt to limit concepts to philosophy. For them, a philosophical "question" is but a name for a philosophical problem that cannot be translated into scientific (or theological) discourse.[19] I would like to reverse this: a problem is something that happens to a thinking subject. A problem is a kind of question that requires thinking, pausing, lingering, and wandering. To someone who thinks, this can also take place in science, in journalism, during a visit to the therapist or to a museum, over morning coffee or in the classroom. And every question that arises can mark a problem, turn into a problem, or hide a problem.

A conceptual statement requires a querying subject. This subject acts: it brackets the term indicating what is to be conceptualized. The use of that term is frozen, stalled, becomes restricted, contemplative, conditioned. The concept bears the unique signature of this querying subject, its style of thinking, and sometimes its style of writing. Descartes's signature is imprinted on the cogito, Kant's on the categorical imperative, Hegel's on Spirit, Nietzsche's on the will to power, and so on. Whoever asks questions about concepts that bear such signatures is destined to move in the space of questioning opened up by those conceptual personae—but there is nothing about the conceptual statement itself that requires this limitation. The discourses of the natural sciences or mathematics tend to refer to concepts by their inventors' names or by the names coined by those inventors, but at the same time they also make an effort to quickly naturalize new concepts and to release them from their inventors' signatures. The same goes for philosophies that adopt scientific rhetoric and modes of thinking, whereas in those philosophies that adopt the rhetoric and modes of thinking of literature or poetry, we find the opposite trend: limiting the conceptual statement to what the undersigned persona could have said. But one doesn't have to choose either one of these poles. For instance, the project of conceptualization developed in this book bears the mark of Foucault's signature: it regards the concept as a statement and places the question "what is a concept?" within Foucault's space of inquiry regarding the production and reproduction of (conceptual) statements. Yet we have no intention of limiting this project to Foucault's questions or ideas, to what Foucault would have said.

No author can be the master of a discourse and sovereignly define the concepts that operate within it. One can offer conceptual "territorializations" (defining lines of closure and demarcation) or disrupt existing territorializations, but one cannot determine these from the privileged viewpoint of a sovereign subject. Even the concept's "author," a subject of privileged authority whose signature marks a singular connection between concepts (e.g., between certainty, the cogito, and an omnipotent God in Descartes and concepts and sensual impressions in Kant), cannot singlehandedly fashion the myriad of other concepts they are related to (Descartes's God is as benevolent and omnipotent as he was to his predecessors; Kant's concept of sense-data is related to receptivity, which is negatively related to freedom, and so on). The author whose signature the concept bears cannot own the semantic field in which the concept operates alongside others, and shape it herself. Even when it comes to concepts that have a distinctive signature, and when the discussion is limited to their history, a conceptual clarification frees us from any pretense of sovereign grip, exposing numerous kinds of connections in the semantic field, which testify to the existence of numerous kinds of coexistence between statements, speakers, and concepts, no matter how much they are at odds with each other. In the community of conceptual discourse, the place of the sovereign remains empty, and no authorial position can fill this void.

The Environment of Statements

Internal Connections

Even the simplest concept requires its other from which it has to be distinguished and through which it is negated; hence, the two are now linked together in a unifying scheme. Concepts always appear in the plural, connected to each other, in need of each other, crossing, confronting, and complementing each other. Between them there are "bridges" of arguments, claims, patterns of opposition, tables of genera and species.[20] But even prior to this multiplicity there is the internal multiplicity of the concept. For a term to become a concept, the answer to the question "what is x?" has to connect at least two terms, each of which is potentially a conceptual statement. A concept is itself a semantic field since it connects within it a multiplicity of terms through a single scheme. This scheme unifies an ensemble of moments, each of which can in principle be a concept itself. For example, each of the four enunciative functions of the statement can be conceptualized in its own right; the concept "state" contains the necessary moments of territory, sovereignty, and so on, each of which is itself a concept; and no concept of infinity can exist without the moments of finitude, negativity, and the like. The collecting of conceptual moments into the concept's ensemble is different from the conjoining of the concept's appearances (in the plane of appearance), where the scheme is repeated in the encapsulated instances.

The multiple moments of the concept are synthetically connected. The conceptual statement is meant to produce and present this connected unity within the act of connecting. "The concept is the unity of multiplicity that develops from it as a law . . . the expression of a multiplicity . . . that is enfolded, like a law, within a unity of content," writes Samuel Hugo Bergmann in a somewhat archaic yet still relevant text.[21] Different theories of the concept look elsewhere for the *relation* (or the "law" that determines the relation) between multiplicity and unity, content and circumference, a single essence and its individuation into particular cases that embody it. Yet no theory of the concept I know of forgoes the bringing together of multiplicity and its connecting in a unifying scheme. When this relation is analytic, it creates an equivalence that renders invisible the specific discursive conditions that stabilize it, and also removes the special excess of the conceptual statement, thereby preventing the appearance of a halo of unattainability and inconceivability around the concept. When the synthetic relation is presented as such, the simple substitution of one term for another never suffices because the substituting term is a moment of the conceptual ensemble, for which the whole is always in excess to the sum of the parts.

This excess, this halo of inconceivability, is the reason the synthetic connection is also restless. Such a connection is a necessary and sufficient condition for the semantic dimension of the concept, for its existence as a distinctive unit in a semantic space. Unlike the alleged "analytic" equivalence created by the dictionary definition, or the transparency implicit in denoting, a concept is neither the result of nor the cause for the serial substitution of one term for another or for a denoted object but, rather, a connection between several terms (or moments), each of which is put into a conceptual statement or a series of such statements, whether real or possible. The terms related by the concept are supposed to be terms whose conceptualization is presupposed or deferred in favor of conceptualizing the concept in question. At any moment, though, a question might arise that would steer the discussion away from one concept and toward another, causing a new concept to appear. The act of conceptualization is supposed to place such distractions under control, to suspend answering new questions that require new conceptualizations, without forgetting that it is committed to going back and addressing everything it bracketed along the way. That means that the work is infinite—a "bad" Hegelian infinity—and that every closure is temporary and tentative. Closure is not the regulative ideal of the act of conceptualization but its mode of progress; its repetition is intertwined with the repetition of its failure, and this goes on as long as there are interested speakers who are not fed up with it yet.

The connection between the moments of the concept is presented in a series of "bridging statements" that make up the conceptual statement, although it is eventually meant to be conceived at once, like a picture perceived in the mind's eye, a presence that seems to freeze time, apparently independent of the time it takes to unfold it in the act of conceptualization.[22] This picture "resides" within the conceptual statement, "lingers over it" as a unifying scheme, even though the statement cannot state the picture without breaking it up into its elements, and without ending up in a to-and-fro motion between the moments and the whole. This motion takes place as a series of reiterations that insert a difference into the unifying scheme, dragging the feeling of presence back into the flow of time. The pictorial presence of the concept is neither a presupposition of the conceptual statement nor its achievement but, rather, its unattainable goal. Aiming for it is a constitutive rule of the language game of conceptualization. Its attainment—were such a thing possible, as Plato foresaw—would be the end of that game; it would drive the concept out of discourse and the querying subject out of the boundaries of language and into a state of pure—and empty—contemplation. Yet pure contemplation would be merely pure staring, and would spell not only the end of the conceptual statement but also the end of thinking.

In the plane of appearance, the concept brings together multiple appearances and frames them within a single scheme. Yet these don't necessarily have to appear together. I don't have to be able to capture in one glance all the recruited soldiers, weapons, vehicles, bases, and posts, even though each embodies for me, with its symbols and uniform, the concept "army." Things are different in the semantic plane, where, in order to understand what an army is, I have to be able to simultaneously connect terms such as state, violence, weapons, war, uniforms, ranks, command, obedience, and the like. I need both to understand each of these independently and to place them in their mutual relations until they form a comprehensive picture of the concept "army." Each of these terms, being a moment of the concept, is necessary for its clarification. But as mentioned, each can be further questioned for what it is, thereby further allowing the original movement of conceptualization to linger, sending our thought spinning in all directions: outward toward new concepts and inward because of the need to use hitherto unexplicated concepts as terms for the explication of the concept in question. The full understanding of a concept requires unfolding the conceptual statement that lies folded in the term. Hence the conceptual statement is doomed to be infinitely restless. In order to gain or simulate control over this spinning, authors of conceptual statements—the present author included—act as if the concept's moments are terms, or as if the question that brings their conceptual excess to the surface can be frozen and bracketed, at least until the conceptual picture becomes clearer. They act as if the interconnected terms are known, allowing the conceptual statement to perform an act of closure.

The connection between the moments of the concept is presented through propositions. This does not entail that a concept can be reduced to a series of propositions.[23] The concept appears through propositions yet is not composed only of them; its unifying scheme "inheres" or "subsists"" in those claims in the same way sense "inheres or subsists in the proposition," according to Deleuze,[24] or the way a square inheres in the space enclosed by four lines and angles. The concept cannot be grounded in propositions—be it a single proposition that ties together all other propositions or the sum of all propositions into which the terms themselves break up when they are treated as concepts—without leading to infinite regress. Propositions connect the different moments of the concept, and this connection cannot be stabilized because no moment (or aspect) exhausts the concept, nor can it be reduced or expressed in terms of another aspect. The concept requires all its moments, and even if there are only two or three of them, the concept has to throw our thinking around from one moment to the other (at an "infinite speed," according to Deleuze and Guattari), in order to contain both without being reducible to either one.[25]

Ever since Plato and Aristotle, philosophers have tended to regard the concept's moments as its subspecies, and the concept as a species of a broader genera. But even this simple scheme is unstable since the concept has to simultaneously contain both the subspecies to which it is individuated and the genera to which it belongs, and which it cannot contain but only illustrate or instantiate as one of its moments. In order to nonetheless stabilize this scheme, philosophers from Aristotle to Hegel were tempted to try and think of a general order in which all concepts participate to varying degrees of abstraction. This logic led Spinoza, Hegel, and others to argue that the complete concept of every essence is ultimately the way in which it is contained within the concept of a certain totality—God, Spirit, or the Infinite Substance. But a taxonomy of genera and species is insufficient (for a concept also appears according to the unique relations between them), and anyway, it is but one kind of individuation. The composition of different moments in a single concept isn't necessarily derived from a previous order, and isn't necessarily differentiated beyond the moments that contain it, even if each moment can itself appear as a concept.

External Connections

As mentioned, the conceptual scheme that brings together a multiplicity of terms is itself connected to multiple terms that are external to it through various kinds of propositions. Some of these propositions connect those terms to the concept as its possible yet unnecessary qualities or manifestations (a relaxing color, an enlightened regime, etc.); others do just the opposite: they negate the possibility of a certain term being a quality or manifestation of the concept (an immortal man, a kosher pig, a resident alien who has the right to vote). This map of interconnections, according to Foucault, is precisely what radically changes when the discursive regime changes: certain connections that previously seemed impossible now appear to be contingent, contingent connections are now necessary, and so on. But what makes the conceptual statement unique is not merely the existence of such a map of connections and the various bridges that are constructed between concepts and terms but, rather, its relentless movement of containing some of the terms it excludes, thereby distinguishing and defining the concept by way of negation. In order for this carving of the concept from its environment not to be arbitrary, the concept must negatively contain whatever delimits it: the Jew must contain the Gentile; the public, the private; the allegedly apolitical and value-neutral science—the political dimension that it excludes and the values with respect to which it is neutral; and so on. When this paradox is taken into account, the concept also appears to be an unfinished work of closure, an effort to bring a multiplicity under a unifying scheme.

Closure doesn't mean closing up. Closure determines the forms of connecting with other terms and concepts, and with the problems and statements they are related to. These problems, like concepts, appear in clusters. The effort to explicate concepts is also the effort to distinguish problems, to take control of the wild, irregular, and unpredictable aspects of the movement between them. But every distinction—between problems as well as concepts—is a kind of connection. The correct carving of the concept should bring about the conjoining of separate moments (which become inseparable once the concept is conceived),[26] and the appearance of unity out of and beyond multiplicity. But this is not enough. Correct carving also means correctly connecting. Both carving and connecting can't take place without repetitions, duplications, and copying from one context to another. The regulation of the relations within and among concepts is temporary, changes from time to time, and is completely dependent upon discourse as an arena of mutual interactions among many participants.

The interconnectedness of concepts means that conceptualization may have far-reaching consequences. "Key concepts" are those whose explication reverberates throughout a relatively wide discursive space. They are the primary interest of historians of concepts, who study them together with entire discursive fields. But one cannot tell in advance which are the key concepts. It requires tracing the effects of conceptual change as it takes place. Hence every effort to intervene in a discourse through the redefinition of key concepts is destined to fail. Key concepts belong to the past and may only be recognized retroactively; in the ongoing, lived present of discourse there are only more or less intensive efforts of conceptualization.

Key concepts and "analytical concepts" are the two ends of a continuum of discursive interconnectedness. A key concept brings along with it a whole network of statements, terms, propositions, and other concepts that spread out across a large space. An analytic concept is a term that can be explicated by exchanging it for another equivalent term without sensing a difference. The analytic substitution seeks to close the question; like the act of denoting, only inside the realm of language, it is the zero point of conceptualization. But sooner or later substitution fails, for a concept cannot be substituted without a remainder by another equivalent term, or by the thing that it denotes. A concept is a term whose semantic and referential excess is manifested by the unfinished work of explication that always fails to exhaust it. With key concepts this excess, this halo of unattainability surrounding the concept, is obvious and cannot be ignored. This halo indicates what is yet to be explicated or understood with respect to the semantic field, to the experienced world, to the subjects the concept is connected to, and to the conditions under which the conceptual statement can be repeated.

Displacement

The conceptual work displaces a term from the context of its use, its natural environment, where its discursive nature usually goes unnoticed, into another context in which its discursivity is thematized and explicated. In other words, the conceptual statement is simultaneously linked to two distinct sets of statements, the distance between which is not fixed and depends on the kind of discourse in which conceptualization takes place. (Herein lies the weakness of the dictionary in explicating concepts. To the extent that it disengages words from their natural environment, it provides them with a very poor alternative environment; to the extent that it leaves them in their natural environment, it provides them a poor explication, for instance, by demonstrating their known uses. The nonspecialized dictionary belongs to no living discourse).

In Plato's dialogues, Socrates acts as if he is after a philosophical dictionary, yet his specialty is the uprooting of terms from their daily usage environment. In the early aporetic dialogues he leaves the interlocutors confused, but in later dialogues Plato provides a new environment of statements, in which some of the terms at stake gradually appear as moments of a concept. This environment is what Plato refers to as "dialectics," and it specializes in making carvings and distinctions, and in reorganizing an entire network of terms, allowing for a convincing re-articulation of the concept in question. What the Socratic dialogue *shows* with respect to conceptual work—starting with stopping of the natural "flow" of language, lingering and wasting time, up to the special attention it gives to the carving of concepts—is far more important than what Plato *says* about concepts (that they are Ideas or pure Forms). The Socratic dialogue functions like a work of art, inviting later philosophers to interpret what it shows.

Nietzsche, and in a more significant way, Wittgenstein, together with numerous intellectual historians and anthropologists who were influenced by them, suggested the opposite movement: from the privileged plane in which conceptual clarification takes place back to "natural language," to those colloquial or professional uses of the term that are specific to this or that context of activity. But no matter how narrow or short lived is the context of use, the terms used may still be conceptualized. There is always a point in asking "what was x?" for the people of this or that culture, period, or language game, over and above the particular, concrete uses x had. There is a point in studying the chronicles of a concept by unfolding the transformations of its use. There is a point in grouping together certain uses as instances of the same usage pattern—for example, the pattern that keeps generating the illusion that the agent is a subject endowed with will, that the aim of punishment is to reform the sinner, or that language is a relation between words and things. Once such a pattern is identified or reconstructed, there emerges a more-or-less determined concept.

The conceptual statement, which copies sections of one environment and plants them in the other (in order to grant them new status and meaning), also bridges the two discursive environments and allows for the movement backward (in order to teach, instruct, correct, or embarrass those who use the term in its "natural" environment). But first the explication of a concept freezes the movement in one discursive environment and generates movement in another. This freezing is also an intervention, an invasion, a viral movement that may spread in every direction without taking over. It is a toiling, restless parasite that may settle anywhere and invite itself to any conversation. It traces a path like water eroding the soil, forming ravines, changing the landscape. Discursive environments differ in how immune they are to invading conceptual work, how much they resist when it appears or, alternatively, the degree to which they invite it, open up to it, and are willing to adjust to its results. In principle, though, there is no discursive environment that the conceptual work cannot join in order to expropriate terms from it and bring clarified concepts back to it.

Colloquial, everyday political discourse in our contemporary, developed societies is among the most resistant to conceptual invasion. The governmentalization of the state and of its politics, together with the "economization" of society and the political, require black-boxing and cannot afford to spend the time needed for the work of conceptualization. Hence the conceptualization of ready-made political terms—regardless of its content—is always already a form of resistance to the powers that be.

The Material Medium

If a conceptual statement is a relation and a movement between two relatively distinct discursive environments (whatever the distance between them), then its material medium, in which it appears and can be reproduced, must enable their bridging. As mentioned, this bridging means freezing movement in one semantic space in favor of movement in another. The request to define, explicate, or reconstruct a sense lingers and defers the use of that term. This lingering and deferring of a linguistic flow in a discursive environment is a primary condition for the conceptual statement. Time, or rather a sense of "having time to spend"—as opposed to some concrete space of speech or writing—is the primary, rather rare, and most important material condition for the occurrence of the conceptual statement.

The interruption to the discursive flow may be momentary. Such interruptions are typical of misunderstandings in daily conversations and point to the need for precision in technical, bureaucratic, juridical, and various scientific discourses. They are parasitic to people's main interest in the exchange, to the demand for efficiency that they invest in it. But conceptual lingering can be discourse's very interest, one common to many speakers. If there is a sense in which it can be argued that concepts only appear in philosophical discourse, it is because only in that discourse is this deferral institutionalized; only in that discourse is the time wasted on postponement and lingering precisely time invested in the very things that are at stake; only there does the enjoyment of the language game derive from what comes about when one defers, and excellence is measured in terms of the virtuosity involved in that deferring. Discourses differ in how tolerant they are to this conceptual lingering: in the way they seek to limit its duration, continuity, frequency, and range, granting it a shelter or withholding their patronage from it. Rather than rely on the idea of a tight relation between conceptual work and philosophy, in order to exclude what is not philosophical enough, we should use this relation to characterize the continuum between an endless deferral and a ready-made answer that never defers.

The activity of conceptualization defers the use of the concept, its naturalization and routinization into language. Therefore every pragmatic discourse (in the juridical, economic, scientific, or political field) tends to develop an allergy to it. This deferral isn't just a waste of time and inefficient but also has a potential for real trouble because of the impact conceptualization may have on an entire discursive field, which may affect the political order itself.

However, the fundamental antinomy between conceptual work and political discourse rests on a common ground. Both the king and the philosopher have interest in definitions. The ruling power wants to define (and delimit[27]) territory and population, goals and means, a structure of hierarchical authority, and occasional zones of liberty within it. The philosophizer wants to define as part of the attempt to understand what it is for something to be what it is. The explicating definition, unlike the governmental definition versus the dictionary definition, is not a means but an end. It does not have a closed horizon, although its permanent aspiration is to close the concept and to correctly distinguish it from others. At any moment it might come into conflict with the effort of the ruling power to impose closure. The former would give way to the latter only when the community of conceptual discourse is ready to sign up for one of the ruling power's projects. If, as Deleuze argues, all philosophers have hitherto been philosophers of the state, it is not because they engaged in conceptual work but because and insofar as they ceased to do so. This does not mean that they have stopped playing philosophical language games; philosophy is exercised through many language games other than the conceptual one, and these may resonate well with the ruling power's interests and goals. But the ruling power can only use these language games by uprooting them from the space in which conceptual thinking moves, or by linking them to an already frozen conceptual movement, that is, by forcing a conceptual closure.

The reproduction of the conceptual statement requires a space in which there would be no interference with conceptual movement. The statement's material is precisely the condition that makes this movement possible. Plato's deep fear of writing has to do with its being seen as a medium that threatens to ossify the movement of thought, embalming it in written signs. There is no need to agree with the Platonic demonization of writing (presented to us via spectacular writing, of course) in order to understand this worry; there is no need to share its admiration for the living voice and to accept its metaphysics of presence in order to confirm the complete priority of the *performative event* over the *desired accomplishment* that is the source of this preference for speech over writing.

What, then, is the performative event of the conceptual statement? It is the opening and response to the "what is x?" question; it is the *ex*-position and an *ex*-plication of what is conceptualized, articulating the moments that make up the concept, and recollecting and recomposing them within a single, unifying scheme. The conceptual statement *shows* the synthetic composition of its individuating moments, presenting, at the surface level of the discourse, the multiplicity of these moments in its coming together. This statement also signifies the space of appearance of the objects that embody or might embody the concept, points to its relation to a question, and through it to the subject who is allowed to ask and to answer. Above all, the conceptual statement presents itself, in public, as an explication of a concept; it is a public exposition of the concept's discursive being and of the fact that it is a discursive entity.

What the discursive statement shows in the presentation of the concept isn't necessarily what it says. What the conceptual statement says usually has to do with unfolding its constitutive moments and describing their interconnections, expressing a "multiplicity . . . that is enfolded, like a law, within a unity of content."[28] In this sense it is like a picture that shows without saying what it shows, and there is always something left to say about what it shows. No narrative, let alone any caption, can exhaust the visible, which is essentially irreducibility to the sayable. The *obligation* to say what has not been said is not self-evident. In a work of art, it derives from the sanctification of the image in a museal display room, a sanctification that adds a halo of excess to the visible, which words are never able to exhaust, and which leads to an infinite task of interpretation, an obligation to bring this excess into language. A similar difference lies between what the conceptual statement shows—in the event of its performance—and what it says. But in this case there is no obligation to bring the excess of the shown into language. In this case there is no institution that sanctifies the excess of the visible, and yet the movement of conceptual thinking can always position itself within this difference, in order to go on asking "what is x?" and to ask it now with respect to the discursive conditions that made the conceptual statement possible in the first place. This question is essential because the discursive nature of the conceptual statement both enables the concept to appear as a unifying scheme and sets its arbitrary limits.

Attention to the discursive condition does not come at the expense of the semantic content, as suggested by the dictionary, for example; rather, it includes and suspends it at the same time. A dictionary definition is a public presentation of a term that directs attention to its semantic content. As a textual institution, the dictionary directs the reader to the meaning of a word insofar as it can be isolated from its context (thereby pushing other properties of the word to the background, for example, its sound, its oral appearance). The explication of a concept is the detachment of a term from its nonproblematic usage environment, displaying it in public in order to direct the theoretical gaze to its *discursive* appearance, insofar as it can be isolated from specific contexts of use. But the performance in which a concept's discursive appearance is displayed has its own conditions.

What defines an object or image as a work of art, namely, a visible object that demands infinite interpretation, is not some essential quality of the object but its *exhibition*—its public display—within an institution that sanctifies images and objects as works of art. This exhibition pulls the image or object out of its natural environment, detaching it from whatever use it may have had. Thanks to the artistic context of the viewing provided by the museal institution (by its very definition), together with the habitus of the trained spectator, the exhibition directs our gaze and attention to the *aesthetic* appearance of the object or image, namely, to the way in which it is present to our senses and the way it acts upon them and, through them, upon our emotions and cognition.

In the same vein we can add that the courtroom, or the Royal Society, which adopted courtlike discursive patterns, has created distinguished places for the public display of proofs regarding factual claims (the courtroom) or causal ones (the scientific experiment). What we have here is the detachment of things and objects, claims and bits of narrative from their natural environment (which might be nature itself or the cultural environment in which they usually appear), rewoven into the structure of an argument in order to generate a proof and display it in public. Unlike the museal exhibition, but similar to that of the dictionary, the juridical or scientific exhibition isn't meant to present its case as an object about which one can talk forever without exhausting its meaning; on the contrary, it is meant to put an end to endless debate, to establish the facts of the matter and to draw the necessary conclusions.

In various philosophical contexts, conceptual statements strive—or seem to strive—to put an end to debates, suggesting standards for how to decide on the matter at hand and to complete the work of conceptualization—and yet they have never succeeded in doing so. The exhibited event always exceeds what is said in it, and there is no effective sanction on someone who keeps asking and interpreting. Unlike aesthetic (museum), semantic (dictionary), factual (courtroom), or causal (scientific experiment) exhibitions, conceptual exhibitions don't have an institution of their own. Certainly the academic department of philosophy cannot and does not serve as an institution of this kind. Conceptual work is just one of its many tasks and not necessarily the most essential one. At the same time, different types of discourse provide different conditions for conceptual work, and they also differ in the degree of allergy they demonstrate when that work stretches for too long, disrupting existing discursive patterns and suggesting others instead. One may distinguish here between three types of discourse. In the more pragmatic discourses, such as administrative or juridical ones, discursive activity presupposes and relies upon extensive definitional activity, which aims at fixing the meaning of terms and easing their uninterrupted use. Second, in the more contemplative discourses, the work of conceptualization frequently interrupts discursive activity. Finally, in philosophy and in the more philosophically prone fields of the various sciences, conceptual work is an end and not only a means; here the movement that takes place within a concept (within its different moments), or between concepts, is the movement of thought itself.

Philosophy and these "philosophically prone" fields tend to welcome conceptual work and be patient with the time it takes. But this patience and tolerance is not enough to compensate for the lack of an institution whose aim is to provide the conceptual exhibition with the kind of conditions the museum provides for aesthetic exhibition, the courtroom for the factual, and the dictionary for the semantic. Plato tried to establish his academy for that purpose, yet it was quickly flooded with other questions and new practices of inquiry. Even before the demand that it should promote faith or prove beneficial to society, the academy failed to provide conceptual inquiry with taken-for-granted institutional conditions that would help direct the attention of viewers, listeners, or readers to the discursive dimension of the concept, to its being a unique statement. The Socratic moment has never been institutionalized. What, then, is required in order to sustain it? All that it would take is the patience of the addressees—in fact, a single addressee, willing to share the question and not stop asking, would be enough—and the existence of a discursive community whose speakers are ready to waste the time required in order to think. These conditions can appear anywhere, at any time, in almost any context, but by the same token also disappear with the least display of intolerance on the part of the powers that be, with every demand for a different kind of attention—practical, aesthetic, religious. Lacking an institution, everything depends on the interlocutors; they, and only they, can serve as the guardians of the concept.

NOTES

I wish to thank Ariella Azoulay, Dikla Bytner, Roy Wagner, Lin Chalozin-Dovrat, Yoav Kenny, and Itay Snir for their comments on previous versions of this text.

1. Gilles Deleuze and Felix Guattari, *What Is Philosophy?* (New York: Columbia University Press), 11.

2. Stephen Laurence and Eric Margolis, eds., "Concepts and Cognitive Science," in *Concepts: Core Readings*, 3–81 (Cambridge: MIT Press, 1999).

3. This typology follows ibid. For a similar typology, see the entry "concepts" in the online *Stanford Encyclopedia of Philosophy*, http://plato.stanford.edu/entries/concepts.

4. The Greek expression became the Latin *essentia*, and Aristotle's definition of "definition" may be read accordingly as "the stating of essence."

5. S. H. Bergmann, *Introduction to Logic: The Theoretical Science of Order* [Hebrew](Jerusalem: Mossad Bialik, 1964), 63.

6. In Hebrew, the expression "to have no idea (about something)" is literally "to have no *concept*."

7. Philosophers tend to regard such "placeholders" as concepts also. But then one should distinguish between two types of concepts: empty placeholders, whose function neutralizes or blurs the unattainable excess of the concept, and terms that the attempt to clarify or define manifests their excess. Only the latter will interest us here.

8. Michel Foucault, *The Archaeology of Knowledge* (New York: Pantheon Books, 1972).

9. Ibid., part 3, ch. 2–3.

10. The Jewish midrash would be an example of a discourse that doesn't require concepts at all. Military discourse, and others that take place under conditions of strict obedience, do not allow for the creation of concepts because they do not allow the freedom and time for the questions that summon them.

11. Foucault, *Archaeology of Knowledge*, 56–63.

12. Deleuze and Guattari, *What Is Philosophy?*, 22.

13. Ibid., 8–9, 33–34, 150.

14. Deleuze and Guattari's idea of the concept relies heavily on Deleuze's reading of Foucault. Gilles Deleuze, *Foucault* (Minneapolis: University of Minnesota Press, 1988).

15. Or "components," to use Deleuze and Guattari's terminology in *What Is Philosophy?*

16. When the question is addressed by a teacher to a student or an examiner to the person being examined, the addressee is simultaneously supposed not to know—so that the term would appear as a concept—and to know—in order to answer correctly. The student who truly understands is not the one who knows how to give the answer that is expected of him, but the one who knows how to relate the answer (the explanation) to the question and why it must be kept open. The role of the teacher is to teach how to keep the questions open.

17. In Hebrew, "concept" (*mussag*) is a passive adjective form of the verb "to attain" (*le-hassig*).

18. Deleuze and Guattari, *What Is Philosophy?*, 42, 79–80.

19. Ibid., 79

20. "Bridges from one concept to another" is an image from ibid., 19, 23.

21. Bergmann, *Introduction to Logic*, 72.

22. "The concept is defined by the inseparability of a finite number of heterogeneous components traversed by a point of survey at infinite speed . . . the concept is . . . thought operating at infinite (although greater or lesser) speed" (Deleuze and Guattari, *What Is Philosophy?*, 21).

23. I am following here Foucault's (*Archaeology of Knowledge*, 80–81) distinction between a statement and a proposition.

24. Gilles Deleuze, *The Logic of Sense* (New York: Columbia University Press, 1990), 31. This, however, does not mean that science contains no concepts, as Deleuze and Guattari argue (*What Is Philosophy?*, 33–34).

25. Deleuze and Guattari, *What Is Philosophy?*, 21–22.

26. Ibid., 21.

27. In Greek, Latin, Hebrew, Arabic, and other languages, to define is first of all the act of fencing, setting limits.

28. Bergmann, *Introduction to Logic*, 72.

Εί δή τις έξ'αρχής τά πράγματα φυόμενα βλέψειν, ώσπερ έν τοίς άλλοις καί έν τούτοις κάλλιστ' άν 'ουτω θεωρήσειεν.

—Aristotle, *Politics*, 1252a.

5

CONSTITUENT POWER

Andreas Kalyvas

Constituent power is the truth of modern democracy for two main reasons, a historical and an analytical one. First, the birth of the modern doctrine of popular sovereignty coincides with the conceptual advent of constituent power. They are co-original and coeval.[1] The political supremacy of the multitude over princes, kings, emperors, and popes was initially formulated in terms of the originary power of a community to determine the political forms of its collective existence. It is during the volatile period between the late Middle Ages and early modernity that the multitude was identified as the sovereign constituent subject and, respectively, democracy was reimagined as the politics of popular foundings. From a historical point of view, constituent power and modern democracy are intrinsically associated from their beginnings in the idiom of popular sovereignty. Second, there is a profound systematic and analytical analogy between constituent power and democracy insofar as they both describe collective acts of self-legislation and public events of self-alteration. From this elective affinity, democratic constituent politics evokes the principle of liberty as political autonomy, whereby the members of a collectivity constitute the political forms of authority in order to organize and institutionalize their common free life.[2] The addressees of the law become its authors. Hence, formulating popular sovereignty as constituent power is to affirm the basic democratic value of self-government.

This mutual historical and analytical articulation of constituent power and democracy must be emphasized. Sovereignty, as the power to constitute, is misrecognized by contemporary democratic discourses, and for this reason lacks a place in our political vocabulary. Often it is regarded as elusive and indeterminate, barely a concept, bordering on the ideological; either a pure fact or a metaphysical fiction, and thus of minor theoretical interest and political significance.[3] "The capital problem in public law," according to Carré de Malberg, it is since then treated as a legal anomaly, a disturbing irregularity, and a political threat.[4]

In fact, over the long history of modern political thought in the Western world, sovereignty as constituent power was systematically overshadowed by the competing doctrine of sovereignty as "the highest power of command," proudly pronounced in 1576 by Jean Bodin in his celebrated treatise.[5] His new absolutist and unitary definition spread quickly across various political and juridical discourses, appearing in diverse historical contexts and the distinct theoretical systems of several canonical thinkers. Thomas Hobbes, for example, concurred that "Sovereign Power" is "this Right to give Commands," a view also propagated by Samuel Pufendorf and Emer de Vattel, among others, and inherited by Jeremy Bentham, John Austin, and Max Weber. This view was even adopted by Baruch Spinoza, who—while discussing absolute democracy—formulated the question of sovereignty in light of whoever "has the sovereign right of imposing any commands he pleases."[6]

This paradigm of sovereignty, which transverses both natural jurisprudence and legal positivism (albeit in diverse ways) identifies the sovereign as the one who commands without being subject to the commands of another, that is, to a superior.[7] Bodin's sovereign is an "uncommanded commander." The essential political relationship is vertical, between "him who commands" and "him who owns obedience," that is, between sovereigns and subjects, rulers and ruled.[8] This power to command is absolute, inalienable, and perpetual, grounded in divine right. It remains subordinated to natural and divine law; it is hierarchical, unitary, and personified; and it is often identified with executive prerogatives. Internally, it cannot be divided or shared; externally, it should not be surpassed or downgraded.

Bodin's theory of sovereignty became paradigmatic for political modernity, an essential property of the modern understanding of the state, its authority, and its unity.[9] In proposing a theory of state sovereignty in the closing of the sixteenth century, he set the foundation for what came to be the exemplary theory of sovereign power in Western political and legal thought. Bodin's sovereign discourse was also consequential for the formation of international law and the European interstate system: the institution of the state is sovereign over its own territory and has absolute jurisdiction over its subjects. The codification of the principle of nonintervention by one state in the affairs of another—brought about by the Peace of Westphalia (1648)—introduced the principle of mutual recognition among sovereign states, thus consecrating the power of command as the organizing norm of international law and politics. Bodin's definition is the first authoritative statement of the modern theory of state sovereignty where a delineated political community possesses supreme political authority—a determinate, absolute, and supreme power of command, which is not itself subject in any way to the command of another.[10]

When it comes to account for the advent of modern democracy, the paradigm of command tends to explain it in terms of a transfer of sovereignty from the king to the people, from the One to the Many.[11] The modern inauguration of democracy qua popular sovereignty amounts to a passage of command from one holder to another, whereby personal rule is transformed into collective rule. In this passage, democratic sovereignty inverts the monarchical paradigm: the people appropriate the king's power, turning the sources of political authority upside-down. Democracy is portrayed as postmonarchical, insofar as the abolition of kingship does not necessarily eliminate the absolutist discourse of sovereignty as command but replaces one supreme commander with another. Sovereignty changes hands but essentially it remains the same. In this manner, the discourse of command not only treats constitutional norms as external constraints, but it also tends to reduce modern democracy to the state form. The doctrine of the nation-state is also a story about the gradual democratization of the absolutism of monarchical sovereignty.

Bodin's theory of sovereignty successfully dominated modern political theory and practice, shaping the prevailing understandings of democracy. Its commitment to the primacy of coercive command suggests a statist, static conception of sovereignty that consists of a repressive force, emanating from the top, hierarchical and unitary, supported by a centralized administration, and in need of external checks and balances. Michel Foucault described this juridical model of sovereignty as "anti-energy . . . a power that only has the force of the negative on its side, a power to say no; in no condition to produce, capable only of posting limits."[12]

The conceptual history of constituent power speaks directly against this grand narrative of command and subjection. It illuminates important but neglected dimensions of the democratic experience and discloses another understanding of sovereignty. Negatively put, the modern advent of democracy cannot and should not be treated as a mere transfer of sovereignty from the king to the people, immanently unfolding within the uninterrupted continuity of the statist paradigm of supreme command. In positive terms, democracy *qua* constituent power discloses a different idea of sovereignty, not only historically prior to but also analytically distinct from the regal paradigm, opposed and antagonistic to it: the power of the people to constitute. Political modernity can thus be viewed as consisting of two rival forms of sovereign power and two competing visions of politics: the democratic and the monarchical, the constitutional and the absolutist, the federalist and the statist, the power of the Many to constitute versus the power of the One to command.

In what follows, I seek to recover this alternative theory of sovereignty as constituent power that significantly departs from the canonical paradigm of command in order to investigate its democratic implications. In the first section I trace the beginnings of the concept, from the etymological meanings of the Latin verb "to constitute" to its initial medieval articulation that was set against the regal model. The second and third sections revisit formative episodes in the conceptual history of constituent power and consider its diverse but overlapping theoretical and political trajectories as they coalesced around the political ideas of disobedience, resistance, and revolution. The last part attempts to reconstruct the discursive rules and immanent principles that organize the intelligibility of the concept over time and consider the challenges they pose to inherited (mis)understandings of democracy.

BEGINNINGS

The verb "to constitute" comes from the Latin word *constitūere*, which is a combination of the prefix *con-* and the verb *statūere*. The prefix *con-* has several grammatical meanings, the most important of which is "with" or "together." The verb *statūere* derives from *stătūo*, which means "to cause to stand," "to set up," "to construct," "to place," "to erect," "to establish," "to create."[13] The word *constitūere*, therefore, literally denotes the act of founding together, creating jointly, or coestablishing.

In ancient Rome, the verb *constitūere* was used to designate an agreement with another on something in the economic vocabulary of exchange relations, an accord among a plurality of individuals. Furthermore, in Roman public law, it named a very specific kind of legislative practice that was regarded as superior to ordinary legislation, that is, extraordinary acts of establishing or altering the fundamental laws and institutions of the republic.[14] For instance, in the juridical form of *rei publicae constituendae*, the verb meant the power to initiate radical legal changes.[15] The office of the dictator, the decemvirs, the triumvirates, and other regular and special commissions were treated as institutions of constituent power. However, because a higher constitutional authority authorized their power as a special commission, these magistracies were not considered sovereign. Likewise, the title of *cōnstitūtor* signified he who establishes, the one who orders, the founder who exercises the power and authority to reform and transform.[16] After the collapse of the republic, the power to constitute was taken by the Roman emperor and came to describe his judicial decisions and higher executive degrees and enactments (*constitutio*).[17]

From these first etymological meanings and its various economic, political, and legal applications, certain preliminary conclusions follow. The first pertains to the term's provenance, which emerges prior to and outside of the theology of the Judeo-Christian imaginary. Deeply embedded in Rome's political and juridical world, formalized in various legal codes and official magistracies, enmeshed in the social wars among patricians and plebeians, and closely linked with the republic's fate, *constitutio* and its uses had strong worldly connotations and were attached to civic values and close to the productive arts. In addition, the word suggests the inescapable semantic presuppositions of a collective practice. It is the practice of a plurality of actors who publicly engage with one another, associating and acting in concert to mutually erect and found something jointly. Finally, the term is historically associated with critical transformative episodes in the history of the Roman republic. Thus, "to constitute" also designates extraordinary acts of founding and refounding, discontinuous events that transformed the constitution of the city by altering the norms, rules, and institutions that determined the space of normal politics.

During the early Middle Ages, the political use of the term "to constitute" nearly disappeared; it lost its ancient legal and political significance and became purely descriptive—in the literary sense, reduced to the faculty of making or constructing. It was also invoked by various medical discourses to describe the anatomical ordering of a living being, its physical body and material constitution.[18] But then it reappears in late medieval political vocabulary, invested with a new meaning: the act of appointment. From the tenth century onward, "to constitute" means to appoint an officer, to invest a person with specific powers, to attribute concrete and particular public functions to an individual, to elect someone into office; in short, to authorize. It is within this conceptual shell of the late medieval use that the concept of constituent power was firstly incubated and formed. Two important innovations, however, were necessary to make this new conceptual formation possible, and both were carried out by Marsilius of

Padua in the early fourteenth century. His contribution laid the foundation for a novel conception of sovereignty and opened the way for the modern reinvention of democracy.[19]

Marsilius's first innovation pertains to the power of appointment and election. His renowned and controversial text, *Defensor pacis*, was completed in 1324, during the turbulent conflict between Louis IV, the Holy Roman Emperor, and Pope John XXII. He meant it as a concrete political intervention in a moment of severe crisis and also as a justification of his unequivocal decision to side with the emperor against the pope and thus to defend secular against spiritual authority.[20] The dispute between the two over the ultimate locus of sovereignty caused a temporary breakdown of legitimacy, creating a fissure, which allowed popular sovereignty eventually to come into being. Marsilius claimed that none of the two could be sovereign since they both lacked the ultimate power to appoint either oneself or the other. Neither the emperor nor the pope could therefore settle this quarrel. In this extreme situation, Marsilius argued, there is always a final authority that decides the matter: it is the multitude, he asserted, that possesses the right to appoint its secular and spiritual rulers, that is, to authorize them to rule. In the space separating the two instituted sovereigns, in the void opened up by their struggle for supremacy—between the secular and the spiritual—a new political subject made its appearance: the multitude with its supreme right to appoint its emperors and popes.

Marsilius attributed the power of appointment to the multitude, rather than to constituted authorities, magistracies, or persons. He articulated this power in terms of a collective right that empowers the ruled to appoint the heads to which they voluntarily submit. The ruled appoint their rulers, the subjects elect their leaders, and the multitude establishes its kings. In addition to the elements of consent and contract that his arguments invoked, Marsilius's intervention had far-reaching consequences, as it directly questioned the normative foundations of the medieval political edifice. Although earlier jurists, canonists, glossators, and theologians had already touched upon this topic, especially since the crisis caused by the Investiture Controversy, Marsilius was the first to explicitly proclaim and systematically present the core principles of a new theory of (popular) sovereignty: "The efficient power to ***establish*** or elect the ruler belongs to the legislator or the whole body of the citizens. . . . And to the legislator similarly belongs the power to make any correction of the ruler and even to depose him, if this is expedient for the common benefit. For this is one of the more important matters in the polity; and such matters pertain to the entire multitude of the citizens."[21]

Marsilius's second novelty marks another contribution. He recognized the multitude not only as the real and true subject with the supreme authority to appoint their rulers; he also extended its scope to include the formation of government, the establishment of its fundamental laws, and the creation of public offices. For, he asserted, "it pertains to the legislator [i.e., the multitude] to correct governments or to *change* them completely, just as to *establish* them." Marsilius, in fact, transforms the act of appointment to an act of founding, thus introducing the idea of sovereignty in terms of a productive multitude, "a universal active causality" that "forms," "establishes," and "differentiates" the parts of the state.[22] He defined this sovereign power, which resides in "the whole body of citizens or of its weightier part," as an originary and productive "power to generate" (*generare formam*) new legal forms and political institutions: "Since, therefore, it pertains to the whole body of the citizens to *generate* the form, that is, the law, according to which all civil acts must be regulated, it will be seen that it pertains to the same whole body to *determine* this form's matter, that is, the ruler, whose function is to order, according to this form, the civil acts of men. . . . For to whomever pertains to *generate* some form, it also pertains to *determine* the subject of that form."[23]

This singular formulation of the sovereign power of the multitude as form-giving suggests an extrainstitutional force that institutes political authority, determines the form of government, and establishes a just constituted order. Marsilius's theory of popular sovereignty, in fact, departs from the theological ideology of the Middle Ages. Instead of relying on the logic of transcendence and the model of a demiurgic divine figure as an external ordering power, he turned to ancient materialist traditions with a strong biological orientation.[24] Creatively blending Aristotle's *On Animals* (*De partibus animalium*) and Galen's treatise *On the Formation of the Foetus* (*De formatione foetus*), Marsilius described the power to constitute in terms of physical natality and compared the creative sovereign act to that of animal birth. The political constitution of a community is similar, "in an analogous manner," to the organic constitution of the animal. The sovereign action, he argued, "in appropriately *establishing* the state and its parts was proportionate, therefore, to the action of nature in perfectly *forming* the animal." Marsilius's incipient theory of the constituent power of the multitude is informed by a physico-biological materialism and grounded on a naturalistic reasoning, devoid of any transcendentalism, challenging the theological and mystical Pauline metaphor of the sacred body politic. In a bold gesture, he described the institution of political community in terms of animal anatomy and physical desire, thus initiating the most ambitious desacralization and detheologization of the political in the context of medieval philosophy.[25] The political body, through the animal metaphor, expresses its immanence to the material and mortal world of living beings and their relationships. With Marsilius, the modern advent of democracy results from a profane theory of politics and is carried out by means of a materialist method.

With these two major innovations, Marsilius introduced the general idea of constituent power as popular sovereignty. It is important, therefore, to clarify these novel elements that remain present in the subsequent political trajectories of the concept.

Marsilius's originality rests first of all on the appropriation of the ancient figure of the legislator, in order to rework it in the direction, not of a mythical lawgiver and founder of cities, but of an actual community, "the multitude of the needy," the "assembled multitude." The "primary legislator" is a "primary authority," and the multitude is always the legislator because it has the supreme power to establish and abolish its governments, to appoint and depose its rulers. Correspondingly, the laws derive their authority from the legislator, that is, from the multitude. With this synthesis he brings together the legislator, the sovereign, and the multitude in the new form of a collective power of the many to constitute their political world. The many, the poor, and the *vulgus* are names interchangeably used to describe the sovereign as a collective founder who can decide the political structure of its common existence, either in a primary assembly of all through majority rule or by its elected representatives.[26]

Moreover, by expanding the faculty to constitute to include the power to form and establish governments, Marsilius suggested a crucial distinction, differentiating between two separate acts: the act of making laws and the act that institutes a government. The latter designates a founding moment, temporarily and ontologically prior to any government. It is the source of authority, the legitimacy of ordinary laws, and the final judge. The distinction between the legislator and the government points to a differentiated binary concept of power divided between the *universitas civium* of the multitude and the *pars principans* of the government. It is in this way that Marsilius anticipates the key distinction between a constituting community and the constituted commonwealth, which will become central in later doctrines of modern constitutionalism as *pouvoir constituant/pouvoir constituée*.

Marsilius, furthermore, asserted the superiority of those who participate in the establishment of a government over those who rule, legislate, and command within a given institutional framework.[27] The act of establishing/forming is superior to the act of commanding. One important reason is that the common life of the multitude does not emanate from or depend on the rulers or the government. It is a shared life that proceeds immanently and self-sufficiently from the many, that is, autonomously from the instituted forms of authority. There is a dimension of externality of the multitude in relation to its institutions as it is recognized as a political subject that can exist outside positive law. While the many can exist apart from the state, the state cannot live apart from them. Additionally, ruling depends on and is inferior to constituting because, as Marsilius states (by deploying Aristotelian categories of causality), the former is subordinate to the latter in the same way that a cause is always prior and superior to the effects it generates. Moreover, the supremacy of the many over the few is supported by the logic that "every whole . . . is greater in mass and in virtue than any part of it taken separately." Finally, he also echoes Aristotle when he claims that the multitude is also superior in terms of its wisdom, better than any part taken separately.[28] In this elaborate defense of the principle of popular sovereignty, the many are treated as supreme because they are antecedent to all constituted authorities, self-sufficient, capable of virtue and wisdom, and for this reason, the authors of their political forms. Marsilius was the first author to define popular sovereignty in terms of the power of the multitude to constitute.

There is one last word to say on the alleged theological provenance of constituent power, powerfully captured by Carl Schmitt's influential claim that it is merely another secularized theological concept of modern state theory.[29] Marsilius's incipient invention of democratic sovereignty challenges this politico-theological narrative and breaks away from metaphysical and transcendent medieval notions of power and politics. His intervention situates the beginnings of modern democracy apart from the religious monotheistic imaginary of Judeo-Christianity. His theory of popular sovereignty operates strictly on the plane of immanence. It is an affirmation of the powers of this world that dispenses with external causation. He understood constituent politics as "those methods of establishing governments which are affected by the human will." The existence of government is not divinely ordained, nor does it rest on ideas of sin and biblical transgression; rather, it emanates materially from the actual social activity of the multitude that desires a free, peaceful, and sufficient life.[30]

ACTS OF RESISTANCE

Two and a half centuries after Marsilius's "discovery" of the constituent power, in the aftermath of the 1572 St. Bartholomew's Day massacre—another time of intense conflict—several French Huguenot writers, known as the Monarchomachs ("those who fight kings"), renewed this proto-democratic discourse of popular sovereignty in order to defend their radical doctrine of tyrannicide.[31] By radicalizing aspects of Marsilius's philosophy, they brought together active resistance and constituent power to advance their doctrines of sovereignty, and eventually laid the foundations for later theories of popular rebellion, revolt, insurrection, and revolution.[32] With the Monarchomachs the constituent power became revolutionary. Active, even violent resistance is treated as a legitimate extralegal force of political change, rightfully exercised by the people or their representatives in exceptional cases of necessity and self-defense. Relying on Marsilius's suggestion that the multitude could depose unjust rulers and suspend the law in times of crisis, the Monarchomachs went further in exploring the disobedient and seditious effects of constituent politics and rethinking the conflictual and revolutionary nature of popular sovereignty.

In fact, their rethinking anticipated the right of democratic revolution. The right of a people to disobey, resist, depose, or kill their (tyrannical) rulers derives from their sovereign power to determine the political forms of their common life. Resistance against tyrannical rule is a manifestation of constituent politics and an affirmation of popular sovereignty. The Monarchomachs, in fact, put forward a new justification, based on the democratic logic that "those who *constitute* one Form, may *abrogate* it," that is, on the principle of popular sovereignty, according to which the people as constituent power are prior and superior to the forms they constitute, including kings.[33] Or, as George Lawson emphatically asserted, "those who have the power to constitute, have also the power to dissolve, when they decide that there is a just and necessary cause."[34] This collective right that trumps monarchical legality rests on the power of the many to constitute. It offers normative and political validity to the exceptional recourse to legitimate resistance on the part of the people. For the Monarchomachs, the sovereign people decide on the extreme situation of tyrannicide. In this way, they can rightly be credited for inventing the first modern democratic theory of resistance.

The emphasis on the revolutionary excess of constituent power carries a double meaning. On the one hand, it reveals the conditional and authorized existence of all constituted powers. It therefore puts limits on the subjects' duty of obedience, which is a conditional obligation that depends on the ruler's performance. Political forms are denaturalized to the extent that they are regarded as human historical creations, the result of collective action, reversible and revocable, to be amended, transformed, and/or replaced. On the other hand, it argues for an extraconstitutional check on the constituted authorities, a just device for maintaining the reign of law and limiting the dangers of arbitrariness and tyranny. Thus, rulers are subject to limitations and constraints established by the many in their constituent capacity. The first traces of modern constitutionalism are already visible in this seditious attempt to determine the limits of institutionalized power and to set up political safeguards against the transgressions of the constituted order. Here, the notion of a limited government ruled by law appears internal to the democratic doctrine of active resistance, that is, intrinsic to the power to constitute.[35]

In 1573, François Hotman asserted "that the People reserved to themselves all the power not only of *creating*, but also of *abdicating* their Kings."[36] One year later, the French protestant Théodore de Bèze proclaimed the first principle of his new doctrine of legitimate (violent) resistance: "they who have the power to *create* a king, have the power to *depose* him," as they also have "the power to *judge* him." This supreme power to judge and overthrow rulers belongs solely to the people because "peoples do not come from the rulers . . . and that peoples accordingly, are not created for their rulers, but rulers rather for their peoples." Politically speaking, the people are above the monarch. The right to disobey and resist that the many possess results from the primacy of the constituent subject over the constituted order. Because the people constitute their rulers, they have the right to resist and depose them. It is the power of constituting that confers to the people the sovereign right to resist.[37] His principle is unequivocal: those who constitute have the right to disobey.

Five years later, in the *Vindiciae contra tyrannos*, Junius Brutus the Celt (Philippe de Mornay) appealed to the same principle by further accentuating the elements of self-determination and externality in popular sovereignty.[38] He succinctly asserted, following Marsilius and Bèze, that "a people can exist of itself, and is prior in time to a king." Their collective existence is superior to and does not depend on the state because they give rather than receive. In fact, the life of the people proceeds immanently from themselves as they are capable of living apart from the state. By recognizing the people's political externality to the instituted forms of government, Brutus exposed their autonomous, extrainstitutional life as the sovereignty of the *populus constituens*.[39] He reached the conclusion that "as kings are *constituted* by the people, it seems definitely to follow that the people is more powerful than the king. For such is the force of the word: one who is *constituted* by another is held to be lesser; and one who receives his authority from another is inferior to his appointer."[40]

Brutus, like other Monarchomachs, treats the right to remove and depose any constituted authority and even to kill unjust rulers as derivative, emanating from the sovereign power of the people to constitute. He also anticipated the idea of the constitutional convention when he acknowledged the exceptional "proviso" according to which established rules and procedures of the normal order are suspended because, "should the need arise, either the whole people, or else a kind of epitome of the whole people, would be convened in extraordinary assembly."[41] In the same year, George Buchanan proposed a democratic justification of the founding act in his vindication of the right to resist: "a decision should be taken in common in matters which affect the common good of all."[42] Likewise, the Calvinist jurist Johannes Althusius, relying on the Monarchomachs' doctrines, affirmed the same principle of popular sovereignty qua constituent power and provided the clearest formulation yet.[43] In *Politica*, published in 1603, he defended active resistance on the grounds that "it cannot be denied that the greater is that which *constitutes* the other and is immortal in its foundation, and that this is the people . . . By nature and circumstance, the people is prior to, more important than, and superior to its governors, just as every *constituting body* is prior and superior to what is *constituted* by it."[44]

For Althusius, "the right of sovereignty . . . does not belong to individual members, but to all members joined together and to the entire associated body of the realm." Sovereign power, therefore, when properly understood as the power to constitute, cannot conceivably reside in any individual or group of individuals less than the whole people. Moreover, as a power that founds/grounds a political and constitutional order, it remains irreducible to and heterogeneous from that order. This collective sovereign right justifies the removal, deposition, and overthrow by the people of the constituted authorities when they become unjust and tyrannical. The exercise of the right of resistance pertains only to the people in their sovereign capacity as constituent power. Althusius, like the Monarchomachs, formulated a democratic theory of resistance based on the primacy of the sovereign power of the many to constitute, that is, their autonomous power of associating "for the purpose of establishing, cultivating, and conserving social life among them."[45]

REVOLUTIONS

By the time of the English civil war (1642–51) and the Glorious Revolution (1688), the basic conceptual attributes of the doctrine of constituent power were set in place and deployed during the heated debates among Royalists, Republicans, Levellers, and Parliamentarians.[46] During this critical period, the concept became widely diffused, was sharpened, and adapted to very concrete and tense political situations. The doctrine of popular sovereignty *qua* the power of the people to constitute was politically asserted and widely disseminated in numerous revolutionary pamphlets, and it was theoretically enhanced in the writings of George Lawson, Algernon Sidney, and John Locke.[47] It erupted on the political scene, exerting a tangible influence over the structures of political rule and the normative development of modern constitutionalism as the "power to constitute," that is, the sovereign power to "abolish, alter, reform forms of government . . . [and] to form a state, where there is none, and if after a form once introduced, the order be not good, to alter it."[48] From that time on, the distinction between constituent and legislative (constituted) power attains its central and indispensable place in constitutional thought, setting the foundation for the superiority of constitutional law over ordinary legislation. While, on the one hand, the delegated power to legislate is conditionally exercised by an elected representative assembly within prescribed limits, on the other, the power to constitute, that is, to form, alter, or dissolve the government, is absolute, vested in the entire community and in the people acting outside the Parliament. As one anonymous author put it a few years earlier, it was "beyond the power of the *constituted*, and only in the *Constitutors* to make such an alteration in the fundamental Constitution."[49] From this distinction grew the idea of a temporary and extraordinary convention, a political device for the institutional expression of popular sovereignty, set against parliamentary supremacy. Lawson was the first to develop a systematic theory of the constituent assembly, empowered by special and temporary mandates to "model a state," because, as he claimed, "What may be done in extraordinary cases is one thing, what may be done in an ordinary way another."[50]

Locke, likewise, argued that below and prior to the "*Constituted* Commonwealth" there is a higher extralegal power, vested in the self-organized original community or civil society, situated between the natural and political state, "which *begins* and actually *constitutes any Political Society*."[51] Surprisingly, it was Hobbes who had explicitly recognized as early as 1642 that all deliberate foundings are democratic in nature, independent of the political forms they erect because they emanate from the constituent power of the people. Democracy lies beneath all regime forms. There is, Hobbes wrote, a mode of political beginning that "originates in the *determination and decision* (*a consilio & constitutione*) of the uniting parties, and that is the *origin by design* (*origo ex instituto*)."[52] And when this happens and "men have met to erect a commonwealth, they are almost by the very fact that they have met, a *Democracy*."[53] Ten years later Hobbes repudiated this earlier position to advocate instead the institutional and political impossibility of democracy. But it will reappear in Locke's description and defense of "the People as Supream Power" with the unalienable right to decide the structure of government. His work renews and strengthens the classic distinction between constituent power and constituted order by drawing a clear line between the "Dissolution of the Government" and the "Dissolution of Society": the first does not affect the second because society exists independently and apart from the political state. For Locke, popular sovereignty is a founding power, an irregular and exceptional insurgent force, antecedent to positive law and external to any state form, justifying legitimate resistance and revolution on the part of the people.[54]

In the following century, the doctrine of constituent power migrated across the Atlantic and found fertile ground in the North American colonies, inspiring the American War of Independence and the revolutionary making of the federal republic.[55] Once more, it was evoked in the language of popular sovereignty and, as a right to revolt, it supplied the normative resources for the revolutionary war against the British Empire and the political legitimacy for the new republican government. As early as April 1777, Thomas Young, a radical patriot from Pennsylvania, in an open letter addressed to the inhabitants of Vermont, urged them to establish their own government and frame a constitution because "they are the *supreme constituent power* and, of course, their immediate representatives are the supreme delegate power; and as soon as their delegate power gets too far out of the hands of the *constituent power*, a tyranny is in some degree established."[56] Most probably, he was inspired by the 1776 Declaration of Independence, written in the language of constituent power: governments are instituted to secure life, liberty, and the pursuit of happiness, and "whenever any form of government becomes destructive to these ends, it is the right of the people to *alter* and *abolish* it, and to *institute* a new government, laying its foundation upon such principles, and organizing its powers in such forms, as to them shall seem most likely to affect their safety and happiness."[57] A few years later, Thomas Paine articulated the democratic logic of constituent power with his exemplary formulation: "A constitution is not the act of a government, but of a people *constituting* a government. And a government without a constitution, is power without right."[58]

Noticeably, for the first time since Marsilius laid the conceptual foundations and Lawson imagined its institutional shape, the constituent power was finally actualized and given political form in the revolutionary conventions, established outside the colonial legal framework, as irregular bodies with an authority superior to the ordinary legislatures.[59] Starting with Virginia, North Carolina, Pennsylvania, and Massachusetts, conventions sprang up throughout North America with the special task of drafting the new constitutions. These political forms superseded royal charters, were often elected by free men, and fell back on the town hall meetings for consultation and legitimacy. They transformed the colonies into independent states, culminating in the 1787 Grand Convention in Philadelphia that drafted the federal Constitution, which it then submitted to the state conventions for ratification.[60] The vexing problem of the Convention's self-authorization, its illegality and arbitrariness, was resolved by an appeal to "the original *constituting power*" of the people in their sovereign capacity.[61] James Madison, for instance, defended the decision of the Philadelphia Convention to meet without a previous authorization, against the rules established by the Articles of the Confederation, in the name of a power superior to positive norms, emanating from "the precious right of the people to '*abolish* or *alter* their government as to them shall seem most likely to effect their safety and happiness.'"[62] The principle of the constituent power generated the democratic legitimacy that was needed to compensate for the legal deficit of the revolutionary break. In the words of James Wilson,

> There necessarily exists, in every government, a power from which there is no appeal, and which, for that reason, may be termed supreme, absolute, and uncontrollable. . . . Perhaps some politician, who has not considered with sufficient accuracy our political systems, would answer that, in our governments, the supreme power was vested in the constitutions. . . . This opinion approaches a step nearer to the truth, but does not reach it. The truth is, that in our governments, the supreme, absolute, and uncontrollable power remains in the people. As our constitutions are superior to our legislatures, so the people are superior to our constitutions. Indeed the superiority, in this last instance, is much greater; for the people possess over our constitution, control in act, as well as right. The consequence is, the people may change constitutions whenever and however they please. This is a right of which no positive institution can ever deprive them.[63]

The conclusion of the American Revolution saw the first examples of codification and integration of the principle of the constituent power *qua* popular sovereignty in a series of founding legal documents, such as the preambles to several revolutionary state constitutions and the U.S. federal Constitution itself (and its amendment provision).

This original constitutionalization, however, revealed some dilemmas. While the newly founded republic recognized the sovereignty of the people as constituent power, it also sought to freeze and neutralize it. In particular, a critical debate ensued over the issue of constitutional revision, that is, of a legally regulated self-alteration, whereby the Constitution incorporates the constituent logic by inscribing it within a juridical norm. It was a debate around the postrevolutionary survival of the constituent power outside the constituted rules. The main question was whether popular sovereignty, that is, democracy, can exist only as a form, a regime, and a constitution or, rather, must retain its informal disobedient, eruptive, and revolutionary powers. This is the dilemma between revolutionary amnesia and a permanent revolution. To address this vexing problem, Jefferson and Paine rethought afresh the constituent power in terms of temporality and intergenerational justice between "the living" and "the dead," while Madison rejected their proposals and instead defended the stability and lasting promises of the newly constituted order.[64] And as Alexis de Tocqueville keenly observed, although "the principle of the sovereignty of the people . . . is always to be found, more or less, at the bottom of almost all human institutions . . . [it] remains there concealed from view . . . [and] if for a moment it is brought to light, it is hastily cast back into the gloom of the sanctuary."[65]

With the closing of the revolutionary era the first reactions against the constituent power were voiced and its insurrectional, seditious, unruly, unstable, and brief nature. Democracy is revolutionary and, therefore, defective in the long term because of its "subverting the foundation of civil government."[66] It is in this way that the constituted order turned against the constituent power. The new republic absorbed the constituent principle to sanctify its foundations, but it did so by repressing its own beginnings and by objecting to the extraconstitutional survival of the power of the many constitute.[67]

A few years later, the concept, now enriched by the experience of the American Revolution, resurfaced on the European continent to shape the discourse and politics of the French Revolution. It was the Marquis de Lafayette and Antoine-Nicolas de Condorcet but, most notably, Emmanuel Sieyès, who ardently propagated the doctrine of constituent power. This rediscovery initiated by Lafayette had a decisive impact on the conceptual history of constituent power and its subsequent ambiguous legacy.[68] Condorcet's effort, in particular, is remarkable because he sought to institutionally realize the democratic content of the concept by advocating popular ratification, citizens' initiatives, multiple primary assemblies, recurrent conventions, and the right of insurrection.[69] In so doing, he sought to formalize the democratic drive of popular sovereignty. His influence was decisive in the 1793 Constitution, but its permanent suspension indicates the unfortunate fate of Condorcet's theory of the constituent power.

By contrast, Sieyès's attempt to reduce the concept to a national homogenous and organic subject, "la Nation," understood as a prepolitical community inhabiting a normless state of nature, proved to be more successful.[70] By doing so, he inaugurated the doctrine of national sovereignty. As he stated, "the *constituent power* can do everything in relationship to constitutional making. It is not subordinated to a previous constitution. The nation that exercises the greatest, the most important of its powers, must be, while carrying this function, free from all constraints, from any form, except the one that it deems better to adopt."[71]

There is, however, an important unresolved tension in Sieyès's famous definition. Selectively blending elements from Rousseau's and Hobbes's political thought, he praised the constituent power's instituting and revolutionary nature even as he juridified it into a purely legal force: "Its will is always legal, it is the law itself." The constituent power becomes the general national will. Thus, on the one hand, he recognized the constituent power as free, unbounded by constituted norms, the extralegal source of all legality, while on the other hand, he treated it as a juridical concept, with a fixed identity, always already mediated by representation.[72] This ambivalence that resulted in undermining the key constituent/constituted distinction he had once formally endorsed played out politically in the self-authorized Constituent Convention (1789–91) and the popularly elected National Convention (1792–95), with pernicious effects.

In the end, Sieyès's version not only displaced and defeated Condorcet's democratic contribution but it also made possible the subsequent national-plebiscitary exploitation and populist disfiguration of the constituent power.[73] With the French Revolution, the concept, caught in the realm of representation, became entangled with intricate logical paradoxes and puzzling legal formulations that produced politically suspicious appropriations and polemical refutations. Thus, in 1830 François Guizot asserted, "this power anterior, superior, and outside the Charter, that is to say, the *constituent power*, sovereign and absolute . . . was like a poison that had mingled with all goods and with all expectations." Likewise, in 1842, he vilified the constituent power because "if we pretend that there exists, or should exist, within society, two powers, one ordinary and the other extraordinary, one constitutional and the other *constituent*, we say something insane, full of dangers and potentially fatal. . . . Be calm, gentlemen, we, the three constitutional powers, are the only legitimate and legal organs of national sovereignty. Beyond us, there is nothing but usurpation and revolution."[74]

During the nineteenth century, in North America and western Europe, the constituent power became misappropriated, domesticated, neutralized, or belittled. Its gradual absorption by the constituted order not only deprived it of its democratic and revolutionary attributes but also degraded it into an abstract, indeterminate ideology, malleable, at the mercy of ruling elites vying for power. Its impact, however, began to be felt elsewhere, in the anticolonial independence movements of South America and the Caribbean, and in the Balkan corner of southern Europe, moving eastward into the Ottoman Empire.[75] These spatial trajectories suggest that concepts have histories and geographies. The political history of the constituent power became almost global in its reach. In fact, the idea that the final power to establish and alter the framework of government belongs to the people, in their sovereign capacity, to erect their own constitutions, unbound by prior instituted norms, has deeply marked the democratic, insurrectional, and anticolonial consciousness of political modernity.

A DEMOCRATIC CONCEPT

This brief, cursory conceptual history of the constituent power, incomplete as it is, suggests a clear distinction between state sovereignty as command and popular sovereignty as the power to constitute. Their differences are substantial as they are separated by distinct histories, ontologies, normative orientations, and political objectives.

As Martin Loughlin has correctly pointed out, "constituent power as a 'power to' is different from 'power over.'"[76] It is very different, indeed. In the statist paradigm the emphasis is on the moment of (coercive) command, while the constituent version privileges the act of establishing and instituting. The one is repressive and static when contrasted to the dynamic and productive dimension of the other. Consequentially, whereas the principle of command is based on the model of *ruling*, that of constituent sovereignty evokes a *founding* event. The sovereign is not a ruler but a lawgiver. Instead of fixating on a superior command emanating from the *top*, the notion of the constituent sovereign redirects attention to the underlying sources of the instituted reality located at the *bottom*. The first relies on a *vertical* structure, while the second operates *horizontally*. Moreover, contrary to the paradigm of the sovereign command that invites personification—from the ancient *imperatore* to the king to the modern executive—the constituent power conveys the collective and impersonal attributes of sovereignty, its associative public dimension, and its federative inclinations. All these contrasts illustrate how the constituent power has, in modern times, reimagined democracy against the regal paradigm of command.[77]

This juxtaposition between the two competing versions of sovereignty makes it hard to miss the regularity in the concept of constituent power. By looking carefully at how it was theorized and evoked, it is possible to outline in a consistent fashion its discursive rules. In the following, I consider some of the themes that recur most frequently in theories of constituent power in order to try and define the rules that account for the semantic continuity, analytical consistency, and normative singularity of the concept. However different its historical experiences might have been, in its numerous trajectories and variations, in the mode of means of its respective realizations formed by diverse intellectual influences, it nonetheless presupposes certain shared meanings and a common orientation that define and organize its intelligibility. I am referring here to the concept's immanent principles. These principles are internal to the concept, which they construct and help to identify.[78]

To begin with, the constituent power speaks of a collective practice, involving a plurality of actors coming together to *co-institute*, to establish jointly. Two crucial aspects are involved in the semantic composition of the concept, indicative of its first two immanent principles. First, there is equality. An emphasis on the prefix "co-" presents the concept descriptively: on the one hand, as a negation, that is, the impossibility that one could ever *co*-institute anything by oneself; on the other, positively, prescribing that if one wants to *co*-institute, one has to do it in *co*-operation with others. Acting together in concert means to "do certain common acts as a society, which are acts not of a certain part but of the whole."[79] These acts point to a federative and associative structure of public authority that defies centralization, hierarchy, and monopoly of coercion. They are egalitarian to the degree that the coming together is articulated in terms of equal participation. In all theories of constituent power, the politics of new foundations are undertaken jointly and voluntarily, free from asymmetrical power relations and arbitrary interferences, that is, free of inequality and exclusion, in true *co*-operation. Sidney accurately grasped this egalitarian presence when he claimed that "every number of men, agreeing together and framing a society, became a compleat body, having all power in themselves over themselves, subject to no other human law than their own. All those that compose the society, being equally free to enter it or not, no man could have any prerogative above others."[80] The egalitarian meaning of the concept indicates how the act of constituting is performed among peers by mutual association.

Second, the concept also consists of a generative principle. By underlying the second component of the verb to co-*institute*, theories of the constituent power saw in sovereignty a creative form-giving power. Popular sovereignty is presented in its instituting capacity, with the faculty to instaure new political orders, to bring into being novel constitutional forms, to enact new beginnings. Sovereignty establishes political and legal orders and determines constitutional forms.

In a word, it is a productive power, often portrayed as the extralegal source of all legality. This positing aspect of the constituent sovereign is fully captured by Schmitt's definition of sovereignty as a "founding power" (*die begründende Gewalt*).[81] The second immanent principle of the concept of constituent power is positive and generative, a productive and instituting norm.

Correspondingly, the power to constitute pertains to relations of mutual association and self-constitution. The subject of the constituent power is not prior or external to the act of constituting. Rather, it constitutes itself as it constitutes for itself.[82] By framing the political forms of its collective existence, it also produces its own public identity.[83] This process of self-formation is immanent to the degree that the constituent power makes both the subject and the object of politics in the absence of an antecedent, external causality. It is best captured by Althusius's definition of constituent politics as "symbiotics," that is, as a horizontal practice of freely associating and dissociating with others, the forming of a commonality through reciprocal promises and pledges for the sake of "mutual communication of whatever is useful and necessary for the harmonious exercise of social life."[84] For the concept, the people are not a natural, homogeneous unity credited with an organic collective selfhood. Rather, they constitute a combined, artificial body, formed outside the instituted commonwealth, inclusively, and vested in common with certain "things, acts, rights, privileges, interests."[85]

The concept, fourthly, consists of a revolutionary principle.[86] It is forged during extreme situations of crisis, conflict, and transformation, designed for resistance and revolution, an exhortation to rebel. It is the principle of disruption: self-authorized, unruly, against the fixity and permanence of the statist *nomos*. There is here a strong "desire for alteration."[87] The concept indicates discontinuities and ruptures in the constitution of the political, it ponders alterity and otherness against legal closure, and is attentive to accelerated temporalities with sudden unpredictable and contingent outcomes. Theories of constituent power expand the boundaries of politics so as to include its own foundations and beginnings. Since Marsilius's original formulation, the people arrive at the moment of a rupture, staging a dispute against tyranny, in times of exception, to constitute anew their political existence and to renew their constitutional identity.[88] For the modern reinvention of democracy, popular sovereignty is revolutionary.[89]

As surprising as it may sound to some, this revolutionary principle coexists with the constitutional dimension of the concept. Democratic revolutions are constitutional, that is, moments of popular sovereignty and genuine constitutional making. The constituent power is certainly one of the main foundations of modern constitutionalism and public law. It consistently treats politics in terms of constitutional politics; the constitution is understood politically, and politics, in turn, is analyzed constitutionally, thereby bridging the unconvincing and politically suspicious distinction between politics as the field of factual power and the constitution as the realm of pure normativity. Any meaningful and compelling distinction between higher, ordinary laws in fact presupposes the constituent power of the people. This distinction, which corresponds to one of the main principles of modern constitutionalism, emanates from popular sovereignty: the people are sovereign by virtue of their power to constitute.[90] The fundamental constitutional law, "the law of lawmaking," enjoys higher and greater legitimacy than normal legislation because it is a sovereign expression of constituent power.[91] This is the modern idea of democratic legitimacy and the democratic foundations of a constitutional order.[92]

"Democratic theory," Schmitt argued, "knows as a legitimate constitution only the one which rests on the constituent power of the people."[93] Karl Marx had already expressed this view in prescient terms. "Democracy is the solved *riddle* of all constitutions," he claimed, because "here, not merely *implicitly* and in essence but *existing* in reality, the core of constitution is constantly brought back to its actual basis, the *actual human being*, the *actual people*, and established as the people's own work. The constitution appears as what it is, a free creation of man."[94]

In a democratic regime, legitimacy depends upon how inclusive, free, and equal participation is during constitutional politics. Precisely because this concept of sovereignty recalls the normative ideal of political autonomy at the center of modern democratic theory, it points to a distinctive theory of political legitimacy, which focuses primarily on the making of higher law. Participation in the founding defines the modern experience of democracy. It is this primacy of participation over obedience that demands from the subjects of a political order to *co*-institute it. The constituent power evokes the general value of political autonomy: to be free is to live under one's own laws. Popular sovereignty qua constituent power reinvents the ancient democratic principle of self-government. It is the explicit, lucid self-institution of society, in Cornelius Castoriadis's apt formulation.[95]

At the same time, the relationship between sovereignty and constitutionalism, democracy and law, proves to be dialectical to the degree that the constituent power supersedes the constitutional universality of the instituted society. As Marx insisted, the "constitution is no longer equivalent to the whole" and does not monopolize the political because it corresponds to "only *one* facet of the people." For the concept, there is an irreducible political outside to the formal organization of the state. Because the constituent power cannot be absorbed or consumed by the order of the constitution, politics escapes its total constitutionalization and full juridical "objectification."[96] It remains both below and next to the constituted powers as a force of innovation, alterity, contingency, and, most important, as a democratic presence.[97] The idea of the constituent power as the excess of constitutionalism is a reminder that politics cannot be reduced to abstract legality and that democracy exceeds its constitutional forms.

Finally, the constituent power enacts a rupture with theological and transcendent notions of power, politics, and subjectivity. A principle of immanence is present in the constituent power. For instance, this concept of power has always been placed underneath the civil and legal edifice, not above or over it, emanating from the bottom, from the many, those who compose a genuine collectivity. Its various names that designate it—the community, civil society, the multitude, the poor, the plebs, the commons, the demos, the people—all suggest that, in the last instance, the many are the ultimate foundation of the political, the utter social limit of any politics that survives the dissolution of governments, the disruption of legal systems, and the collapse of instituted powers. This persistent constitutional externality is due to the immanence of constituent power to social life. It is internal to concrete relations of mutual association, formed by actual pledges and promises; in exchanges, agreements, covenants, and contacts; in corporations, alliances, and federations. The concept is relational and plural and operates strictly on the plane of historicity and immanence. It is profane and material, the affirmation of the powers of this world, of change and contingency, of beginnings and ends, and the recognition that the political world is made by its participants.

Although it is true that during its long history this worldly concept was periodically tainted by elements of political theology, these remained extraneous, later additions, which never coalesced with the conceptual core to become a constitutive part. By the third quarter of the eighteenth century, Hamilton could proclaim in the opening lines of the *Federalist Papers* "that it seems to have been preserved to the people of this country, by their conduct and example, to decide the important question, whether societies of men are really capable or not of establishing good government from reflection and choice, or whether they are forever destined to depend for the political constitutions on accident and force."[98] Political authority, the grounds of ruling, the government itself, are not inaccessible, beyond judgment and contestation; instead, they are relativized and decentered, regarded as human, that is, mortal artifacts, without extrasocial support, lacking banners of truth or markers of certainty, open to questioning, and thus provisional and revocable, conditional and frail.

Intractable as it may seem, the concept of constituent power possesses its own logic. Its immanent discursive principles define the democratic content of popular sovereignty, which is both revolutionary and constitutional. This reorientation of modern democratic theory toward the power to constitute initiates a shift from the logic of determination to the principle of self-determination, from immobility to movement, from the One to the Many, from the transcendent to the immanent, from heteronomy to autonomy. It is a shift that marks the modern birth of the democratic project and the "modern social imaginary of autonomy."[99] With the constituent power, democracy exists in the radical event of its self-alteration. It is a politics of becoming, the movement of political transformation and constitutional change. Hannah Arendt, following Machiavelli, described this constituent politics as the "augmentation of foundations . . . this notion of a coincidence of foundation and preservation by virtue of augmentation."[100] The constituent power inaugurates a fascinating, unprecedented exploration into the radical nature of democratic politics, that is, a politics that revisits its foundations and politicizes its origins. Democracy, in short, begins democratically.[101]

NOTES

1. Ernst-Wolfgang Böckenforde, "Die Verfassungsggebende Gewalt des Volkes-Ein Grenzbegriff des Verfassungsrechts," in *Staat, Verfassung, Democratie: Studien zur Verfassungstheorie und zum Verfassungsrecht* (Frankfurt am Main: Suhrkamp, 1991), 11–12; Andrew Arato, "Forms of Constitution Making and Theories of Democracy," *Cardozo Law Review* 17, no. 2 (1995): 202–54; Antonio Negri, *Insurgencies: Constituent Power and the Modern State* (Minneapolis: University of Minnesota Press, 1999), 1; Martin Loughlin, "Constituent Power," in *The Idea of Public Law* (Oxford: Oxford University Press, 2004), 100; Martin Loughlin and Neil Walker, eds., introduction to *The Paradox of Constitutionalism: Constituent Power and Constitutional Form* (Oxford: Oxford University Press, 2007), 6.

2. Carl Schmitt, *Constitutional Theory*, trans. Jeffrey Seitzer (Durham, N.C.: Duke University Press, 2008), 101–2, 105, 112, 115, 120–21, 128–29, 136–39, 145–46; Cornelius Castoriadis, "What Democracy?," in *Figures of the Thinkable*, trans. Helen Arnold (Stanford, Calif.: Stanford University Press, 2007), 122–24.

3. Hans Kelsen, *Pure Theory of Law*, trans. Max Knight (Gloucester, Mass.: Peter Smith, 1989), 204; Hans Kelsen, *General Theory of Norms*, trans. Michael Hartney (Oxford: Oxford University Press, 1991), 256; Jacques Derrida, "Force of Law: 'The

Mystical Foundation of Authority,'" in *Deconstruction and the Possibility of Justice*, ed. Drucilla Cornell, 3–67 (New York: Routledge, 1992); Claude Klein, *Théorie et pratique de pouvoir constituant* (Paris: Presses Universitaires de France, 1996), 194–99.

4. Raymond Carré de Malberg, *Contribution á la théorie générale de l'état,* vol. 2 (Paris: Librairie de la Société du Recueil Sirey, 1922), 483.

5. Jean Bodin, *On Sovereignty*, trans. Julian Franklin (Cambridge: Cambridge University Press, 1992), 1; Julian Franklin, *Jean Bodin and the Rise of Absolutist Theory* (Cambridge: Cambridge University Press, 1973), 23, 54–68.

6. Thomas Hobbes, *On the Citizen*, ed. Richard Tuck (Cambridge: Cambridge University Press, 1998), 73; Benedict de Spinoza, *A Theologico-Political Treatise*, trans. R. H. M. Elwes (New York: Dover, 1951), 207.

7. Antonio Negri and Michael Hardt, "Sovereignty," in Antonio Negri, *Reflections on Empire*, trans. Ed Emery, 48–59 (Cambridge: Polity, 2008).

8. Bodin, *On Sovereignty*, 49. Hannah Arendt, *The Human Condition* (Chicago: University of Chicago Press, 1958), 234–35. "The doctrine of sovereignty," according to L. H. A. Hart, "asserts that in every human society, where there is law, there is ultimately to be found latent beneath the variety of political forms, in a democracy as much as in an absolute monarchy, this simple relationship between subjects rendering obedience and a sovereign who renders obedience to no one. This vertical structure composed of sovereign and subjects is, according to the theory, as essential a part of a society which possesses law, as a backbone is of a man." L. H. A. Hart, *The Concept of Law*, 3rd ed. (Oxford: Oxford University Press, 2012), 50.

9. Otto Gierke, *Natural Law and the Theory of Society, 1500–1800* (Boston: Beacon Press, 1957), 40; Julian H. Franklin, "Sovereignty and the Mixed Constitution: Bodin and His Critics," in *The Cambridge History of Political Thought, 1450–1700*, ed. J. H. Burns (Cambridge: Cambridge University Press, 1991), 307.

10. Bodin, *On Sovereignty*, 11.

11. Hannah Arendt, *On Revolution* (New York: Viking Press, 1963), 154–58.

12. Michel Foucault, *The History of Sexuality*, vol. 1, *An Introduction* (New York: Vintage Books, 1990), 85.

13. *Stătūo* is itself derived from *stăre*, that is, to stand firm and still.

14. Theodore Mommsen, *Le droit public Romain,* vol. 4 (Paris: Thorin and Fils, 1884), 425–70; Carl Schmitt, *Die Dictatur* (Berlin: Duncker and Humblot, 1994), 127–49.

15. Marcus Tullius Cicero, *De re publica*, trans. Clinton Walker Keyes (Cambridge, Mass.: Harvard University Press, 1994), 264–67; Livy, *History of Rome*, trans. B. O. Foster (Cambridge, Mass.: Harvard University Press, 1997), 333–34; Appian, *Civil Wars*, trans. Horace White (Cambridge, Mass.: Harvard University Press, 2002), 185; Lucius Ampelius, *Liber memorialis*, (Leipzig: B. G. Teubner, 1873), chapter 29, http://penelope.uchicago.edu/Thayer/E/Roman/Texts/Ampelius/home.html.

16. Karl Ernst Georges, *Ausführliches lateinisch-deutsches und deutsch-lateinisches Handwörterbuch aus den Quellen zusammengetragen und mit besonderer Bezugnahme auf Synonymik und Antiquitäten unter Berücksichtigung der besten Hülfsmittel* (Leipzig, 1869), 1151–52.

17. Justinian, *The Digest of Justinian*, trans. Alan Watson (1985; repr., Philadelphia: University of Pennsylvania Press, 2009), 1.1.6, 1:2.18.

18. Ulrich Preuss, "The Constitution as the 'Object of All Longing,'" in *Constitutional Revolution* (Atlantic Highlands, N.J.: Humanities Press, 1995), 27.

19. Otto Gierke, *Political Theories in the Middle Age* (Cambridge: Cambridge University Press, 1987), 46–47; Charles Howard McIlwain, *The Growth of Political Thought in the West: From the Greeks to the End of the Middle Ages* (New York: Macmillan, 1932), 305; Alexander Passerin d'Entrèves, *The Medieval Contribution to Political Thought* (Oxford: Oxford University Press, 1939), 59; Walter Ullmann, *Principles of Government in the Middle Ages* (New York: Routledge, 2010), 282.

20. In 1327, this oppositional and dissident stance caused Marsilius of Padua's condemnation as a heretic by the Catholic Church.

21. Marsilius of Padua, *Defensor pacis*, trans. Alan Gewirth (Toronto: University of Toronto Press, 1956), 61; emphasis added.

22. Ibid., 87, 26, 63–64; emphasis added.

23. Ibid., 62, 64, 65; emphasis added.

24. Alan Gewirth, *Marsilius of Padua: The Defender of Peace* (New York: Columbia University Press, 1951), 50–56.

25. Marsilius, *Defensor pacis*, 63, 64, 62, 27.

26. Ibid., 53, 27–28, 52, 54–55, 48, 64, 87–88, 45–46. Marsilius also anticipated the revolutionary idea of the constitutional convention.

27. Gewirth, *Marsilius of Padua*, 167–225.

28. Marsilius, *Defensor pacis*, 46, 49–55.

29. Carl Schmitt, *Political Theology: Four Chapters on the Concept of Sovereignty*, trans. George Schwab (Cambridge, Mass.: MIT Press, 1988), 51, 36; Schmitt, *Constitutional Theory*, 126–28; Ulrich Preuss, "Constitutional Powermaking for the New Polity: Some Deliberations on the Relations between Constituent Power and the Constitution," in *Constitutionalism, Identity, Difference, and Legitimacy: Theoretical Perspectives*, ed. Michel Rosenfeld, 144–45 (Durham, N.C.: Duke University Press, 1994).

30. Marsilius, *Defensor pacis*, 29, 89–97.

31. The Scottish Catholic jurist William Barclay coined the name "monarchomach" in his polemical pamphlet, *De regno et regali potestate adversus Buchanum, Brutum, Boucherium et reliquios monarchomacos* (Paris: G. Chaudière, 1600).

32. Julian Franklin, *Constitutionalism and Resistance in the Sixteenth Century* (New York: Pegasus, 1969), 11–12; Antonio Negri, "From the Right to Resistance to

Constituent Power," in *The Porcelain Workshop: For a New Grammar of Politics*, trans. Noura Wedell, 109–26 (Los Angeles: Semiotext(e), 2008).

33. This is Sidney's classical version, almost a century later, which exemplifies the normative meaning of popular sovereignty based on the power to constitute. It also testifies to its discursive permanence beyond and after the Monarchomachs. Algernon Sidney, *Discourses concerning Government*, ed. Thomas G. West (Indianapolis: Liberty Fund, 1996), 20.

34. George Lawson, *Politica sacra et civilis*, ed. Conal Condren (Cambridge: Cambridge University Press, 1992), 48.

35. Franklin, *Constitutionalism and Resistance*, 37, 42–45.

36. François Hotman, *Fraco-Gallia; or, An Account of the Ancient Free State of France* (Cambridge: Cambridge University Press, 1972), 82; emphasis added.

37. Théodore de Bèze, "Rights of Magistrates," in Franklin, *Constitutionalism and Resistance*, 124, 126 (emphasis added), 104, 106.

38. Junius Brutus the Celt (most probably Philippe du Plessis-Mornay), *Vindiciae, contra tyrannos; or, Concerning the Legitimate Power of a Prince over the People, and of the People over a Prince*, ed. George Garnett (Cambridge: Cambridge University Press, 1994), 68–76.

39. Ibid., 71, 156, 99–102, 75, 169.

40. Ibid., 74 (emphasis added), 68–74, 92, 94, 130.

41. Ibid., 78, 82.

42. George Buchanan, *A Dialogue on the Law of Kingship among the Scots* (Edinburgh: Saltire Society, 2006), 72.

43. Gierke, *Natural Law*, 241, 244, 257.

44. Johannes Althusius, *Politica methodice digesta*, trans. Frederick S. Carney (Indianapolis: Liberty Classics Edition, 1995), 72–73 (emphasis added), 93, 96–97, 110–11. For Althusius's theory of active resistance and tyrannicide, see 191–200.

45. Ibid., 70, 72–73, 17. Althusius's refutation of Bodin in the name of popular sovereignty *qua* constituent power not only challenges the monarchical paradigm of sovereignty, it also questions the legitimacy of the modern state. In fact, the development of sovereignty as the power to constitute forms of government passes through the rediscovery of the federation as a superior alternative to the unitary and indivisible authority of the modern state. Althusius is both a thinker of the constituent power of the people and the first modern proponent of federalism, understood as the mutual binding of families, cities, guilds, communities, and provinces that associate together through mutual promises into a constituting body, outside and prior to any state form. With Althusius, therefore, the federation becomes the most appropriate and natural expression of constituent politics; the state, by contrast, appears as its enemy.

46. Edmund S. Morgan, *Inventing the People: The Rise of Popular Sovereignty in England and America* (New York: W. W. Norton, 1989), 55–121; Martin Loughlin,

"Constituent Power Subverted: From English Constitutional Argument to British Constitutional Practice," in Loughlin and Walker, *Paradox of Constitutionalism*, 27–48.

47. Lawson, *Politica sacra et civilis*, 21–30, 41–76, 88–125, 218–51; Sidney, *Discourses concerning Government*, 20–23, 30–32, 46–52, 69–76, 91–92, 97–107; John Locke, *The Second Treatise of Government*, ed. Peter Laslett (Cambridge: Cambridge University Press, 1991), 318–74, 406–28.

48. Lawson, *Politica sacra et civilis*, 47, 46; emphasis added.

49. Anonymous, *Exercitation concerning Usurped Powers* (London, 1650), 8, 73; emphasis added. See also *A Plea for Non-Scribers* (London, 1650), 26–27.

50. Lawson, *Politica sacra et civilis*, 48–49, 107–8.

51. Locke, *Second Treatise of Government*, 333.

52. Hobbes, *On the Citizen*, 74. See Murray Forsyth, "Thomas Hobbes and the Constituent Power of the People," *Political Studies* 29, no. 2 (1981): 191–203.

53. Hobbes, *On the Citizen*, 94.

54. Locke, *Second Treatise of Government*, 366–67, 427–28 (emphasis added), 406–28.

55. R. R. Palmer, *The Age of the Democratic Revolution: A Political History of Europe and America, 1760–1800,* vol. 1 (Princeton, N.J.: Princeton University Press, 1959), 213–38; Gordon S. Wood, *The Creation of the American Republic, 1776–1787* (Chapel Hill: University of North Carolina Press, 1998), 306–89; Richard B. Morris, *The Forging of the Union, 1781–1789* (New York: Harper and Row, 1987), 115–16; Arendt, *On Revolution,* 145, 154, 165–71, 179–85; Larry D. Kramer, *The People Themselves: Popular Constitutionalism and Judicial Review* (Oxford: Oxford University Press, 2005).

56. Thomas Young, "To the Inhabitants of Vermont, a Free and Independent State, Bounding on the River Connecticut and Lake Champlain (April 11, 1777)," in Zadock Thompson, ed., *History of Vermont, Natural, Civil and Statistical, in Three Parts* (Burlington: Chauncey Goodrich, 1842), 106; emphasis added.

57. U.S. Declaration of Independence (July 4, 1776); emphasis added.

58. Thomas Paine, "Rights of Man: Part II," in *Thomas Paine: Collected Writings*, ed. Eric Foner (New York: Library of America, 1995), 572; emphasis added.

59. Thomas Paine, "Common Sense," "The Forester, Letter IV (May 8, 1776)," and "Rights of Man, Part I," in *Collected Writings*, 32–34, 85–90, 469, respectively; Thomas Jefferson, "Notes on the Virginia Constitution: Query XIII," in *Jefferson: Political Writings*, ed. Joyce Appleby (Cambridge: Cambridge University Press, 1999), 327–31; James Madison, *Federalist* No. 37, in Alexander Hamilton, John Jay, and James Madison, *The Federalist: A Commentary on the Constitution of the United States* (New York: The Modern Library, 1935), 224–32.

60. John Alexander Jameson, *The Constitutional Convention: Its History, Powers, and Modes of Proceedings* (New York: Charles Scribner, 1867); Clinton Rossiter, *1787:*

The Grand Convention (New York: W. W. Norton, 1987); Michael Allen Gillespie, *Ratifying the Constitution* (Lawrence: University Press of Kansas, 1992).

61. On "the original constituting power," see Paine, "Rights of Man, Part II," in *Collected Writings*, 579, 537, 545–58, 572–79. James Madison, *Federalist* No. 40, in *The Federalist*, 250–59. On this point, see Arendt, *On Revolution*, 179–214; Jacques Derrida, "Declarations of Independence," *New Political Science* 15 (1986): 7–15; Bruce Ackerman, "Neo-Federalism?," in *Constitutionalism and Democracy*, ed. Jon Elster, 153–94 (Cambridge: Cambridge University Press, 1988); Frank Michelman, "Constitutional Authorship," in *Constitutionalism: Philosophical Foundations*, ed. Larry Alexander, 64–98 (Cambridge: Cambridge University Press, 1998); Andrew Arato, *Civil Society, Constitution, and Legitimacy* (New York: Rowman and Littlefield, 2000), 170–75; Jason Frank, "Unauthorized Propositions: *The Federalist Papers* and Constituent Power," *Diacritics* 37, nos. 2–3 (2007): 103–20.

62. James Madison, *Federalist* Nos. 40 and 39, in *The Federalist*, 257, 258, 243 (emphasis added).

63. James Wilson, quoted in Jonathan Elliot, *Debates in the Several State Conventions on the Adoption of the Federal Constitution as Recommended by the General Convention at Philadelphia in 1787*, vol. 2, ed. James McClellan (Cumberland, Va.: J. River Press, 1989), 432.

64. Thomas Jefferson, letter to James Madison (January 30, 1787), letter to William Stephens Smith (November 13, 1787), letter to James Madison (September 6, 1789), letter to John Wayles Eppes (June 2, 1813), letter to Major John Cartwright (June 5, 1824), in *Jefferson: Political Writings*, 107–11, 593–604, 382–88; Paine, "Common Sense," 16; Paine, "Rights of Man: Part I," 438–42, 518.

65. Alexis de Tocqueville, *Democracy in America*, trans. Henry Reeve (New York: Vintage Books, 1990), 55.

66. James Madison, letter to Thomas Jefferson (February 4, 1790), in *Jefferson: Political Writings*, 608; James Madison, *Federalist* Nos. 49–50, in *The Federalist*, 327–55.

67. Arendt, *On Revolution*, 215–81; Negri, *Insurgencies*, 1–35, 103–36; Horst Dippel, "The Changing Idea of Popular Sovereignty in Early American Constitutionalism: Breaking Away from European Patterns," *Journal of the Early Republic* 16, no. 1 (1996): 21–45.

68. Marquis de Lafayette, *Mémoires, correspondance et manuscrits*, vol. 4 (Paris, 1837–38), 36; vol. 2, 263; vol. 5, 445.

69. Marquis de Condorcet, "On the Influence of the American Revolution on Europe," "Essay on the Constitution and Functions of the Provincial Assemblies," "On the Principles of the Constitutional Plan Presented to the National Convention," in *Condorcet: Selected Writings*, ed. Keith Michael Baker (Indianapolis: Bobbs-Merrill, 1976), 71–83, 84–87, 143–82; Marquis de Condorcet, "Sur la nécessité de faire ratifier la

Constitution par les citoyens," in *Oeuvres de Condorcet,* vol. 9 (Paris: Firmin-Didot, 1847–49), 413–30.

70. Emmanuel Sieyès, *Qu'est-ce le Tiers État?*, ed. Roberto Zapperi (Geneva: Librairie Droz, 1970), 180–91.

71. Emmanuel Sieyès, "Reconnaissance et exposition raisonnée des droits de l'homme et du citoyen," in *Orateurs de la Révolution Française: Les constituants*, vol. 1, ed. François Furet (Paris: Bibliothèque de la Pléiade, 1989), 1013; emphasis added.

72. Sieyès, *Le Tiers État,* 180, 184–86.

73. On becoming emperor in 1804, Napoleon declared, "I am the constituent power." *Correspondance de Napoleon I*, vol. 3 (Paris, 1859), 314. However, it is under the rule of his nephew Louis-Napoléon Bonaparte that the constituent power was converted into national plebiscites from above and turned into a proto-populist instrument of ruling that became almost synonymous with Bonapartism.

74. François Guizot, "L'esprit d'insurrection est un esprit radicalement contraire à la liberté," in *Discours à la Chambre des Députés (29 Décembre 1830)*; emphasis added; François Guizot, *Le moniteur universel (20 Août 1842)*, 1807.

75. The modern rediscovery of democracy is anticolonial. It predates the age of world conquests but, most important, it challenges normatively and analytically any attempt to impose a political order on those who do not participate in its establishment and institution. In fact, five centuries of Western imperial attempts demand the elaboration of a critical discourse, as the one provided by the constituent power, to understand and oppose the democratic deficit of such imperial discretionary attempts at global command. In this sense, the doctrine of the constituent sovereignty of the people is deeply anti-imperial and anticolonial at its core.

76. Loughlin, *Idea of Public Law*, 112.

77. Andreas Kalyvas, "Popular Sovereignty, Democracy, the Constituent Power," *Constellations* 12, no. 2 (2005): 223–44.

78. On the normative content of these immanent principles, see Andreas Kalyvas, "The Basic Norm and Democracy in Hans Kelsen's Legal and Political Theory," *Philosophy and Social Criticism* 32, no. 5 (2006): 587–92.

79. Lawson, *Politica sacra et civilis*, 24.

80. Sidney, *Discourses concerning Government*, 99.

81. Carl Schmitt, *Die Diktatur* (Berlin: Duncker and Humblot, 1994), 134, 137–38; Carl Schmitt, *Über die drei Arten des rechtswissenschaftlichen Denkens* (Berlin: Duncker and Humblot, 1993), 21, 23–24. Accordingly, the French constitutional scholar Maurice Hauriou has described the constituent power as "a founding legislative power." Maurice Hauriou, *Précis de droit constitutionnel* (Paris: Sirey, 1929), 246.

82. Sheldon S. Wolin, "Collective Identity and Constitutional Power," in *The Pres-*

ence of the Past: Essays on the State and the Constitution, 8–31 (Baltimore: Johns Hopkins University Press, 1990).

83. Antonio Negri, "Political Subjects: On the Multitude and Constituent Power," in *Reflections on Empire*, translated by Ed Emery, 96–113 (Cambridge: Polity, 2008), 109–10.

84. Althusius, *Politica methodice digesta*, 17.

85. Lawson, *Politica sacra et civilis*, 24.

86. Paine, "Common Sense," 42, 52; "Last Crisis XIII," 348–54; "Rights of Man," 512–13, 536–40, 547–51, 572–79, in *Collected Writings*; Thomas Jefferson, "Letter to James Madison (January 30, 1787)," and "Letter to Stephens Smith (November 13, 1787)," 107–11, in *Political Writings*.

87. Lawson, *Politica sacra et civilis*, 227.

88. Even contemporary liberal thinkers have come to realize that democratic legitimacy presupposes a break with the inherited legality. John Rawls, for instance, acknowledges that the "constituent power of the people sets up a framework to regulate ordinary power, *and it comes into play only when the existing regime has been dissolved*." John Rawls, "The Idea of Public Reason," in *Political Liberalism* (New York: Columbia University Press, 1993), 23.

89. Pierre Rosavanlon, "Revolutionary Democracy," in *Democracy Past and Future*, ed. Sam Moyn, 79–97 (New York: Columbia University Press, 2007); Sheldon Wolin, "Norm and Form: The Constitutionalizing of Democracy," in *Athenian Political Thought and the Reconstruction of American Democracy*, ed. J. Peter Euben, John R. Wallach, and Josiah Ober (Ithaca, N.Y.: Cornell University Press, 1995), 29, 37–41, 47–48, and 53–57.

90. For a detailed distinction of this point, see Raymond Carré de Malberg, *La loi, expression de la volonté générale* (Paris: Economica, 1984), 103–39.

91. Frank Michelman, *Brennan and Democracy* (Princeton, N.J.: Princeton University Press, 1999), 48.

92. According to Maurice Duverger, "It is the constitution that derives its authority from the constituent power and not the constituent power that derives its authority from the constitution." Maurice Duverger, "Légitimité des gouvernements de fait," *Revue du Droit Publique* (1948): 78.

93. Schmitt, *Constitutional Theory*, 143, 112, 120–21, 136–39, 255–67. To the question "Do the people have the right to make a new constitution?," Marx unreservedly answered in the affirmative, "for a constitution that has ceased to be the real expression of the will of the people has become a practical illusion." Karl Marx, "Critique of Hegel's Doctrine of the State," in *Karl Marx: Early Writings*, trans. Rodney Livingstone and Gregor Benton (New York: Penguin Books, 1975), 120.

94. Marx, "Critique of Hegel's Doctrine," 87.

95. Cornelius Castoriadis, *The Imaginary Institution of Society*, trans. Kathleen Blamey (Cambridge: MIT Press, 1987), 369–74.

96. Marx, "Critique of Hegel's Doctrine," 87, 88, 80, 90.

97. Schmitt, *Constitutional Theory*, 268–79.

98. Alexander Hamilton, *Federalist* No. 1, in *The Federalist*, 3. Madison concurred and explained "the improvement made by America on the ancient mode of preparing and establishing regular plans of government" as "a revolution by the intervention of a deliberative body of citizens." James Madison, *Federalist* No. 38, in *The Federalist*, 235, 234. From the seventeenth century onward, the term "constitution" came to designate a written document and a set of explicit superior, higher, fundamental legal norms and procedures instituted by human beings in opposition both to customs or conventions and to a transcendental natural law. Gerald Stourzh, "Constitution: Changing Meanings of the Term from the Early Seventeenth to the Late Eighteenth Century," in *Conceptual Change and the Constitution*, ed. Terence Ball and J. G. A. Pocock (Lawrence, Kan.: University Press of Kansas, 1988), 43–44.

99. Castoriadis, *Imaginary Institution*, 135–59, 353–68.

100. Arendt, *On Revolution*, 201, 202.

101. Today, with the project of a European constitution facing major challenges, the problem of democratic foundings is topical again. Similarly, the American appropriation of constituent power to establish new regimes demands the elaboration of a critical discourse against the democratic deficit of imperial attempts at global command. The democratic concept of popular sovereignty as constituent power prescribes that not any act can claim to be constituent and not any actor can contend to be a founder, even if the actor and the act have been successful—that is, effective in creating a new political order. Should a person or group appropriate the power to constitute a legal order at the exclusion of all those who will be its addressees, the government should be regarded as invalid, the result of an act of usurpation. Such an act is undemocratic, a repressive command, an expression of coercive imposition. As Carl Friedrich correctly observed, "To make the constitutional decision genuine it is also necessary that it be participated in by some of those who are being governed as contrasted with those who do the governing. This differentiates such a constituent act from a coup d' état." Carl Friedrich, *Constitutional Government and Democracy: Theory and Practice in Europe and America* (Boston: Ginn, 1950), 128.

6

DEVELOPMENT

Gayatri Chakravorty Spivak

A gradual unfolding, a bringing into fuller view; a fuller disclosure or working out of the details of anything, as a plan, a scheme, the plot of a novel. Also quasi-*concr.* that in which the fuller unfolding is embodied or realized.

The economic advancement of a region or people, esp. one currently underdeveloped (sense 3b).

1902 *Daily Chron.* 25 Nov. 4/5 This consideration leads us to what is the supreme need for all parts of that country, namely, economic development. "Development first" was the formula for the moment used by Lord Milner in his latest speech. What South Africa . . . needs above all is . . . the primary plant of civilized development.

1945 *Polit. Q.* Oct.–Dec. 359 Economic development has benefited large sections of the people in Anatolia.

1982 *Dædalus* Spring 133 All African countries lack sufficient managerial, administrative, and technical skills to undertake the massive task of development contemplated at independence. (*OED*)

Why is "development" a political concept? The historical answer might well be that we should plot it on a chain of displacements beginning perhaps with the notion of the possibility of the perfectibility of humankind, a conviction not necessarily confined to Europe, but most publicly associated with the Encyclopaedist strain of the French Enlightenment.[1] Upon this chain of displacements, Kant has been marked as inaugurating modernity.[2] In our reading, Kant binds free will as a programmed necessity within practical reason; the necessity to declare freedom to be taken as constituting human agency. This *Anlage* or program is irreducible and can be called a nuanced "fatalism," within which the Kantian critique exemplifies the acting out of an unavoidable desire for philosophy. This declaration of free will by a structurally determined necessity leaves fatalism as such unguarded in the persistent structures of history. The force of the Kantian critique is counterintuitive and has idled as a guide to practice. In the lay reading, he has been seen only as an implacable moralist. Rather than Kant's taxonomy of *Anlage* and "fatalism," we have fallen back or into or yet forward to a race-class–determined binary opposition of free will and fatalism that writes our world today. The so-called abstract workings of capital operate a deconstruction—fatalists to be folded together (made com-plicit, a typical deconstructive move) with capitalist petty bourgeois ideology (everyone can be a captain of industry)—which is called "development."

Ranajit Guha has allowed us to plot development in a chain of displacements applying to India, as I have noted recently, in the following way:

> the converted Buddhist Emperor Asoka (304–232 B.C.)'s new imperial-universal notion of *dhamma*, not to be found in the *Arthasastra* (150 B.C.–300 A.D.)—the classic text of Indian economic and military practice—was in its turn miscast into the older Hindu notion of *dharma*, both instruments of class reconciliation between sovereign and subject. Historical change, class accommodation, not "Indian" psychological essence. A chain of displacements again: *dharma-dhamma-dharma*; with colonialism, "Improvement," "civilizing mission"; in general theory, today "Development." *All these words utilize invented "tradition" for the sake of reconciling established class/caste convictions in the lower social strata.*[3]

I believe one could find corresponding chains and linkings in other parts of the world.

In the last century, Michel Foucault taught us to think about politics as a heterogeneous insertion into the play of power. Although Foucault was not specific about race and class, I can summarize his position as follows: access to power positions is not initially deliberate but rather an "insertion" by virtue of what an older language would call "social formation." Within a single social formation, such access is necessarily heterogeneously determined by race-class-gender as the condition and effect of inequality. In my estimation, the diversity involved in the field of application of "development" pulls Foucault's analysis beyond its own empirical limits.

One can come to this conclusion by attending to questions Foucault himself famously posed about conceptualization: "conceptualization should not be founded on a theory of the object—the conceptualized object is not the single criterion of a good conceptualization. We have to know the historical conditions that motivate our conceptualization. We need a historical awareness of our present circumstance. The second thing to check is the type of reality with which we are dealing."[4]

In our reality, wherein states have been usually undermined with reference to capitalist globality, some of us might think of politics by going back to the word *politeia* or, roughly, constitutionality. Although most new nations are tremendously interested in new constitutions, and European nations are also concerned about constitutions because of the precariousness of the euro zone, in fact we know that the charge of the state for redistribution and constitutionality has been taken elsewhere: the human rights lobby, the various United Nations organizations from peacekeeping to language protection, and the international civil society in general. The state now operates by the unconstituted "rule of law" required for the management of global capital, preserving its ideological frame: neoliberalism. On this agreement, economic growth is the main index of what is called "development." The measuring site of economic growth, nonetheless, remains the state, and with it there is also an increasing awareness across the political spectrum that economic growth is not an adequate gauge for development in the qualitative/affective sense.[5] The historical conditions of our conceptualization of "development" must take into account a change in the electronic capitalist management of capital, where economically restructured states take on a managerial role. Thinking capital's social productivity as "development" is now more apposite than "improvement" or "civilizing mission." The contradiction between state-by-state measurement of economic growth and the decimation of the stately function (neoliberal governance by unconstituted "rule of law"), the increasing use of "cheap labor" (heterogeneity of labor) leading to massive labor export understood as migration, legitimized by tremendously expensive tax-dodging "V.I.P. migration" required by the same "rule of law," the preservation of differences in foreign exchange to protect one of the mainstays of finance capital and innumerable other details in order to grasp that "development" as a word hides the gap between a statistical measure and a trained epistemology. This is supported by private sector voluntarism of heterogeneous sorts: from international civil society through corporate social responsibility into the antics of the World Economic Forum and its reactive double, the World Social Forum.

This constellation enables the word "development" repeatedly to cross the aporia between mathemata and pathemata, statistics and affect. Marx's use of the word "social" shares the same problem—a quantified definition that seemed useful and a fuzzy qualitative idea. The first leads to the hope that "socialization"—using abstract average labor power with worker-owned means of production—would lead to a just society; the second to an unexamined and vague idea of a humanistic good society that Marx himself left untheorized as "the realm of freedom."[6] Some of us are trained into an intellectual style that welcomes such openings, but the traditional imperative to theorize considers all openings to be loopholes to be closed off. Hence the unexamined, fuzzy connotative field is simply taken for granted or ignored, ripe for political mobilization and poetry, sometimes indistinguishable, that cannot be satisfactorily thought through and therefore can destroy the clear outlines of a conceptual field.[7] It is because this muddle between affect and statistics cannot be satisfactorily theorized—that we can have moralistic, descriptive books, but no discussion of solutions.

Reviewing Jean Drèze and Amartya Sen's *An Uncertain Glory: India and Its Contradictions*, Jyoti Thottam writes, "Drèze and Sen might have devoted more thought to how to make India's existing social-welfare initiatives work better. They describe successes in a few forward-thinking states, but it is not clear how to replicate those results on a national scale. The section on discrimination against girls—an issue on which Sen is an unquestioned expert—also cries out for a more prescriptive analysis."[8] And Robert Shiller makes the same complaint in the pages of the same newspaper: "In his monumental new book, *Capital in the 21st Century*, Thomas Piketty of the Paris School of Economics documents a sharp increase in such inequality over the last 25 years, not only in the United States, but also in Canada, Britain, Australia, New Zealand, China, India, Indonesia and South Africa, with people with the highest incomes far outstripping the rest of society. The book is impressive in its wealth of information but it is short on solutions."[9]

Put another way, "development" is an insertion into the circuit of capital, without developing the subject of its ethical, or even appropriate social, use. The development of the subject is apparently in the self-interest of the "underdeveloped," but the larger pattern is in the interest of developed capital, as will be clear from the clinching concluding module of this sample of a "sustainable development" syllabus:

> **Module 1:** Introduction to sustainability management: What is it? How can we achieve it?
> **Module 2:** The public policy and regulatory framework of sustainability: How can this speed transition to sustainability?
> **Module 3:** A sustainably built environment: How can we plan for, design, and operate green workplaces, buildings, and infrastructure?
> **Module 4:** Sustainable financing and investment: How can we fund sustainability initiatives?[10]

This is designed for the subject of *developed* capital, whose force is larger than the undoubted personal goodwill of teacher and student. But the underdeveloped hastily trained into self-interest or self-interested income-production remains incapable of capital management, especially in its global form. Therefore, if we credit the abstract power of largely more and more unregulated capital, what is ultimately sustained is minimum "development" and maximum accumulation and surplus for financialization. Let us call this "sustainable underdevelopment."

In a popular essay on "development," a successful transformation of the gendered subject in Peru is described as follows: "Between 200,000 and 300,000 persons have been sterilized in the course of the program, 90 percent of whom were women. The government thus managed to restructure the field of action predominantly of its female population in the area of reproduction in a way that led to the desired change in behavior—not through the direct use of force, but through positive reinforcement and disciplinary measures (incentives offered for compliances and sanctions used against dissident conduct)."[11]

"Gendering," also the subject of micro-credit, is always the paradigm case of the inefficient production of the subject of development, whereby the provision of unmediated economic independence—let us forget global control—is a guarantee of victory in the gender struggle.

At the developed end, the management of subject production in the citizen—as well as the global citizen—an oxymoron—is guided by timid invocations of behaviorist economics, assuming a precritical theory of the subject that takes a step or two beyond rational choice. A "global citizen" is an oxymoron in the strict sense because there is no constituted global state. It uses the fuzzy connotative field around the word "citizen" as if it is conceptualizable. "Behavioral" economics, like behaviorism itself, conceptualizes the affects as leaders of "motivation" and thus ignores the complexities of the human mind. I use the term "precritical" in relationship to the outlines of the Kantian critique that I attempted to summarize above; because these motivations are argued by "mere reason"—Kant's phrase for reason defined by its lowest common denominator—behaviorist economics seems a modest modification of rational choice. Thus, its attempt to solve the problem of the muddle between statistics (rational choice) and affect (behavior) remains inadequate. I am still with Foucault's warning about the conditions of conceptualization. Among the many implications of explicit electronification of globalization is the setting-to-work of the rusing potential of language in its normal mode of existence: "development"—as "improvement" and "civilization" in previous formations.[12] One of the conjunctural contradictions thus glossed over by the nature of words is the obvious existential impoverishment of abstract calculation—the distance between capital measurement and the task of subject-formation that defines "development" in our conjuncture, as I have already suggested.

What follows is an example of advancement in statistics inadequate even to understanding the task of subject-formation:

> The Human Development Index, devised by Mahbub-ul-Haq, and used by the United Nations since 1990, has fallen upon bad days, as I have pointed out on various occasions, since the last report of the Human Development Index came out. The two items which transformed mere development into human development—education and life expectancy—were about to be discarded by the statisticians who put together the HDI, because they wanted to try for more efficient statistical production.[13] Thus indirectly we get a critique of the sentimental obstreperousness of affect-measurement by statistics; although to prove my point was not the statisticians' goal of course. "Development," with the affective paleonymy of the word, invariably taken seriously by top and bottom alike, cannot be conceptualized without theories of democratic subject-formation that require alternative disciplinary formations.

We must now confront the fact that "development" might top the list of a generic change in global index-making since the tremendous advance in statisticalization brought in by the silicon chip: the measure of affect by numbers, as it affects our everyday: please "like" this, please be my "friend." Presidents blog and tweet. Development is on the cusp of this loosening of the conceptualization of the political. When such measurement began, in the aftermath of the Great Depression and World War II, the idea was, as Yeats put it, "Measurement began our might."[14] After Bretton Woods, "GDP becomes the standard tool for sizing up a country's economy."[15] Now, as we notice in the module for sustainable development training, we must consider investment, for finance capital is more important than industrial. And, the bull market is constantly dependent upon affect: not even the most mathematical textbooks can escape the fact that the bull market is dependent upon investor confidence. It is therefore dependent upon an interested subject-production.

The relationship between affect and its statistical legislation can also be seen as a displacement of the concept-metaphor argument made in Derrida's "White mythology," that the concept erases within itself the fabulous scene that persistently produces it. Derrida does not see this erasure as sequential.[16] Although worldwide policy on many angles is made on these existentially impoverished statistics, the word "development" is used and felt by people even at the bottom of the pile to describe a general condition of human value. It is this that the concept erases by the general law of abstract measurement. For whom is the definition to be made? The way in which the policy makers use it? The way in which among the policy makers there is still a group that thinks economic growth is not, in the human sense, development? The efforts at nuancing the concept simply by adding myriad items is an example of Kant's long ago indication that "mere reason" reduces responsibility to ***Zurechnungfähigkeit***, or reckoning. Similarly, the desire to measure "happiness" ignores the condition of subalternity: the subaltern as such—not yet in crisis/struggle—thinks objective wretchedness is normal; how shall we measure "happiness" here? (Let us remember Kant's displacement of "fatalism" in his bound conception of freedom—the misfired mark of a misfired philosophical modernity that was replaced by a race-class–determined binary opposition of free will and fatalism that runs our world today.) I refer the reader to the more extended discussion above. These, then, are the "fatalists" at the bottom. Should the definition accommodate the way in which large sections of the population use it at present, as what Raymond Williams would call a "residual," hanging on from the sense of being a second-class culture that came with colonialism? If you think I am beginning to suggest that this is a word that would be better off without the convenience of adequate conceptualization, you are correct. (I realize I am interdisciplinary here. No doubt the qualitative social sciences must aim to conceptualize seamlessly; the quantitative ones statisticalize; the qualitative are most often a combination of the two. The humanities break them open to consider the incalculable when we speak "development." Can a lexicon allow for this?) The task is to translate the word into many different languages and see how it is understood and internalized by the class that cannot access worldwide quantification—and by gender singled out as an alibi for intervention. For this persistent opening up, the baseline concept will suffice:

the economic transition into the circuit of capital with insufficient attention to subject-formation.

It is the task of such a supplementation of the word "development" to make the apologists or organic intellectuals of capitalist globalization think development as subject-formation and dismiss this "real" definition of development as only "economistic." Development as such moves at best toward fostering the justified self-interest of groups often in opposition. As Marx already knew, it is not enough to wish to end exploitation for one's own group. The point is to foster an international will for social justice in general. There are many reasons why this does not happen. The failure does not require us to fall back into unexamined liberalism. I can repeat here what I said to the World Economic Forum: knowledge depends on cooking the soul with slow learning, not the instant soup of a one-size-fits-all toolkit. The world is not populated by humanoid drones. You cannot produce a toolkit for "a moral metric," or if you do you will be disappointed.

Cooking the soul = subject-formation. "Development" as a political concept ignores this. That the World Economic Forum has no interest in this does not mean that the readership of this critical lexicon also should not!

"Development" as a concept is understood by ordinary people differently from the statistical understanding available to competitive national governments and international finance. The word in my mother tongue is *unnayan*. As a noun, it works fine—it is understood as various good things like schools, bridges, hospitals, or trees coming our way. For "developing" there is no colloquial word. For "undeveloped," a word routinely chosen for self-description, we have *anunnoto*. Paradoxically, this adjective is usually applied by my clients—landless and ill educated, often illiterate, men—to describe India, of which they have a somewhat vague idea. To represent themselves, they use the colloquial version of this adjective—*pichhiye pora*, held back—which is also routinely used by so-called radical intellectuals to describe them.

Many years ago we read Walter Rodney's *How Europe Underdeveloped Africa*.[17] I am proposing that that story, although signaling a rupture, could take hold because it is also a displacement of the general dominating practice of precolonial conjunctures. Benevolent or malevolent or in-between or indeed not-bothered-to-be-volent-precolonial power groups unevenly enriching themselves at the expense of the postcolonial groups inheriting older hierarchies share that logic. This gives us a premodern clue to the word "underdevelopment" as it spread to varieties of the class-apartheid present in all polities, cutting across gender-apartheid and group-apartheid, where the usual overflowing of something like "class" in the everyday must be allowed to contaminate the disinfected house of scientific socialism.[18] The Dalit leader Bhimrao Ramji Ambedkar suggests, in a graduate seminar paper written by him as a student at Columbia, and intended therefore for a non-Indian audience, that the difference in the treatment of surplus men and surplus women, present in all societies, is the motor of group-formation, including caste.[19] In other words, the essay acknowledges reproductive heteronormativity as the matrix within which the history of all apartheid is held.

If we allow the concept of development to overflow the interplay of capital and colony, we will see this matricial role more clearly. This requires allowing reproductive heteronormativity itself to overflow the outlines of sexual reproduction and be thought as the possible unacknowledgeable antonym of the autonormativity that is the authoritative self-representation of ideology as Idea. I will unpack this by way of Marx's discovery of surplus-value.

Marx describes the secret of surplus-value in *Capital I* as the *Sprengpunkt* or "the 'pivot' of his critique."[20] In surplus-value, discovered during the composition of the *Grundrisse*—he discovered the secret of reproductive heteronormativity, that everything human and upper primate emerges out of the difference between needing and making. He described it in human terms—the worker advances the capitalist his laborpower and the capitalist repays less than he gets out of it; and he also describes it in rational terms—laborpower is the only commodity that, when consumed, produces value. Yet this discovery of human and top primate hetero-norm (that the contingent surplus produced in the difference between need and the capacity to make runs the world), was seen subsequently as lodged in the autonormative idea, identical with itself, scientific socialism. Hence Antonio Gramsci's word, "gnoseological"—neither "psychological," for the logic of the psyche is at the mercy of the individuated contingent, nor "moral," although consciousness and morality are at issue. The tremendous discovery of the heteronormative as the source of simple as well as expanded reproduction was put in the service of autonormative gnoseology—gnosis, diagnosis, prognosis: scientific socialism. Marx gives enough signs that he is aware this can go beyond the economic sphere. However, tying it to the economic has prevented us from noticing that this is how all intuitions of the transcendental also come forth, including any possible acknowledgment of complicity with the anthropocene. Here, however, we are on the track of the rich potentiality of Ambedkar's early reckoning of reproductive heteronormativity as the matrix within which the history of apartheid, consistent in race, caste/class, and gender—most damagingly marked in access to educational quality, subject formation—is held.

If we open up this autonormative drive to deny the heteronormative—that everything emerges in the difference of self-adequate need-satisfaction and excessive capacity to produce—the trivial Euro-sequential truism that time moves from the premodern to modern through colonialism into globality (spiced up by "culture" as invented by anthropology and now bowdlerized by UNESCO and the Nara Document on Authenticity of 1994) that runs the world can be revised. To conceptualize development as freedom in capitalism without the task of subject-formation will then have to acknowledge the incalculable in what is in excess rather than narrow it down only to the economic sphere. It is clear that this acknowledgment requires the rethinking of political concepts. To make the possibility of the anthropocene visible in the ceaseless turning of capital into capitalist implementation is well-nigh impossible. Here socialism and capitalism are themselves complicit in their will to knowledge, full control through concept.

With colonialism came, unevenly, the social productivity of capital and the inbuilt mechanism for the disavowal of the imbricated increased subalternization. I am asking for an acknowledgment of "development" as a task—understood from the subject-formation rather than the capitalization angle—diversely neglected also in precolonial time and space worldwide. It is not "individualistic" to teach the elite as well as the subaltern/proletarian to think, in a complicit and gendered manner, that "development" is not necessarily tied to that Euro-sequential truism; that interested underdevelopment rather than development has forever made the world turn and inhabits the persistent structures of contemporary globality; that rogue capitalization, as it is now indicated by more and more people at the center, could inhabit those structures not only as rupture but as repetition.

Once again, then, I am asking us to allow the concept of development to overflow the interplay of capital and colony. This makes room for an acknowledgment of complicity—folded-togetherness—rather than see "development" to be conceptualized as good or evil or both *after* colonialism. I am asking for us to see that development as sustainable underdevelopment has a longer history and perhaps even that this history is beginning to make itself visible as the pattern of globalization explodes economic growth into developing inequality. I am suggesting that the conceptualization of development must be unevenly interdisciplinary—statistics and political science folded together, complicit—with the disciplines of subject-formation, the humanities.

Globalization requires a change in ourselves as instruments of knowing. Those wonderful historical approaches, "culture wars" approaches, critique of Eurocentrism approaches, the modernity/tradition approaches, postcolonial approaches, will not serve if you're doing the contemporary as such. That's the epistemological challenge: How do we construct our objects of knowledge now, in the moving global now-time?

The question, for us, is, how to "determine" a "people," in order to decide development. I use "determination" in the sense of *Bestimmung*, and I thank Werner Hamacher for long ago endorsing enthusiastically my emphasis on *die Stimme* (tune or voice) in *Bestimmung*.[21] Determination is also a resonance, as in a keynote: "The unfolding of the qualities or capacities of a musical phrase or subject by modifications of melody, harmony, tonality, rhythm, etc., esp. in a composition of elaborate form, as a sonata [or a raga]" (*OED*).

To conceptualize development, the intellectual must be in tune with, enter the *Bestimmung* of "the people," from top to bottom, elite to subaltern, capitalist to client, and rearrange desires, our own among them. This supplementation is so slow and painstaking—the world has such a wealth of languages—that it is impossible for this to be a general agenda, such as the globalization of capital or the social must be. This is why, once again, this kind of linguistic commitment must work as an unceasing supplementation of the work of the qualitative social sciences, which must in turn supplement the quantifying work of sociology and economics, continuing on to the development indices. Practically speaking, as a woman persuaded of the humanities' supplementary potential, I must think that development might be a word that would be better off without strict conceptualization. With the inauguration of this new genre, where the affective part is socially mediatized, we might, rather, engage in an admittedly (rather than disguised as correcting others' mistakes) persistent effort at the questioning of conceptualizations in this stage of capital. Concepts of development are needed here and now as methodological practical necessities, not as governing ideas. If you stick to classical concept production in development, you remain with the fiscal and the juridico-legal, tax reform and enforcement, and, of course, the sentimental statisticalization of affect.

We should recognize that development is in complicity with what it endangers, that "the opposition of intuition, the concept, and consciousness at this point no longer has any pertinence."[22] Resist the will to conceptualize as you develop yourself. To misquote a classic, "Conceptualization is its own resistance."[23]

NOTES

1. For the most interesting discussion of perfectibility, see *L'homme perfectible*, ed. Bertrand Binoche (Paris: Editions du Champ Vallon, 2004).

2. Foucault hailed Kant as the inaugurator of modernity for a somewhat different reason. See "What Is Enlightenment?," in *The Foucault Reader*, ed. Peter Rabinow, 32–50 (New York: Pantheon, 1984).

3. Gayatri Chakravorty Spivak, "A Penny for the Old Guy," *Cambridge Review of International Affairs* 27, no. 1 (2014): 184–98, accessed May 28, 2014, http://www.tandfonline.com/doi/abs/10.1080/09557571.2014.877262#.U8afU_ldXTo. For invented tradition, I am using the introduction to *The Invention of Tradition*, ed. Eric Hobsbawm and Terence Ranger, 1–14 (Cambridge: Cambridge University Press, 1983).

4. Michel Foucault, "The Subject and Power," *Critical Inquiry* 8 (1982): 778.

5. An excellent account of this in the African context can be found in Thandika Mkandawire, *Africa: Beyond Recovery* (Legon-Accra: Sub-Saharan Publishers, 2015), 16–18.

6. Karl Marx, *Capital: A Critique of Political Economy*, vol. 3, trans. David Fernbach (New York: Penguin, 1992), 958.

7. Following from these general presuppositions I had written in the first, strictly twenty-minute, paper: the muddle between statistics and affect cannot be satisfactorily noted. These now disclosed presuppositions will, I hope, make clear that we literary folk are satisfied with that connotative muddle. However, the too tightly packed earlier version called forth a reader's question: "Who or what prevents it from being noted?" Alas, the answer is: the nature of words. They offer meanings, the simpler the better. And today these meanings can be extremely satisfactorily measured. We are trained to ignore what cannot fit into the measurement. Knowledge management skills stop the contingent, and there is no computer that can catch the contingent. The ruse of single words—to close off resident contradictions—is such an everyday phenomenon that to bring in arguments from the hermeneutics of suspicion and/or the trivialization of the humanities would be, as the saying goes, to use cannonballs to kill mosquitoes.

8. Jean Drèze and Amartya Sen, *An Uncertain Glory: India and Its Contradictions* (Princeton, N.J.: Princeton University Press, 2013); Jyoti Thottam, "Two Indias," *New York Times*, September 6, 2013, BR10.

9. Thomas Piketty, *Capital in the Twenty-First Century* (Cambridge, Mass.: Harvard University Press, 2014); Robert J. Shiller, "Better Insurance against Inequality," *New York Times*, April 13, 2014, BU6.

10. The Earth Institute, "Sustainability Essentials Training (SET) Program," Columbia University, accessed September 3, 2016, http://earth.columbia.edu/sections/view/9.

11. Aram Ziai, "Development: Projects, Power, and a Poststructuralist Perspective," *Alternatives* 34 (2009): 190.

12. V. N. Volosinov, *Marxism and the Philosophy of Language*, trans. Ladislav Mateijka and I. R. Titunik (Cambridge, Mass.: Harvard University Press, 1986).

13. United Nations, "The Rise of the South: Human Progress in a Diverse World," 2013 Human Development Report (New York: United Nations Development Program, 2013).

14. William Butler Yeats, "Under Ben Bulben," in *The Variorum Edition of the Poems of W. B. Yeats*, ed. Peter Allt and Russell Alspach (New York: MacMillan, 1957), 638.

15. Elizabeth Dickinson, *GDP: A Brief History*, in *Foreign Policy* 184 (2011) 37.

16. Jacques Derrida, "White Mythology: Metaphor in the Text of Philosophy," in *Margins of Philosophy*, trans. Alan Bass (Chicago: University of Chicago Press, 1982), 213.

17. Walter Rodney, *How Europe Underdeveloped Africa* (London: Bogle-L'Ouverture, 1972).

18. National liberation is freedom from colonial rule but cannot necessarily create a rupture from the old precolonial structures of sustainable underdevelopment. The nation that is liberated is often a product of orientalist historiography. Ama Ata Aidoo's "For Whom Things Did Not Change," in *No Sweetness Here* (New York: Feminist Press, 1995), 8–29, captures this.

19. B. R. Ambedkar, "Castes in India: Their Mechanism, Genesis and Development," in *The Essential Writings of B. R. Ambedkar*, ed. Valerian Rodrigues (Oxford: Oxford University Press, 2004), 241–62. My remark is the gist of a complex argument.

20. Karl Marx, *Capital: A Critique of Political Economy*, vol. 1, trans. Ben Fowkes (New York: Penguin, 1977), 132; translation modified.

21. Personal communication after my paper "The Dimension of History and the Political," at the Conference on Critical Philosophy and Critical Theory: The Wake of Kant's Third Critique, at the University of Minnesota, April 1986.

22. Derrida, *Margins of Philosophy*, 270.

23. Paul de Man, "The Resistance to Theory," *Yale French Studies* 63 (1982): 20.

7

EXPLOITATION

Étienne Balibar

When I proposed "exploitation" as a contribution for this volume, I thought I would vindicate the political character of Marxism in the framework of an encyclopedia of "political concepts" in the making, since everybody knows that this is one of Marxism's central notions and that it characterizes Marxism's way of overcoming separations between disciplinary fields and idioms.[1] Hence, the concept of exploitation underpins our conviction that Marxism is an important reference for critical theory. For political theorists, exploitation appears as an "economic" concept, or is at least fraught with economicism. It is much less easily incorporated in debates on "justice" than inequality or discrimination. For economists, even if they are not "orthodox" or mainstream, it is a political and ideological concept, which relies more on partisan choices and humanist assumptions than verifiable hypotheses. But isn't it precisely this kind of nondialectical alternative that Marxism wanted to overcome? However, this is also what constitutes its fragility in today's conversations, insofar as the technical support for a theory of capitalist exploitation—namely, the concept of *surplus value* (in German, *Mehrwert*) that Marx coined in his "Critique of Political Economy"—seems to rely on a prerequisite that is either too speculative or too narrow to account for contemporary manifestations of social domination and alienation in our societies, namely, what falls under the *labor theory of value*.

Addressing this difficulty from a broader point of view, which, for want of a better etiquette, I will call "anthropological," I am convinced that concepts only work in correlations whose displacements and condensations make it possible to insert them in different *problematics*, and this is in fact what we want to investigate in our encyclopedia. My objective will be to discuss the unstable correlation of *exploitation*, *domination*, and *alienation*. The Marxist problematic of exploitation has been oscillating between tendencies to essentially read it as domination, and tendencies to read it as alienation. I submit that it is inasmuch as we reopen the question of their overlapping and their interdependencies that we may reach a better understanding of what Marx contributes and what he leaves open for a critical articulation of the economic and the political in the present. I will try to do it in two steps, limiting myself to very schematic and provisory indications indeed.

My first point begins with etymologies and uses. Allow me to recall two famous jokes. One is a Soviet joke, alluding to quasi-official mantras at the time of "really existing socialism." It goes like this: "What is capitalism?" asks a student or a child. The father or the teacher answers: "It's the exploitation of man by man." "And what's communism, then?" Answer: "It's the opposite!" Note that no woman is there, or if there is, she is subsumed under the name "man." I will return to this. The second joke is a "Bushism" that my compatriots heard with some surprise when George W. Bush was president of the United States (but perhaps they were too quick to laugh). "The French really don't understand economic matters," Bush explained; "they don't even have the word *entrepreneur*." But maybe "entrepreneur" became a different word when migrating from French to American English?[2] Terms such as "exploiter" or "expropriator" might also lead to surprises. So let's turn to etymology. I believe that Marx's notion of exploitation comes immediately from the opposition between *les exploitants* and *les exploités* that the Saint-Simonians made use of, and which they applied to individuals—but especially to classes—and associated with a notion of antagonism.[3] Note that, in French as in English, you can say "the dominants" and "the dominated," changing an adjective into a noun in certain contexts, but not really "the alienants" and the "alienated." All this seems to locate a problematic of exploitation on the "political" side, a master-slave relationship or *Herrschafts- und Knechtschaftsverhältnis*, as Marx would write in Hegelian language, which is not "impersonal" like commodity fetishism. This was the reason the Saint-Simonians argued that exploitation essentially characterized pre-bourgeois societies and would wither away in the industrial society. Marx precisely objected to that, and he "reversed" the use of the opposition, to show that in capitalism the degree of exploitation is in fact *increasing*, leading to a historical climax, and not decreasing. But *exploitant* in French (especially in agriculture, where as a name it practically means a farmer) has a very wide use extending to any situation where you can say that you materially, economically, or morally draw on a resource for your own benefit. So you can "exploit" someone (or someone's labor, skill, qualities, but also defects and weaknesses: vulnerability, poverty, naïveté, and so on, of which you *take advantage* strategically), but you can also "exploit" a generic material resource (e.g., the fertility of the earth, or the ocean full of fish, or a rich mine, etc.) from which you extract a product through labor or appropriation. The Saint-Simonians were industrialists who thought that the trend of modern history was to shift from the exploitation of men to the exploitation of nature, also called in a later jargon "the administration of things." And although Marxism later resumed this formula to define socialism, it began with a more symmetric view, where capitalism exploits persons and things at the same time. Hence a famous passage in volume 1 of *Capital*, which says that "capitalist production only develops the techniques and the degree of combination of the social process of production by simultaneously undermining the original sources of all wealth: the soil (*die Erde*) and the worker."[4]

This leads me to a first consideration: any rigorous use of the category "exploitation" should be subjected to a syntactic and semantic question that is a logical preliminary: *who or what exploits whom or what?* There is ambiguity both on the side of the subject and on the side of the object. On the side of the subject, the issue may seem relatively innocuous, at least from a Marxist point of view, since we have become accustomed to thinking that, essentially, it is a system or a structure called capitalism or capital that causes exploitation and the benefits that arise from it, for the sake of its accumulation, Capitalism's agents—the capitalists—are mere instruments, even when they enjoy privileges linked to their function. I will return to this.

The issue of the object is far more sensitive and complicated. Our political uses of the language of exploitation impose the idea that it is human beings or persons that are exploited, insofar as they must serve others or work for others, or for a system that dominates them. But the Marxist critique explains that what is in fact exploited is the *labor force* that the workers or the proletarians possess within themselves, and which they must sell to capital. Hence it is in fact a *thing* that their person "harbors" or contains. But this formulation is too naturalistic or mechanistic: more properly, for Marxism, what is exploited is a *part* of the workers—a living capacity that, for the sake of this exploitation, becomes *reifed* or transformed into a "thing"—both in the sense that it is legally owned, sold, and bought, and in the sense that it is technically shaped, controlled, and manipulated. Here we see the understanding of exploitation as essentially a form of domination, projected into the field of economic relations, shifting toward a more specific and more profound understanding as a *process of alienation*. This is exploitation as an inversion of personal relations into relations among things, as Marx notoriously explained in the chapter on the fetishism of commodities.

But this beautiful demonstration also leads to problems, which become very apparent today. It is an essential part of Marx's demonstration in *Capital* to explain that the only source of surplus-value, *Mehrwert*, is surplus-labor, *Mehrarbeit*, which is to say, surplus-value only arises through the alienation and domination of human productive activity. There can be no other source because "value" itself is the expression of an expenditure of labor that is socially necessary. This explains why, however eloquent it sounds, the phrase on the destruction of the "two sources of wealth"—human labor force and the earth—remains isolated. It is a moral judgment on the effects of capitalism, but it is not integrated into the axioms of the theory. However, this formula sounds prophetic today because we discover that the destruction of the environment is at the same time intrinsic to the mode of production and a major threat to the life of humans themselves (and needless to say, their productive capacity as well). We are thus tempted to *broaden the notion of exploitation* in order to incorporate an exploitation of nature as well as an exploitation of the human labor force within its range. But here we face a dilemma. For this to have a Marxist sense, it is necessary that the phenomenon of the exploitation of nature, or the natural "things," is also an intrinsic part of the creation and accumulation of capital, that is, of the production and valorization of value. Nature has to be productive, even if it is not the only productive force, as in the old "physiocratic" theory. This makes no sense within the theory of Marx's *Capital*, since these natural things are used, appropriated, and ultimately destroyed by labor, but they are not themselves "living" labor. So we must either drop the notion of exploitation or drop the notion of value, unless we find a way to *transform the concept of "labor" and "labor force"* in order to incorporate in its definition something like a *reciprocity* of natural and human actions (which would no longer be a "humanist" concept of labor): a "third way," as it were, which is the most difficult, but also in my eyes the most promising. This is what, in the excellent formulation of David Harvey, I would call a *point of stress* of Marxist theory, or Marxist axiomatics.[5]

In the same spirit, let me now examine a second question. According to Marx, exploitation indeed has a history. In fact, it means nothing outside of its history: the emergence, development, and transformation of its forms, arising from their internal and external contradictions. Already the famous phrase at the beginning of the *Communist Manifesto* (which has a direct Saint-Simonian ancestry) expresses this intrinsic historicity, in that it identifies every past and present history with the history of class struggles, and is then followed by an enumeration of the typical figures of a relationship between exploiters and exploited, which are each time depending on a new mode of production. As I mentioned earlier, this served to reverse the progressive vision of the history of human emancipation shared by the Saint-Simonians and other Enlightenment philosophers and replace it with a different concept of progress, whereby—as Marx also wrote in a contemporary text—*l'histoire avance par le mauvais côté*.[6] As we know, this was developed later in the complete problematic of the modes of production, which are also, each time, modes of exploitation in a new form, or even in a new sense. I am not interested in discussing the details of the modes of production now, however important this may be for the social sciences, nor in criticizing the scholastic aspect of the typology of modes of production in historical Marxism, which, we should not forget, has never been independent of its political uses. But I am interested in highlighting two conceptual implications and, once again, a point of stress.

The two implications are linked: they concern the articulation of *exploitation and overexploitation*, and the distinction (or nondistinction) of the political conditions and the economic modalities of exploitation. Exploitation and overexploitation are distinct notions, abstractly speaking, and this distinction really matters because, as Marx is never tired of explaining, exploitation in capitalism is not the result of an injustice, in the sense of violating legal and moral norms; it is not a fraud or an arbitrary violence. The violence is already involved in the "normal" exploitation wherein workers are paid wages that correspond to the value of their labor force. It is the result of a "fair" contract. However, as every reader of *Capital* knows, the distinction of exploitation and overexploitation is difficult to inscribe in the pragmatic organization and history of labor because every method for the production of surplus value, which means a specific modality of extracting surplus labor beyond necessary labor, either leads to overwork and overexploitation (Marx particularly refers to the endless prolongation of the working day) or always already introduces forms of overexploitation *inside* the organization of the productive forces. This latter point can be seen, for example, in the combined intensification and increased productivity that characterizes all phases of the industrial revolution (there are amazing anticipations of Taylorism when Marx describes the "factory system" in volume 1 of *Capital*). This means very concretely (and tragically) that the physical, moral, and psychic integrity of the human workforce is continuously threatened by the conditions of its capitalist use (without which it is not even a workforce).

I propose to express this situation by saying that what characterizes capitalism is a *normalization of overexploitation*. The reverse side of this is a class struggle that tends to impose limits, establishing, as it were, "normal conditions of exploitation," which for that reason are deprived of any technical or economic objective criterion but merely express an unstable relationship of forces between the tendency toward overexploitation and the countertendency or resistance that reduces it. The same idea could be expressed in terms of violence, extreme violence, and antiviolence.[7] It is important to understand the anthropological meaning of the historical perspective on the succession of modes of production. We do not have criteria to compare the degrees of violence linked to exploitation in different historical periods or societies in an absolute manner, but we have the possibility to demonstrate that there is no such thing as a law of irreversible progress: there is no spontaneous economic development that would result in a progressive civilization or humanization of exploitation in history, except and inasmuch as a collective capacity of resistance is built and is favored by external conditions. Suffice it to look at the contemporary examples of forced labor during the construction of the World Cup stadiums in Qatar,[8] or the suicides of overworked technicians in French and Chinese electronic factories, to illustrate this remark.

This leads me to a second consideration. A crucial aspect of Marx's *Darstellung* of capitalism in his work relies on comparisons between the capital-wage labor relation and the corresponding relations among "immediate producers" and "owners of the means of production" in other modes, particularly *slavery* (ancient or modern), and *feudalism* (based on the imposition of "corvée" on peasants or valets). The immediate aim of these comparisons is to single out the permanence of a distinction between "necessary labor" and "surplus labor" in every form of exploitation, with or without a transformation of labor into a commodity. A further aim is to highlight aspects of capitalist exploitation (and overexploitation), which are either akin to a perpetuation of feudalism, or to a reproduction of slavery in a new form. And as a consequence they help us to understand which aspects of capitalism are better analyzed in terms of domination, and which in terms of alienation, since feudalism or bondage is the archetypical form of a process of exploitation whose condition is the institution of an anthropological hierarchy. Slavery (especially chattel slavery), conversely, is the extreme form of alienation, in which the person not only harbors a capacity that becomes reified as a labor force; more radically, the labor force becomes a thing, juridically and fantastically.

But, as Emmanuel Terray explains in a remarkable essay on "Exploitation et domination dans la pensée de Marx," this comparison is also the key to understanding the articulation of the "economic" and the "political" aspects in the analysis of modes of exploitation and their transformations.[9] Terray's discussion is based on the famous passage in volume 3 of *Capital*, where Marx asserted that "The specific economic form, in which unpaid surplus labor is pumped out of the direct producers, determines the relation of rulers and ruled, as it grows immediately out of production itself and reacts upon it as a determining element. . . . It is always the direct relation of the owners of the conditions of production to the direct producers, which reveals the innermost secret, the hidden foundation of the entire social construction, and with it of the political form of the relations between sovereignty and dependence."[10]

As Terray explains, the apparent thesis is that what distinguished capitalism from previous modes of production is that they always needed an *external political* (and ideological) *constraint* to impose the domination of the exploiters on the exploited, an element that capitalism does not need (or only in a secondary manner, to control class struggles after the event), inasmuch as it relies on the *alienation* of the labor force, which is not political, but economic. But a more profound or virtual thesis is that capitalism *interiorizes the political conditions* to the economic process itself: its "material" basis, the collective labor force with a "value" corresponding to necessary labor, is never a physical or natural element but a social and cultural factor determined by class struggles, in a conflictual manner. To which I might add, in the spirit of the "workerist" analysis (from Italian *operaismo*), that the political state has roots in the "plan of capital" in the factories, or is less and less discernible from the modalities of "governance" of the class struggle within production itself.[11] Domination and alienation are thus once again dialectically combined.

However, there is something, strangely, missing from Terray's discussion when he comes to the issue of the historical reproduction of the labor force, again signaling what—after David Harvey—I call here a point of stress. This is the function of domestic labor, or in other terms, the articulation of exploitation with sexual difference, whose symptom is the double meaning of the name "reproduction" in our anthropological language, as indicated in particular with great clarity by Alys Eve Weinbaum.[12] Of course, this symptomatic omission is largely the result of Marx's blindness to this question in his analysis of exploitation, which is the object of Terray's commentary. But let's see schematically how it affects the axiomatics of Marx's discourse in significant developments.

I will refer first to the *Communist Manifesto*. As I recalled, the enumeration of modes of exploitation and class struggles which form the entrance gate of its philosophy of history directly echoes similar typologies of *exploitants et exploités* in the Saint-Simonian doctrine. However, the Saint-Simonians (and more generally the romantic "utopian" socialists) always included the *émancipation de la femme* in the same vindication as the *émancipation du prolétaire*, which should have led Marx to include a patriarchic structure of domination and a domestic form of exploitation (both the exploitation of services and the exploitation of sexual and reproductive capacities) in his typology. But, in spite of later developments in the *Manifesto* on the fact that the bourgeoisie has perpetuated the enslavement of women and transformed marriage into a form of legal prostitution,[13] Marx dropped this form of exploitation from his canonic series. It is not difficult to understand why: patriarchy and domestic exploitation have a historicity and temporality that completely differ from the class structures described by Marx, one that cannot become inscribed in a *successive order*, whether linear or not, where they would feature as *prior to something and posterior to some other thing*, or as "dialectical" conditions for the emergence of certain political-economic forms of production, while resulting from the decomposition of others. So, if the domestic forms of exploitation had been kept in Marx's scheme, his teleological philosophy of history or his alternative notion of progress would have been destroyed *ab initio*.

From there we can pass to the even more enigmatic symptom of the missing articulation in *Capital*. To put it simply, Marx's definition of capitalist exploitation in terms of the conversion of surplus labor into surplus value (which in turn can become accumulated, provided it is "realized" in the circulation of commodities, making it possible to subject present or living labor to the rule of past or dead or accumulated labor), relies on the idea that, on average, capitalists pay wages that correspond to the "value of the labor force."[14] Most commentators focus on the question of the expression of living labor as value and surplus value. This expression depends on the length, intensity, and productivity of labor that is "socially necessary," and therefore already involves serious problems of calculation, if it is to be understood in quantitative terms—which the very notion of "value" seems to impose. Others are concerned with the fact that, in Marx's presentation, which relies on the idea of the "double character of labor," every productive activity has a double function: on the one hand to "preserve" the value of the means of production, including the machinery; on the other, to produce a *new* value, which includes both the value of the labor force and the surplus value. But nobody discusses the idea that "value of the labor force" and "value of the means of reproduction" are equivalent, if not identical, notions and necessarily express the same magnitude. This is, of course, an idea that comes from classical political economy. But there is more than that: to understand such an equivalence, we must suppose that the actual *process of consumption* (i.e., *usage*), where means of reproduction such as food, housing, education, love and care, birthing and nursing, and so on, are "incorporated" into the capacities of a worker. This incorporation is theoretically (and therefore also politically) neutralized as an activity, an experience, a use of time and a kind of social co-operation. It is as if these moments and *dispositifs* did not exist, or their result would be automatic. Of course, this is not the case, but the theory does not see it (except *negatively* inasmuch as the period of "individual" consumption necessary for the reproduction of the labor force cannot be used for labor, or is "useless" for the capitalist, and therefore must be reduced to a minimum), which is important nevertheless.[15] Why this invisibility? Because an axiomatic distinction between *productive and unproductive labor* is featured among the axioms of the theory, which comes from Adam (Smith), and in fact erases Eve, or ejects her own life from consideration as falling under the category of "unproductive labor"—a "labor" or a service without which, however, no consumption and no reproduction of the labor force would have taken place in the anthropological structures of bourgeois society, and others (insofar as there would have been no cooking, no sewing, no pregnancy, no child rearing, no consolation of the exhausted and humiliated worker, etc.—not really "minor" *conditions* for the mode of production).

This is the point of stress I was talking about: for the sake of the consistency of Marx's demonstration in *Capital*, it is necessary to assert a distinction between productive and unproductive labor, while at the same time, this distinction is incoherent from the perspective of the *general* notion of exploitation that is implicit in his comparisons and articulations of diverse modes of production. So, again, different "solutions" are possible, and they have been partially tried, of course. One of them is to jettison Marxism or declare it irrelevant because Marx had expelled the exploitation of women from his vision of politics and history—a rather harsh punishment indeed. But perhaps this is paying too dear a price if it leads to abandoning an analytic instrument that, after all, has something to say about capitalism that no other discourse really explains, to my knowledge, and which also will concern women. Another possibility that enjoyed a good reputation among Marxist anthropologists some decades ago, in the wake of remarks by Louis Althusser and Claude Meillassoux in particular:[16] to develop a theory of the "social formation" as an *articulation of modes of production*, which would also be an articulation of different modes of historicity, whereby every form of economic domination (including the capitalist one) also presupposes a form of domestic domination that reproduces it. This is also, of course, a way of reopening the syntactic question of what or who exploits what or whom, not only on the side of the objects but also on the side of the subjects (including the disturbing question about whether exploited subjects can be also exploiters, even if on behalf of others). And it changes our anthropological image of a "system." But perhaps it does not go far enough to analyze alienation, which includes dominations in the plural.

My guess—not really more than a guess—is that we should question the axiom itself, namely, the distinction of *productive and unproductive labor* (which is, obviously, profoundly linked to Marx's articulation of philosophical anthropology and politics since it does not only concern a distinction of "social spheres" in which social activities are displayed but also the intrinsic affinity of the worker and the revolutionary, or the agent of *poiēsis* and the bearer of *praxis*).[17] To articulate modes of production, of which one is a mode of producing the producer through the operations or *uses* of consumption, is of course a way to *broaden* and *differentiate* the very notion of labor, as was already the case with the destruction and productivity of nature in my first example. Feminists tended to express this differentiation in the form of a vindication: "we are productive too, if not more productive, since we 'reproduce.'" I understand that kind of *counterinterpellation* very well. Maybe the reverse operation, which is worth thinking about, is worth attempting as well, namely, reflecting on the unproductivity of social labor, without which there is no productivity or reproductivity in general. This seems to evoke Georges Bataille, for whom expenditure is essentially unproductive, *neither for "use" nor for "exchange value,"* but it is also compatible with much that is written today on the notion of "care," although—compared to Marx's articulation of the political, the economic, and the anthropological—the first seems very metaphysical, and the second often very psychological.[18] Suffice it to have located as precisely as possible the theoretical point of stress and the bifurcations that it makes possible from within the Marxist problematic itself.

POSTSCRIPT

As a consequence of the discussions and afterthoughts that occurred to me during the conference at Brown University, I want to add three remarks, which will serve only to remind us of the necessity of a more complete development.

First, what I have been trying to illustrate is indeed a *relational* conception of "concepts." This is not incompatible with the idea that concepts require "proper names" that serve to attach (provisionally) an effort of definition and a movement of problematization (therefore different, if not divergent temporalities and intentionalities). A distinction of *concepts* and *terms*, as proposed by Adi Ophir, seems to me very useful here, provided we agree to incorporate into its elaboration not only the articulation of a *performance of concepts* and the *circulation of terms*, but also an articulation of their respective multiplicities. To elicit a single concept for definition or investigation (as proposed by the *Lexicon* in its charter, and as we all agree to do it, following the rules of the game) is always to make a *strategic choice* in the field of theory, for which the multiplicity of terms offered by the historical "uses" or "language games," is the only possible experimental terrain. It is not, therefore, to identify an "idea" or "essence" with an ontological foundation—unless we move toward an "ontology of relations" in the epistemological field as well.

Second, in the current essay (very imperfect, I am aware), the underlying network of notions (each susceptible to become selected as a concept for definition and problematization), which was suggested by the reading of Marx (rather: by successive readings of Marx), can be presented as a crossing of two axes that intersect in a "point of condensation" marked by the name "surplus-value" (more precisely: the *doublet* "surplus-value"/"surplus-labor," which already indicates a complexity, an internal dialectic of terms). One axis joins the question of "domination" to the question of "alienation"—which is a great antithesis of modern political philosophy (since Hobbes and Rousseau). The other axis joins the notions of "exploitation" to that of "accumulation" (or *capital*), which arises from the critique of political economy. The indicative topography is therefore something like this:

Exploitation
*
Domination * surplus-labour/value * Alienation
*
Accumulation (capital)

Third, the antithesis of domination and alienation (which crystalized in the philosophical tradition with Hobbes and Rousseau, passing to Hegel and Marx himself, but also Simmel, Weber, and Lukács, etc.) represents an opposition of two modes of subjection: one centered on persons and the other centered on things or reified actions and agencies. It is an extremely general one, which can be retrieved in many different domains of politics, anthropology, and culture. It also has affinities with other antitheses around which the discourses of political philosophy become organized: I am thinking in particular of the recent (but in fact already classical) discussion of justice as redistribution and justice as recognition, illustrated by the Honneth-Fraser debate.[19] Conversely, the antithesis of "exploitation" and "accumulation," whose genealogy I have partially reconstructed through the indication of the shift in semantic content and pragmatic orientation, and which took place in the transition from the Saint-Simonian to the Marxian discourse, is a very specific one, linked to the critique of political economy (which is itself, of course, at the same time a *political* and an *epistemological* critique). As I was retrieving the "points of stress" that affect the Marxian construction of surplus-value as an expression of the exploitation of labor for the sake of accumulation (with the help of various debates where the "unthought" of Marx's axioms became perceptible), I became more aware that what is at stake is the sheer possibility of offering a political theory (even a political theory for the emancipation of all forms of domination and alienation) on the basis of the analysis of the *exploitation of labor*, which is what Marx selected as the foundation for his critique. This is a *strategic choice*, which determines the way in which the concepts are defined. If one asks whether this is the only possible choice (or even the best in every circumstance), the answer is clearly no. One could also relate this situation to the fact that, in Althusser's terms, Marxism is a "finite theory."[20] However, the "limits" of that theory are not given in advance. They vary (shrink or expand) with the possibilities of making *labor* (with its correlatives) a *political concept*. The same is true for the possibilities of this theory's application, which depend on changes in the historical realities themselves. One must be aware that a Marxist problematic of "exploitation" is not the only possible one, and that it is an *open* problematic, an instrument of problematization. Hence the importance of such thought experiments as carried on in this essay, which attempt a reconstruction that is also a variation.

NOTES

1. This essay was originally presented at Brown University, Cogut Center for the Humanities, on November 15, 2013, as part of the Political Concepts Conference.

2. Its intellectual history is a fascinating chapter, particularly investigated by Hélène Vérin, *Entrepreneurs, entreprises: Histoire d'une idée* (Paris: Presses Universitaires de France, 1982).

3. Saint-Amand Bazard et Olinde Rodrigues, *Exposition de la Doctrine Saint-Simonienne*. Première Année, 1829. Nouv. éd. publ. avec introd. et notes par C. Bouglé et Elie Halévy, Paris, Marcel Rivière, 1924.

4. Karl Marx, *Capital: A Critique of Political Economy*, vol. 1 (New York: Penguin, 1992), 638.

5. David Harvey, *A Companion to Marx's Capital, Volume 2* (London: Verso, 2013), 173, 188, and throughout.

6. The full sentence reads: "C'est le mauvais côté qui produit le mouvement qui fair l'histoire en constituant la lutte" (It is the bad side that produces the movement which makes history, by creating the struggle). Karl Marx, *Misère de la philosophie: Réponse à la philosophie de la misère de M. Proudhon* (1847; repr., Paris: Éditions Sociales, 1961), 130.

7. See my Wellek Library Lectures from 1996, now published with other essays in *Violence and Civility: On the Limits of Political Philosophy*, trans. G. M. Goshgarian (New York: Columbia University Press, 2015).

8. Pete Pattison, "Revealed: Qatar's World Cup 'Slaves,'" *Guardian*, September 25, 2013, https://www.theguardian.com/world/2013/sep/25/revealed-qatars-world-cup-slaves; Bobbie Johnson, "Former France Telecom CEO Indicted over 35 Suicides," *Gigaom*, July 5, 2012, https://gigaom.com/2012/07/05/former-france-telecom-ceo-indicted-over–35-suicides; Aditya Chakrabortty, "The Woman Who Nearly Died Making Your iPad," *Guardian*, August 5, 2013, http://www.theguardian.com/commentisfree/2013/aug/05/woman-nearly-died-making-ipad. See also Christophe Dejours and Florence Bègue, *Suicides au travail* (Paris: Presses Universitaires de France, 2009).

9. The essay is now reproduced in his book *Combats avec Méduse* (Paris: Galilée, 2011), 149–67.

10. Karl Marx, *Capital: A Critique of Political Economy,* vol. 3, trans. David Fernbach (New York: Penguin, 1992), chapter 47, "The Genesis of the Capitalist Ground-Rent," §2, "The Labour-Rent" (here is the corresponding German: "Die spezifische ökonomische Form, in der unbezahlte Mehrarbeit aus den unmittelbaren Produzenten ausgepumpt wird, bestimmt das Herrschafts und Knechtschaftsverhältnis, wie es unmittelbar aus der Produktion selbst hervorwächst und seinerseits bestimmend auf sie zurückwirkt . . . Es ist jedesmal das unmittelbare Verhältnis der Eigentümer der Produktionsbedingungen zu den unmittelbaren Produzenten . . . worin wir das innerste Geheimnis, die verborgne Grundlage der ganzen gesellschaftlichen Konstruktion und daher auch der politischen Form des Souveränitäts- und Abhängigkeitsverhältnisses . . . finden."

11. See Mario Tronti, "Il piano del capitale," in *Operai e capitale* (Turin: Einaudi, 1966), 60–85. Passages from Tronti's major work translated into English are available on the web at https://operaismoinenglish.wordpress.com/category/mario-tronti/page/2. An important critique of Tronti's views is included in Bruno Trentin, *La cité du travail: La gauche et la crise du fordisme* (Paris: Fayard, 2012).

12. Alys Eve Weinbaum, *Wayward Reproductions: Genealogies of Race and Nation in Transatlantic Modern Thought* (Durham, N.C.: Duke University Press, 2004). She was preceded in particular by Gayatri Chakravorty Spivak in her seminal article, "Scattered Speculations on the Question of Value," *Diacritics* 15, no. 4 (1985): 73–93

(who also asks about the relationship between "domination" and "exploitation"). See also the recent work by Silvia Federici, in particular, *Caliban and the Witch: Women, the Body and Primitive Accumulation* (New York: Autonomedia, 2004).

13. An idea that, as we know, originally came from Mary Wollstonecraft's *Vindication of the Rights of Women* from 1792.

14. Or, even more exactly, the "social capital," *das Gesamtkapital*, continuously acquires the social labor force for its value, which is the value of all means of reproduction consumed by the labor force.

15. It is reduced to a minimum as long as consumption itself does not become an important source of profit through the development of mass consumption: the capitalist imperative is then to have workers (or, rather, certain workers, concentrated in the affluent regions of the world) consuming as much as possible in as little time as possible. Together with the introduction of "indirect wage," consisting of welfare benefits, this leads to a profound transformation of the "social relation of production" itself.

16. Claude Meillassoux, *Maidens, Meal and Money: Capitalism and the Domestic Community* (Cambridge: Cambridge University Press, 1981); for Althusser I rely on personal communication; cf. Emmanuel Terray, *Marxism and "Primitive" Societies: Two Studies*, trans. Mary Klopper (New York: Monthly Review Press, 1972).

17. It is on this point that Hannah Arendt, not usually considered either a feminist or a Marxist but an avid reader of Rosa Luxemburg and influenced in her critique of Marxism by the rejection of a "violent" notion of labor, advocated a return to the classical, Aristotelian, disjunctions of production and action. See Hannah Arendt, *The Human Condition* (Chicago: University of Chicago Press, 1958), 188–95, 294–304.

18. For expenditure in Bataille, see Georges Bataille, *The Accursed Share: Consumption*, vol. 1, trans. Robert Hurley (New York: Zone Books, 1988). One could argue that this is precisely the dilemma that Michael Hardt has avoided through his concept of "affective labor," elaborated in cooperation with Antonio Negri; see Hardt's "Affective Labor," *boundary 2* 26, no. 2 (1999): 89–100, which takes distances from Spivak's notion of "affectively necessary labor." Gayatri Chakravorty Spivak, "Scattered Speculations on the Question of Value," *Diacritics* 15, no. 4 (1985): 73–93.

19. Nancy Fraser and Axel Honneth, *Redistribution or Recognition: A Political-Philosophical Exchange* (London: Verso, 2003).

20. Louis Althusser, "Le marxisme aujourd'hui," in *Solitude de Machiavel et autres texts* (Paris: Presses Universitaires de France, 1998), 292–310; translated by James H. Kavanaugh as "Marxism Today," in *Philosophy and the Spontaneous Philosophy of the Scientists* (London: Verso, 1990).

8

FEDERATION

Jean L. Cohen

Two developments call for creative thinking about constitutional and political forms.[1] The first is the universalization of the political form of the sovereign national state—in the aftermath of formal decolonization and then with the decomposition of the great land-based empire of the Soviet Union (post-1989). Rules against conquest and forced annexation and the decline of violent state death seem to indicate that the self-determining sovereign national state with internationally recognized borders, autonomous constitutional and political structures, and international legal standing has become the norm today.[2] There are now 192 sovereign states recognized by international law and enjoying U.N. membership, each of which clings tenaciously to its sovereignty. Yet the legitimacy and efficacy of state sovereignty seems to be undermined by undeniable ideological transformations, legal developments, and structural trends.

Indeed, and second, the nation-state and the traditional conception of sovereignty that went with it (absolute, comprehensive, supreme, autonomous, with the *jus belli*) came under great stress in the same period as its universalization. The ideal of "one nation—one state" linked to the principle of self-determination was already unobtainable for the newly emerging polities in the period of decolonization. The "cleansing" of ethnic/religious/linguistic plurality that would be required to realize this ideal is now deemed unacceptable. Instead of nation-states as sovereign "state-nations," multinational, multilinguistic states are the norm today. The homogeneous nation-state, always a myth, is clearly an anachronistic and destructive ideal.

From another quarter, the economic and geopolitical imperatives of globalization and the pressures of size they generate seem to render the idea of sovereign states (except for great powers or very large polities) as anachronistic today as the city-state became in an earlier period of globalization and state making (the end of the sixteenth century). The realities of international interdependence, of transnational risks requiring regional or global "governance," and of ideological challenges to the classic "Westphalian" conception of absolute state sovereignty and exclusive domestic jurisdiction are just a few of the forces one could mention. None of the innovative modes of governance on regional, global, or transnational levels fit the model of the sovereign state "writ large," and many seem to undermine it. From this optic too, the classic ideal of the sovereign state is deemed to be a problematic, and for most states an unrealizable, ideal. Contemporary geopolitical and economic pressures of size imply that for a polity to remain autonomous and efficacious it must grow larger or merge with others. However, the idea of creating a world of sovereign, regional megastates (*Grossraume,* or new imperial formations), or a world-state is objectionable for normative and pragmatic reasons. Yet the proliferation of concepts like post-, supra-, or transnational to refer to emergent political formations and talk of regional and global "governance" all lack political-theoretical precision—and give us few clues regarding the question of political and constitutional form for the new political communities and/or proliferating regulatory regimes that are neither states nor their creatures.

Two conceptual responses to this conundrum have emerged. One resurrects the discourse of empire as an analytic, a descriptor or prognosis; a second weds the discourse of global governance to various new cosmopolitan theories of a multileveled yet legally integrated world order, to a normative ideal of a cosmopolitan constitution. I propose a third approach: the revival and reconceptualization of the concept of federal union or federation. I find the thesis of postmodern empire in the influential form presented by Hardt and Negri confused and premature.[3] But I also find the idea of a cosmopolitan, multileveled world order of constitutional quality (assuming these are not the same as postmodern empire) to be incorrect as an empirical description and unfeasible and weirdly apolitical as a project.[4] Both of these are too quick to relegate to the dustbin of history the idea of a plurality of autonomous self-determining and self-governing (sovereign) political communities and international relations. Both responses to the geopolitical problematic of size and to economic globalization are too totalizing: there is no outside to the world empire or to the global cosmopolitan world order being imagined and, despite disclaimers, both are ultimately monist conceptions.

Here's one way to think about the conundrum we now face: if the political and personal freedoms we associate with constitutional democracies are at risk the greater the size of the polity, then what chance is there for liberal democratic republics—already enlarged through the device of representation—to avoid evisceration by centralizing distant executives and administrations of the now proliferating regional and global institutions? Is there a way to theorize a mode of political integration (growing larger) and a type of polity that is normatively attractive and feasible on the regional or even on the level of functional global governance, to which the discourses of constitutionalization and democracy would be analytically adequate? I suggest that there is and that we proceed by rethinking the concept of federation as a type of union of states and peoples, a type of constitutional polity that is not itself a state. Reworking the concept of federation may allow us to construct the appropriate political referent of these processes and thus to address the legitimacy problematic of regional and global "governance" in creative ways. The federal principle, appropriately analyzed, can do justice to the dual trends mentioned above. In other words, the concept of a federal union of states (and peoples) involves a way of making the external internal, and allows one to conceive a political structure that enables both self-rule and shared rule, autonomy and participation of discrete (even "sovereign") political entities within an overall polity under its public constitutional law whose legal and political orders are pluralistic rather than monistic, heterarchical rather than hierarchical.

RETRIEVING THE CONCEPT (*RETTENDE* CRITIQUE)

Federation has to be retrieved and reconceived as a concept because ever since the sovereign state won out against its competitors in Europe, it has been captured by and studied through the lens of the modern statist paradigm, that is, as a type of state structure. At the onset of the modern epoch in Europe, federation reappeared—as an alternative to the state-making logic initiated in France and carried out by centralizing monarchies mobilizing for war, territorial conquest, and dominion. The latter involved the expansion of power radiating out from a center and coercively incorporating territories, cities, peoples, and all formerly independent authorities into its structure, annihilating their political and legal autonomy. Once one polity succeeds in such state making, others have to follow suit to survive geopolitically and to compete economically. The classic state-making logic carried out by absolute monarchies in Europe proceeded via mobilization for war, as Tilly argues, and it seemed to require absolute sovereignty, as theorists from Jean Bodin toThomas Hobbes insisted.[5] The expansionist logic of this process unleashed the imperative of size and control that had to be faced for all those in proximity, creating a strong incentive to reproduce the political form and regime of the absolutist sovereign state. This logic of annexation, hierarchy, and rule over subject populations was projected outward by each state in their imperialist quest for colonies and rule over subject populations once the system of states established itself on the continent and no one of them could gain imperial control over the others.

But the logic did not go unchallenged. One alternative was to federate: small polities could defend their autonomy if they pooled their resources, acted together for collective security and welfare, and created common institutions for that purpose. Federations did emerge as an alternative to state making in the eighteenth century—think of the United Provinces of the Netherlands (1759–1795), the old Swiss Confederation (from the later medieval period until 1789 and renewed in 1815–48), the German empire/federation and the United States Federal Union—until 1865.[6] Moreover, federation had its own supporters—political theorists who challenged the political theology of absolutist sovereignty propounded by advocates of the centralized state form, such as Bodin and Hobbes. Johannes Althusius countered Bodin, Samuel Pufendorf challenged Hobbes, opposing the "sovereignty" of the people—the conglomerate of the varied and stratified population of the cities and provinces of the compound polity—to that of the monarch or state, insisting on the possibility of a complex and heterarchical and freedom-preserving union as an alternative to leveling centralized administrative and political forms. Montesquieu proposed federation as a way for republics to grow larger, that is, superior to imperial expansion because it did not involve the sacrifice of the freedom of citizenry. Of course the context and debates surrounding the most enduring experiment in federal union—the United States—generated the most innovative theorizing of federal union, culminating in the work of John C. Calhoun.[7] But the success of the state-making project, first in Europe and then ultimately worldwide, is undeniable. The federal alternative seemed to lose out to its statist competitor thanks to the apparently inexorable dynamic of either centralization or dissolution. Hannah Arendt was the most important twentieth-century theorist to revive the republican approach of Montesquieu, and to link it to a democratic theory of federation as an alternative to empire and to nation-states for postcolonial societies, including the Middle East.[8] Drawing on her work, Fred Cooper and Gary Wilder show that the federal alternative did indeed come up in the context of decolonization of overseas empires of France and Great Britain, but for the most part, these too lost out to the sovereign nation-state form.[9] Nonstate federations of states until very recently have been judged to be exceptions and/or unstable, conflict-ridden and transitional political forms, way stations en route to consolidated federal and/or centralized sovereign statehood.

Even sophisticated analysts of the distinctive constitutional and political features of federalism such as Daniel Elazar construe federations in terms of the binary—federal versus unitary states—and thus screen out the idea of federating as a way to grow larger that does not culminate in a megastate or an empire.[10] Most analyses of federalism, in short, operate with two dichotomous frameworks: federal versus unitary states and confederations of sovereign states versus federal states.

According to the second binary, confederations are merely treaty organizations in which states remain sovereign. On the statist paradigm, ideal-typically, a confederation is an international law creature—a contractual arrangement whose legal basis is a treaty that does not alter the constitutional structure or international legal standing of the sovereign states that comprise it. Confederation is a way for states to cooperate for limited purposes: it is not meant to be permanent; its jurisdiction is limited and delegated; its legislative/administrative bodies are no more than a board or a congress of the executives of the state parties, retaining their international character; rules are enacted on the basis of unanimity, and this holds for any alteration of the treaty; the confederation itself is not a subject at international law; and its rules do not have direct effect within the member states. Member states remain sovereign subjects of international law. The territories and citizens of the member states do not become the territory or citizenry of the confederation, for the latter has no demos. Relations among the states are international. Since it is not a permanent arrangement, states can exit at will, assuming they fulfill their contractual obligations.

By contrast, a modern (federal) state typically is a sovereign, political, territorial entity that has the internal monopoly of the use of force; a hierarchically supreme coercive and comprehensive domestic constitutional legal order and governing apparatus, no matter how decentralized or delegated some of its competences are; and it has the *jus belli*, control over armed forces, treaty-making power, international legal standing, and full diplomatic power internationally within a system of sovereign states. Thus in a consolidated federal state, as in any state, sovereignty is vested in the center. This means that the state as a whole is sovereign, not its component parts, however decentralized it may be. Unlike a confederation, a federal state has its legal basis in a constitution, not a treaty. It has original, direct, and comprehensive jurisdiction, its own system of courts with direct effect, a real legislative body typically consisting of two houses, both proceeding on the basis of majority or in some cases supermajority decision but not unanimity, thus divesting the legislative organ of any international character. Based in a constitution, the federal state is deemed the political expression of a single people to whom the constitution is ascribed, and which the constitution helps to construct through its electoral and amendment rules—in other words, it rests on the constitution-making power of one individualized demos. The law of the federal state is supreme, citizenship is nationalized, and the component member states are states in name only. A federal state monopolizes external affairs and member states typically have no international legal standing, no treaty-making powers, no diplomatic capacities, and armed forces are under the command of the federal head of states. No subunit has the right to exit even if there once was a confederal origin to a federal state. So, the distinction between a federal and a unitary state, or among different consolidated federal states, is primarily a matter of the mode of organizing a state.

Clearly this taxonomy screens out the very idea of a composite, constitutional nonstate federal polity that bridges the domestic/international divide. Yet this is, I argue, a political and constitutional form that is on the agenda for the twenty-first century. It is time at least for democratic and republican theorists to recuperate insights of the federal vision while freeing it from the statist paradigm since it may offer a distinctive answer to the problems of size facing states under pressures of globalization and to legitimacy problems created by regional and/or global governance institutions.

THE NONSTATIST CONCEPTION OF FEDERATION

What is the ideal type of nonstatist model of a federation? The point is to screen in what statist, cosmopolitan, and imperial approaches to political forms screen out: namely, the idea of a discrete, territorially based political and legal group of communities that is neither a state nor a classic international organization, yet which has international legal personality, its own public legal order of constitutional quality, internal legislative capacity, legal autonomy, and is composed of member states with similar characteristics. Nonstate federations are unions of states and peoples that are dualistic political formations that bridge the international and the national, the foreign and the domestic, treaty organizations and constitutional polities in ways that require careful conceptual (and normative) analysis. Sovereignty does not describe their internal relations, if by sovereign one means legal hierarchy, supremacy, comprehensive control, and political rule by the center. But sovereign states are members of such federations and can remain sovereign with respect to the outside and retain international legal standing: even without this, they can resort to the discourse of sovereignty regarding actual or potential conflicts of jurisdiction, over the competence to decide jurisdictional competence, or over the ultimate locus of constitution-making power inside the federation. Disputes about the relevance of sovereignty discourse remains today one of the key issues in conceptualizing federal unions. But to grasp what is distinctive ideal-typically to a federal union and the federal principle, one has to eschew the sovereigntist statist frame.

What are the distinctive features of such a polity? I draw on the work of the few theorists who are trying to rethink federation outside statist frame.[11]

Most of these agree that the point of creating or joining a federal union is to establish a structure in which the independence and political existence of member states of the federation is maintained yet serves their common goals. The duality of particular and general (community) purposes is characteristic. The idea is to find a form of political association that guarantees the political existence and autonomous status of member states (the particular purpose) by federal law while creating a political entity, a federal union that is able to secure the collective goals of the union, that is, of its members in their status of forming a community of communities. Thus the autonomy of the federation in relation to the member states must also be institutionalized. The structure of "shared rule and self-rule" that ensues involves complex relationships of independence and interdependence of a plurality of political and constitutional legal orders.

Federal unions of states are ideal-typically based on a *consensual foedus*—a pact or covenant—that articulates the purposes of federating and establishes a totality, a polity that has its own distinct representative body and within which each of the member states are represented. This enables the federation to present a common face to the outside, but, in so doing, a transformation of the external into the internal occurs. By virtue of joining a federal union, international relations among foreign states become internal relations between member states with respect to the relevant purposes of the association.

Ideal-typically, a federal union is meant to be a permanent, albeit initially voluntary, association. By federating, states enter into (and willingly construct) a new and autonomous constitutional legal and political community. Entry into a federation thus entails a change of each member state's constitution, irrespective of whether or not any word is altered. The states become transformed into members of a new political totality, but they remain states, and may even retain international legal standing, depending on the design of the new federal polity they join. Federation is a way of growing larger that involves extension through iteration, such as is found in republican federations or federations of constitutional democracies. Unlike the statist imperial or imperialist logic of expansion through domination and centralized rule, the federal principle involves a process of inclusion without annexation, iteration of the republican or democratic constitutional form as a condition of entry without leveling diversity in other respects, with guarantees of autonomy and equality that constitute a noncentralized or polycentric matrix structure quite distinct from the sovereign state form. But this is also distinct, pace Hardt and Negri, from empires past and present, which always have centers/peripheries and violent or coerced alliances and annexations. In this sense, federation is the alternate route (to empire) for a republic to grow larger while retaining its constitutionalist and republican or democratic freedoms.

To see what is distinctive here, one has to grasp the special dualist nature of the federal pact. The federal pact is a constitutional treaty or contract that creates a unique order that accommodates a dual set of goals characteristic of every federation of states: to maintain the political existence and legal autonomy of its members while creating a new political unity with its own political existence and purposes.[12] The duality is evident in the terms "contract" and "constitutional." The contractual (treaty) dimension pertains to the voluntary decision of each state to join and become a member of the federation. This is the international law component. The constitutional dimension refers to the product—the treaty is the federation's constitution along with the institutions and new relations it establishes, that is, once they join up, states are integrated into a politically comprehensive structure/polity with respect to general purposes. This is why their sovereign decision to join entails domestic constitutional change. This dimension escapes the "free contract" aspect, for the pact does not simply regulate discrete and definable individual relations as per ordinary international treaties. The constitutional contract is, rather, an "interstate status contract" since it changes the status of states into member states. This is the internal public constitutional law component (The constitutional component also refers to a compound constituent power or a special type of demos as its referent, as I will discuss below.)

The constitutional contract constructs an autonomous, constitutional, legal, and institutional order for the organized federal polity such that conflicts over jurisdictions, competencies, and so on, must be resolved through law. The law (and relations) of the federation is internal, public, domestic, and constitutional, not external, international, or foreign. Its legal order is autonomous, supreme in its specified functional domains, endowed with the competence to use its powers enumerated in the constitutional treaty, and the member states are bound by its decisions. Federation law has direct effect. Indeed, the federation constitution is a component of each member state's constitution. Moreover, the federation may intervene in member states to enforce its law with regard to its specific functions. In this respect the internal orders of the member states are no longer impermeable because they are in a treaty organization. Yet the constitutional orders of the states and of the federation are not merged; instead, there is a composite, constitutional pluralist arrangement that links them while leaving their autonomy intact.

The federation also has a dual institutional makeup. As a political unity, the federation must be represented. Representation is no insignificant matter. The federal political community thereby attains a political existence internally and externally. Furthermore, the federation must have a territory, consisting of the territories of the member states, and, within or alongside these, its own territorial possessions involving, at the very least, the seat of government. This means that the institutions and being of the federation exist *alongside* those of the member states.

One of the prime purposes in federating, and hence a key goal of a federation, is to guarantee the political existence of each member state and to provide internal peace, welfare, and in many but not all cases to protect members against the outside. The federation can obtain the *jus belli* via the federal pact (but need not: think of the EU if member states had ratified the constitution in 2004). Internally the federation ensures civil peace: federation members permanently give up self-help and the *jus belli* vis-à-vis one another, and war may not take place between federation members; otherwise, the federation will be destroyed. Internally there is only federal enforcement action or execution of federal law against a recalcitrant state: that is partly what I mean by saying former external international relations among member states thereby become internal. Insofar as the federation acquires the *jus belli*, it has an obvious independent political existence and is a subject at international law. But even if a federation has a *jus belli*, this need not mean that it has an exclusive *jus belli* vis-à-vis the outside. In other words, this does not preclude the possibility that member states retain the *jus belli* vis-à-vis nonmembers alongside that of the federation.

Crucially, member states retain their autonomous legal and political existence. It is the express purpose and constitutive nature of a federation that it should preserve and respect their political self-determination, constitutional legal autonomy, and territory. Accordingly, from their own point of view, the member states' political existence does not derive from—nor does the validity of their legal systems and constitutions inhere in—the federal constitutional contract. The latter is not in a hierarchical relation to the former despite its supremacy with respect to law making within its constitutionally specified domain, and despite having direct effect and even implied powers. Disputes over the scope of that domain are hence possible and likely. Within the federation, the political status quo must be guaranteed, meaning the guarantee of territorial integrity of each member state: no federation member can have a part of its territory taken, nor its political existence, nor its voice in the federal organ eliminated without its consent. This is evidence of the contractual dimension of a federal constitutional order. These guarantees stem from the goal of self-preservation and the concept of duration (permanence) that is essential to a federal union.

This is so irrespective of the fact that there can be no federation without involvement in the affairs of member states. Indeed, precisely because the federation has a political existence, it must have a "right of supervision" and a right to intervene. Conflicts over competences, implied powers, and jurisdictions are inevitable, including conflicts over the competence to decide upon competence.

It would thus seem logical that the ideal-typical amendment rule of a federation should reflect its position between a confederation and a federal state. Whereas for a confederation the amending powers, the states, are outside the treaty, and amending the treaty typically requires unanimity, in the case of a federal state, the "states" are within the constitution and can be treated as organs of the federal union with respect to the federal constitution. Thus an ideal-typical federal state constitutional amendment rule could involve the use of a federal senate, but its ratification would rely on individual voters of the federal state. For a federation of states, the amendment rule, as for a confederation, would have to maintain the states as the sources of fundamental legal change (the treaty component), but the constitutional dimension of the pact would have to entail that a qualified majority of these formally equal states (one state, one vote) would be able to bind the minority. This is a way to bring all the states into the constitution while ensuring that they remain in some sense the authors of it.

So what about sovereignty? What about constituent power? If sovereignty is indivisible, entails autonomy vis-à-vis the outside, and supremacy is on the inside and pertains to the self-determination of a political community, a state, how can one account for such dualisms of political existence within a polity? Foreigners cannot determine the regime or law of a *sovereign* state, but membership in a federation renders the external internal, the foreigner into the friend. Yet sovereignty cannot be divided or shared. We face the old Calhounian dilemma: mustn't sovereignty be located either in the member states or in the union? Sovereignty, as I said, does not describe the internal relations of a federation: these are characterized by heterarchy not hierarchy, by noncentration, not decentralized or delegated rule. Nevertheless, it is not a solution to try to banish the issue of sovereignty as irrelevant to a federation because, thanks to its dualistic structure, sovereignty discourse and fundamental conflicts remain possible. In a *genuine* federation, "sovereignty is not absent"; instead, the locus of sovereignty remains undecided.[13] As long as the federation is a general federal union rather than a consolidated state, as long as the member states and the federation exist alongside one another in a nonhierarchical relationship, the sovereignty question is *permanently deferred*. The practice of constitutional pluralism and the efforts to resolve conflicts by law mean a commitment to the federal polity by all parties such that "neither the federation in regard to the member states nor the member state in regard to the federation *plays the sovereign*."[14]

This brings me to the final and most crucial issue: namely, whether a federation has a demos and how to conceptualize it. To whom is the constituent power that pertains to the constitutional (status-altering) dimension of the constitutional compact to be ascribed? I argue that there is a federal demos, but it is a compound one. A federation is a union of states and peoples. The duality of political existences means the doubling of the referent "the people," such that the demos must mean something different than what it means in a state. In the latter it is a unity of individuals; in the former, "the people," the federal demos, is a composite: the federal "people" is composed of peoples in the plural—it is a demos of demoi. Thus the peoples of the member states (the citizens) can exercise a constituent power on the level of the member state by giving themselves a constitution or by changing it, but they can also do so on the federal level, by participating in the formation of the federal constitution through ratification of the federal pact as citizens of member co-states and hence as co-constituents. The constituent power of the federation must be postulated as a composite or compound political community of political communities.

Hence the typical paradox inherent in every federation, namely, that the federated peoples protect their political existence by creating or joining a federal polity and participating in the exercise of federal constituent (as well as constituted) power. The constitution-making power of a federation is thus a mediated one: it is as members of a compound demos that they participate in constitution making and in constitutional change.

So what are the gains of this political reconceptualization? Federation of the sort I imagine has a way of growing larger that delivers on the pragmatic reasons why independent polities would seek to unite: security, defense, and welfare. But there are also normative justifications: arguments from constitutionalist principles, from freedom (republican/democratic), the argument from peace, and the argument from diversity and from legitimacy. Unlike sovereign nation-states, coming-together federalism does not have a homogenizing logic and it does not entail leveling or eradication of difference. Constitutionalist principles entail that public powers must be under public law—if regional associations were to federate, their executives would be inside the constitution, unlike treaty organizations where they remain outside. A constitution-making process would certainly enhance legitimacy and open up the possibility for democratic participation and internal reform. Inflexibility of unanimity requirements for treaty change would be replaced by a more flexible amendment rule that also facilitates reform when necessary. The internal plural, nonhierarchical relations pertain to the argument from republican freedom. A federal constitutional treaty can provide individual rights protections, stipulate a republican or democratic form of constitutionalist government for members and for itself, protect minorities, and militate against parochialism. But the plural matrix structure of a federation would allow for democratic experimentalism on the state level and for compounding majorities, that is, more consensual majorities on the federal level. The argument from diversity is interesting, too: unlike status-based legal pluralism typical of empire, and unlike consociational arrangements, "coming together" in federation accommodates diversity without freezing identities, without freezing private hierarchies or elite forms of rule on the local level or reproducing them on the federal level, and without reifying the cleavages that may involve language, religion, culture, and ethnicity, because in a federal system individuals can vote with their feet.

It would be absurd to argue that federations are intrinsically liberal, democratic, republican, tolerant of diversity, respectful of rights, or that all of these must go together. There have been monarchical federations, imperial and imperialist federations, illiberal and undemocratic republican federations, hegemonic federations, asymmetrical federations, and polities that are federal in form only, such as *grossraume* or empires with a paper federal constitution. Elites in member states may choose to federate and create institutional rules in order to entrench their local powers, hegemony, and local tyrannies. The point is not that federal unions of states are necessarily superior to large states along these normative dimensions. And of course, federal unions can change and morph into federal states or even into centralized states. Nevertheless, they do involve a mode of growing larger: of structuring institutions and power relations among parts that avoid the problems of top-down hierarchical rule and reified group identities. At the same time, they can create a federal constitutional polity that hews to democratic and liberal constitutional principles and insists on these as conditions for membership in the effort to preserve diversity while creating or enabling commonalities and transnational solidarities, thus remaining true to the principles of human rights and democratic participation.

NOTES

1. This article is part of a larger piece in Jean Cohen, *Globalization and Sovereignty: Rethinking Legality, Legitimacy and Constitutionalism* (Cambridge: Cambridge University Press, 2012), 80–158.

2. Tanisha Fazal, *State Death: The Politics and Geography of Conquest, Occupation, and Annexation* (Princeton, N.J.: Princeton University Press, 2007).

3. Michael Hardt and Antonio Negri, *Empire* (Cambridge, Mass.: Harvard University Press, 2000).

4. For the best version, see Matthias Kumm, "Who Is the Final Arbiter of Constitutionality in Europe?," *Common Market Law Review* 36 (1999): 351–86.

5. Charles Tilly, *The Formation of the National States in Western Europe* (Princeton, N.J.: Princeton University Press, 1975).

6. Charles de Secondat, baron de Montesquieu, *The Spirit of the Laws*, trans. and ed. Anne M. Cohler, Basia Carolyn Miller, and Harold Samuel Stone (Cambridge: Cambridge University Press, 1989), chapter 9.

7. Jean Bodin, *Six Books of the Commonwealth*, originally published in 1576, is the classic source along with Thomas Hobbes, *Leviathan* (1651) of the absolutist concept of sovereignty attached to the developing theory of the state first in France, then in England. Johannes Althusius's *Politics*, originally published in 1603, is the source of the constitutionalist theory of (popular) sovereignty and the beginning of a line of federal thinking that was developed more consistently and systematically by Pufendorf in a body of works culminating in *The Law of Nature and Nations* (1729), which may be said to be the first sustained theoretical analysis of the nature of a confederation of states. See Murray Forsyth, *Union of States* (New York: Holmes and Meier, 1981), 74–85. See also John C. Calhoun, *Union and Liberty: The Political Philosophy of John C. Calhoun*, ed. Ross M. Lence (Indianapolis: Liberty Funds, 2010),

for a full-fledged theory of confederal union of independent polities that creates a polity, rests on a constitutional contract, yet does not create a nation. Finally, see also Carl Schmitt, *Constitutional Theory*, trans. Jeffrey Seitzer (Durham, N.C.: Duke University Press, 2008), part 4, for a highly influential discussion. Needless to say, I do not embrace either Calhoun's proslavery, antiunionist motivations or the contemporary states' rights revival found in his rhetoric, on the part of the American Tea Party movement—or, for that matter, his disparaging assessment of the federal unions and his preference for *grossraume*.

8. Hanna Arendt, *On Revolution* (New York: Penguin Books, 1963); *The Jewish Writings* (New York: Shocken Books, 2007).

9. Frederick Cooper, *Citizenship between Empire and Nation: Remaking France and French Africa, 1945–1960* (Princeton, N.J.: Princeton University Press, 2014); and Gary Wilder, *Freedom Time, Negritude, Decolonization, and the Future of the World* (Durham, N.C.: Duke University Press, 2015).

10. Daniel Elazar, *Exploring Federalism* (Tuscaloosa: University of Alabama Press, 1987).

11. For the best jurisprudential reworking of the concept, see Olivier Beaud, *Théorie de la fédération* (Paris: Presses Universitaires de France, 2007), and Forsyth, *Union of States*.

12. The idea of a federation as based in a constitutional contract comes from Calhoun and is adopted by Schmitt.

13. See Schmitt, *Constitutional Theory*, 389.

14. Ibid., 395. On the meaning of "constitutional pluralism," see Cohen, *Globalization and Sovereignty*, 66–80.

9

IDENTITY

Akeel Bilgrami

What is it for an individual person to be a social type, a Muslim, say, or a white male, a Québécois, gay or lesbian, and so on? This sort of question about identity has come to have an urgency because of the rise of identity politics in the past many decades. But there has been very little rigorous theoretical elaboration on answers to such a question.

An initial step toward imposing some theoretical order on the notoriously haphazard concept of identity in politics is to distinguish at the outset between its subjective and objective aspects. When a person is said to have a certain identity owing to some characteristic she has, and with which she iden*tifies*, then we are thinking of identity in its subjective aspects. If a person is said to have a certain identity owing to some characteristic she has, but with which she does not necessarily identify, then we are speaking of her objective identity.

SUBJECTIVE IDENTITY

Subjective identity is most immediately relevant to politics because people sometimes allow themselves to be mobilized in the public arena on its basis. It is not—by any means—that subjective identity is always mobilized in politics. It is more that, where it exists, it is poised so as to be mobilized if other conditions, which I will not discuss here, are present.

Subjective belonging to a social group, when it is longstanding and deeply rooted, is un-self-conscious and unarticulated. Only people who undergo some sort of dislocation from their deep and long-standing roots ask questions such as, "Who am I?" or "To which group do I belong?" Of course, the dislocation that makes them raise these questions about identity or belonging, though it is often so, need not always be physical or geographical (as in migration) but can also occur when one is sedentary—as a result of unsettling (material, psychological, and cultural) conditions owing to a variety of either external influences or internal transformations.

Often, subjective identifications are formed under conditions of defeat and feelings of powerlessness and helplessness. Thus, much of Muslim identity in the Middle East today has been formed under (explicitly articulated) anti-Western feelings of being subjugated by what is perceived as a long history of colonization that continues in revised forms to this day, despite decolonization. Islam, under such conditions, came to be seen by a demoralized population as a source of autonomy and dignity. But sometimes identities are formed through triumphalist feelings as well. Linda Colley describes how Scots came to endorse a British identity only when Britain became a great Empire, and much identification of American Jews with Israel occurred in the aftermath of Israel's smashing victory in 1967.[1] Also, some Jihadi identifications with Islam formed through triumphalist feelings in the light of what were felt to be "Mujahideen" victories after the Soviet withdrawal from Afghanistan.

Nationalism has played a role in the formation of identities. In Europe, many religious and other types of identity were formed as a result of nation-building exercises after the Westphalian peace. Nationalism of this kind was based on a self-conscious majoritarian identity-formation—finding an external enemy within, despising and subjugating it, and claiming that the nation is "ours," not "theirs" (the Jews, the Irish, Protestants in Catholic majority countries, Catholics in Protestant majority countries, and so on). Often this resulted in a backlash that created self-conscious minoritarian identities among these populations. (In fact, secularism, as a doctrine, was formulated to repair the damage of religious and civil strife caused by conflicts among religious identities formed by these nation-building majoritarianisms and the minoritarian reactions against them.) A familiar form of identity formation of majorities and minorities also grew out of colonial policies of "divide and rule" in countries of the south, importing European nation-building ideas into the colonies.

But quite apart from the sources that give rise to it, there is the prior theoretical question about what *is* subjective identity? How shall we characterize or define it?

There is a tendency by some social theorists who shun identity politics to confuse normative and descriptive questions and take a skeptical stance on the very idea of subjective identity, claiming that any given individual subject cannot be said to have a firm or clear singular identity because he or she identifies with far too many wider groups—gender, family, profession, religion, nation, class, caste, company of people with shared mutual interests, and so on indefinitely. But this skepticism, though it may have a normative point in commending those who have an ecumenical and flexible social outlook, cannot be grounds to dismiss the importance of notions of subjective identity since for many subjects, descriptively speaking, one or the other of these identifications will be far more important and loom larger in certain contexts, and, when that is so, they will be much more likely to mobilize themselves in public life and politics on the basis of that identity. Thus, a Muslim may also be an Iranian, a father, a doctor, but in certain contexts (such as those mentioned above), it is his Islamic values that he elevates above his nationalist, family, professional values, and he mobilizes himself on that basis and not others in public and political life. Such a strongly felt singular identity, and the politics that is sometimes based on it, has been an undeniable descriptive fact in our social and political lives, however multiple one's identities may be—and ought to be.

But to say that subjective identity is not thus dismissible is not yet to define it. And defining it is no easy matter. We have said that subjective identity usually consists in *endorsing* certain facts about oneself—one's nationality, race, gender, caste, class, and so on—and in doing so allows oneself to be poised to be mobilized in public and political life on its basis. So the question is what sort of state of mind or commitment is this endorsement? At first sight, the answer might be that these endorsements are simply one's valuing one's nationality, religion, and so on, more strongly or intensely than other things one values. However, "intensity" (with which one holds a value) is not exactly a theoretically tractable idea, and even if it were, it is not sufficient to define subjective identity since one may have these intensely held values and find that they are not quite rational in oneself, even often wishing one didn't have them. If so, it would be perverse to define subjective identity in terms of it. Some further constraint must be added to the presence of these values to reveal identity in the subjective sense. It is tempting to think that the further constraint is simply a second-order attitude of valuing one's first-order values. That would rule out the cases in which the first-order values seem unwanted and alien to oneself. But this is insufficient too because our second-order states of approval and disapproval of one's first-order states may also seem irrational or neurotic—to one—as, for instance, when one thinks that one's second-order disapproval of some first-order value or disposition is too prim, too much of a superego phenomenon. And suggesting a step up to the third order threatens to merely render an infinite regress. What other constraint, then, might help to characterize subjective identity?

One possible answer is to see these values as accompanied by a very specific sort of property, the property of viewing them as something one ought not to revise—as in the case of Ulysses and the sirens, whereby one ties oneself to the mast of these values so that even if one were tempted by circumstances to cease to have these values or commitments, one would still be living by these values. This analytically elaborates upon the intuition that subjective identity consists in one's self-conception, how one conceives oneself to be. Such self-conceptions are often intuitively expressed in such remarks as: "I wouldn't recognize myself if I betrayed my country" (or my family, or class, etc.), or even as in the British schoolboy identity expressed by E. M. Forster: "I wouldn't recognize myself if I betrayed my friends." In other words, one views departures from these values as moral or political weakenings and, therefore, departures from one's identity. Values held in this way may properly be thought of as identity-imparting values. So, for instance, the Iranian clergy in Iran might—in this Ulysses fashion—think of Islamic values in such a way that they are willing to entrench Islam in their society so that if they were to weaken in the face of what they conceive to be the pernicious siren songs of modernity, they would still be living by Islamic values. This idea of subjective identity cannot be dismissed as a form of fanatical irrationality since even those with a liberal identity share this constraint on how they hold their values. This is evident in the fact that liberals elevate some of their values (such as freedom of speech) to fundamental rights, the point of which is precisely to prevent themselves from acting when they weaken in their resolve and wish to censor some odious viewpoint (neo-Nazism, say) that has surfaced in society. This echoes exactly the same structural constraint on how values are held, as in the case of the Islamic clergy mentioned above. Such a constraint (of holding values in the Ulysses and sirens form) captures how deeply one identifies with some point of view (Islam, liberalism, etc.) at any given time and may properly be thought to be a reflection of subjective identity (at that time). Much more can be said to elaborate upon this but will not be pursued here.

As I said earlier, the notion of identity came into prominence with the rise of the identity politics of race, gender, caste, language, and so on, since the 1960s and 1970s, and which has been with us ever since in many parts of the world. A good deal of this was necessitated by the fact that standard universalist formulations of liberal ideals refused to acknowledge these particular identities, dismissing them as parochializing public life in one form or another. More interesting was their refusal by traditional leftist politics that claimed that class identity was the more fundamental identity, not race or gender or linguistic identities, and that a lofty focus on class struggles would usher out the other deprivations that each identity politics was seeking to remedy with more specific struggles of its own. There was undoubtedly something blinkered about this refusal, too, since they refused to recognize the extent to which disrespect can come from sources other than class distinctions. Even so, there is a sense that it seems as if the category of class is more basic, and one needs to find a way of expressing it without failing to recognize the point about the multiple sources of disrespect. A way to approach how it is more basic is by pointing out the following. Though substantial gains have certainly been made on the racial, gender, caste, and so on, fronts in past years as a result of identitarian struggles, these gains would never have been allowed if they had deeply undermined the basic structure of the capitalist society and, in particular, if they had jeopardized the key interests of corporations, which have such a sway on policy makers nowadays. This is, of course, speculation. But given the conspicuous power of vested corporate interests, we can make the speculation with confidence. If so, there is no gainsaying the fundamental importance of class identity over others, and this speculative formulation is the right way to present it rather than a formulation that does not recognize the importance of other forms of identity. (Of course, one should also explore parallel speculations, for instance, by speculating that if any gains have been made on the class front, they would not be allowed if it deeply undermined patriarchy. But although it is certainly worth exploring, it is not perhaps as immediately obvious that one has as full a grip on what such a speculation would be based on.)

OBJECTIVE IDENTITY

When we turn to the objective aspects of identity, identification on the part of the subject in question with the identity-imparting characteristic(s) is not a necessary condition. Biological criteria for identity such as, for instance, chromosome-based definitions of gender identity, are frequently considered objective or *given* to one (which does not mean that they do not leave one with a subjective choice about the matter since—increasingly—one's biology may be altered by one's own voluntary decision). However, though gender and racial identity were once considered to be objective and based purely on biological considerations, in the past few decades the very idea of a purely objective criterion of identity of this kind has been put into question, and gender and race and a variety of other such forms of identity are thought to be "socially constructed." This does not necessarily mean that they are not objective. They may still be more on the objective than the subjective side of identity, especially if the process of social construction occurs independently of subjective endorsement and choices on the part of the individual agents. The entire question of social construction is a complex and interesting topic that cannot be pursued here in any detail, except to say that it complicates the notion of objective identity and to that extent qualifies the distinction between objective and subjective identity or belonging.[2]

Objective identities are much more interesting when they are social rather than biological, and in a way even more problematic; this bears some detailed discussion. Perhaps the most classic and frequently discussed example of this is class identity. One familiar way of understanding class identity is owed to Marx, but how exactly to understand what Marx said about it is a matter of interpretation and dispute. An objectivist reading of Marx goes roughly like this: one's class belonging or identity is not a matter of subjective identification but an objective given that derives from history, and history is to be understood by an objective account of it found in what has come to be called "historical materialism"—though that is not an expression in Marx's own writing.[3] On this account, which class one belongs to has nothing to do with one's identifying with any given class. Whether or not one identifies with a given class, one belongs to it simply because of the objective unfolding of successive economic formations in history. Thus, for instance, proletarian identity is entirely a matter of specific forms of class employment (working class) in a certain economic formation (capitalism) in a certain period of history (modernity). One may have no commitment to that class, have no class consciousness or solidarity with other working people, pursuing only what Marx called "bourgeois" aspirations—still, one's true identity or "self" or consciousness is proletarian even if, in such cases, it is hidden from oneself by layers of ideology or false consciousness. It is the task of revolutionary social transformation to mobilize the proletariat to overcome this false consciousness and to realize their true "selves," their proper or objective revolutionary class role in history.

Such a view has given rise to much anxiety, especially in liberal thinkers such as Isaiah Berlin, who saw in such an ideal of emancipation or self-realization a form of liberty—what he called "positive" liberty—which he thought to be tyrannical because someone can be "forced to be free" (to be someone other than what one subjectively views oneself to be) by a vanguard, armed with an objective theory of history.[4] Though in Berlin's case this was a cold warrior's anxiety, there is a deeper, more theoretically motivated, underlying worry about such objectivity, which is that someone is being attributed a self or identity and belonging that he or she may explicitly disavow or—as is perhaps more often the case—about which they may have no self-knowledge. That is to say, nothing whatsoever in someone's behavior reflects the identity being attributed, not even in one's unconsciously motivated behavior (in this respect, Marx—on this objectivist reading—is distinguishable from Freud, who at least insisted on unconscious behavioral manifestations of identity). The intuition against objectivism of this sort in the matter of identity is that to attribute a self or identity or belonging to someone when there is no behavioral sign of it nor any self-awareness of it (perhaps even disavowal of it) is to disregard the agency of the subjects, seeing them merely as reflections of an objectively conceived theory of history. The intuition in favor of the objectivist side arises most pressingly when subjects of a group are deeply oppressed and yet acquiescent in their oppression. The intuition is that such subjects are oppressed despite their acquiescence in the oppression, oppressed by standards that have nothing to do with the behavior, the awareness, or the avowals of the subjects.

One possible solution to the difficulty is this. Frequently, in history, populations that have been acquiescent in their oppression have transformed abruptly and in very large numbers and joined movements of social and political transformation and even revolution. This could, of course, be a change of mind on their part, a change from acquiescence to dissatisfaction and revolutionary consciousness. That is how the opponent of objectivism would insist on presenting it—one subjectivity being replaced by another. But both the abruptness and the large numbers to whom this sometimes happens suggests that a "change of mind" is not a plausible explanation since changes of mind tend to emerge through deliberation or acculturation toward something new—processes that are slow and proceed from small numbers of people to larger numbers via a variety of accumulated efforts at public education. A better explanation of the volatility and numerical strength of such transformations is to attribute retrospectively a latent dissatisfaction among the population, even when they were explicitly acquiescent in their behavior and avowals. This solution does not give up the link between agency and behavior. It simply does not require that the link be simultaneous. It may be thought that if there is this link to behavior, something of the "objectivity" in the objectivist position is compromised. But it should not be seen as a wholesale cancellation of objectivity since objectivist positions that do not require even this minimal theoretical link with behavior and agency are, in any case, marred by an ulterior form of transcendence in the understanding of identity that seems irrelevant to the study of society and history.

This essay on identity has distinguished fundamentally between the subjective and objective aspects of the concept. To a considerable extent, which of these two aspects we emphasize in our study of the concept will be a matter of theoretical decision, a decision which, in turn, depends on nonarbitrary philosophical considerations having to do, as we have just seen, with themes at some distance from identity, such as autonomy and moral reasons but also questions of politics and social oppression. This is to be expected not only because self, freedom, and reason have been closely connected themes in both analytical and European traditions of philosophy ever since Kant, but because our notion of identity gains so much of its interest from the fact that identities get mobilized in politics under conditions of oppression.

NOTES

1. Linda Colley, *Britons: Forging the Nation 1707–1837* (New Haven, Conn.: Yale University Press, 1992).

2. For an illuminating discussion of the issues around "social construction," see Ian Hacking, *The Social Construction of What?* (Cambridge, Mass.: Harvard University Press, 2000).

3. A clear statement of what has come to be called "historical materialism" may be found in Karl Marx, "Preface to a Contribution to a Critique of Political Economy," in Karl *Marx and Friedrich Engels, Selected Works*, vol. 1 (Moscow: Foreign Languages Publishing House, 1955), 362–64.

4. Isaiah Berlin, "Two Concepts of Liberty," in *Four Essays on Liberty* (Oxford: Oxford University Press, 1969).

10

THE RULE OF LAW

J. M. Bernstein

NAZI LAW AND THE RULE OF LAW

Gustav Radbruch twice served as the minister of justice for the Social Democratic Party during the Weimar period. The final version of his *Legal Philosophy* was published in 1932. He went to ground during the Nazi reign of terror, only to resurface in 1946 with an essay entitled "Statutory Lawlessness and Supra-Statutory Law,"[1] that, in response to the gross perversions of Nazi law, argues that a statue, despite being on the books, can be so unjust that it no longer should count as law at all, and conversely, there are norms—say those that form the core of the consensus about fundamental human rights—that although not actual statutes can and should be used by judges. The essay immediately became a fount of postwar German law and jurisprudence. Lon Fuller began teaching the essay at Harvard Law School, where it quickly became a prime node in the debate between Fuller's defense of law as having an "inner morality" and the legal positivism of H. L. A. Hart, who argued there was an uncrossable abyss separating positive law and morals: the law is the law whatever its moral merits. Some aspects of this debate will concern us later.

It is, however, not his effort to demonstrate the outer limits of positive law in the idea of statutory lawlessness with which I wish to begin; rather, it is the conclusion of Radbruch's essay, with its sweeping encomium to the rule of law: "We must seek justice, but at the same time attend to legal certainty, for it is itself a component of justice. And we must rebuild a *Rechtsstaat*, a government of law that serves as well as possible the ideas of both justice and legal certainty. Democracy is indeed laudable, but a government of law is like our daily bread, like water to drink and air to breathe, and the best thing about democracy is precisely that it alone is capable of securing for us such a government."

"Legal certainty" refers to the social actuality of law—the certainty of the ordinary citizen that the rule of law prevails practically, in everyday life, and procedurally in the courts and government administration. Democracy is indeed laudable, but our daily bread is legal order, without which democracy is meaningless. Thus, despite Radbruch's urgent justification of justice as forming the moral horizon of intelligibility for any legal system, it is finally his vision of a modest utopia of legal certainty, of everydayness under the rule of law, the rule of law's own deflationary utopia that concludes his essay. The rule of law (within the horizon of justice), Radbruch presumes, possesses a utopian kernel, an ethical ideal intended to govern and depict the determining moment of an intrinsically valuable form of life. Thus Radbruch's contention must be that the rule of law possesses a utopian ethical content and ideality that is nonetheless compatible with the fact that governance by the rule of law does not itself preclude the obtaining of unjust laws. I further take it as essential to Radbruch's thesis that there is an emphatic but unelaborated dialectic between law and democracy; if pressed into a formula, we might say democracy without rule of law is empty; the rule of law without democracy is blind.

Although going back to the Greek notion of *isonomia*, the equality of all under law, the rule of law receives its clearest modern formulation—contrasting the coercive or forceful rule of one person over another with the rules of law themselves—in Locke's *Second Treatise*. Locke's formulation significantly *identifies* the meaning of "law" as such, what having a legal system is, with the rule of law: "Freedom of men under government is to have a standing rule to live by, common to every one of that society, and made by the legislative power erected in it; a liberty to follow my own will in all things, where that rule prescribes not: and not be subject to the inconstant, uncertain, unknown, arbitrary will of another man."[2] Locke's clinching last clause, as we shall see, sets in place a foundational element in arguments for the rule of law, namely, what is to be escaped from through it: a disorderly, threatening, fearful world in which what others will do (to me) is unregulated and unpredictable. Legal positivists and antipositivists alike strike this note; here is Judith Shklar turning to the rule of law as a form of negative ethics after excoriating affirmative views of it: "If one then begins with the fear of violence, the insecurity of arbitrary government and the discriminations of injustice one may work one's way up to finding a significant place for the Rule of Law, and for the boundaries it has historically set upon those most enduring of our political troubles."[3] One patent extension in Shklar's formulation in contrast with Locke's is that the threat of the unregulated behavior of others is matched by the arbitrariness and violence of government action. These two sources of arbitrariness, private and state violence, should be thought of as equally threatening and equally demanding of response. The stakes of arguments for the rule of law will turn on what affirmative provisions are necessary in order for those negative determinations to have normative authority.

While the notion of attaining meaningful freedom through ascension to life under law is palpable in Locke (as it is in Rousseau), so is his emphasis on "a liberty to follow my own will in all things." It is this latter emphasis that forms the cornerstone of the skeptical regard in which the rule of law is held by socialists and radical democrats. Their suspicion is that the rule of law is nothing but the legal veneer and framework for capitalist economic relations—a suspicion that receives a modest confirmation by the rule of law's eager embrace by conservatives and (some) libertarians. So Friedrich Hayek argues that the kind of rules appropriate to the rule of law are "*formal rules* which do not aim at the wants and needs of particular people. They are intended to be *merely instrumental* in the pursuit of people's various individual ends."[4] He further contends, "any policy aiming at a substantive ideal of distributive justice must lead to the destruction of the Rule of Law."[5] Not only does the rule of law foster an instrumentalist conception of law and seek to protect existing inequalities but, its critics argue, the requirements for stability and an enduring framework of action must curtail and inhibit radical democratic practice, while its formality is morally indifferent to significant differences in the life conditions under which certain groups of individuals suffer, making equality under the law in practice a right to inequality.[6] Nor can it be denied that under even the most progressive legal systems individuals will be required to follow some laws that they regard as unjust, and that, as the history of slavery, woman's suffrage, criminal law, and the treatment of the poor amply demonstrate, most otherwise constitutional and legal states have tolerated large swaths of significant injustice throughout their history. *How can the rule of law spell out even a modest utopian ideal if legality so easily consorts with injustice?*

Legal positivism has the singular virtue of being able to license the actuality and continuing possibility of there being unjust laws because it insists upon the clean separation of law from morality; indeed, legal positivism takes the inevitability of unjust law as a weighty argument in its favor. The positivist appropriation will be a running theme in sections 2–4 of this essay. Section 2 offers an examination of Radbruch's theory since his argument against the extremes of Nazi law was, rightly, a pivotal moment in the re-emergence of antipositivist conceptions of legality. In section 3, I elaborate Lon L. Fuller's account of eight constitutive, formal features of law that, he contends, begin to get at the "inner morality of law." While important, these features of law are too formal in Fuller's characterization to carry the weight he assigns to them. Arguably, the modern commitment to the idea of the rule of law has its genealogical source in the eighteenth-century decision throughout Europe to abolish first all judicial and then all penal torture. The argument connecting the abolition of judicial and penal torture with the rule of law is found in Caesar Beccaria's *On Crimes and Punishments.* Section 4 offers a version of Beccaria's argument that the formal and procedural elements constituting the rule of law should be conceived as, on the one hand, generating the necessary conditions for relations between the citizen and the state and, on the other hand, among citizens themselves that will be sufficient to free individuals from coercive, force-based relations both among themselves and between themselves and the state. The rule of law spells out the minimum institutional forms necessary to escape from arbitrary, dependent relations grounded on force alone. If this is true, then it follows that the rule of law makes possible horizontal relations among citizens and vertical relations between citizens and the state that recognize, protect, and foster a conception of humans as vulnerable and mutually dependent centers of self-determining agency. The rule of law thus projects a conception of dignity-preserving relations among citizens and between citizens and the state using solely the modest means implied by the original contrast between coercive and lawful relations between persons. This is the claim that, however different, both Radbruch and Fuller were searching after. It is a modest, even deflationary utopia of everydayness in that mutually respecting lives governed by the rule of law does *not* necessarily free the citizen from either injustice or tragedy.

RADBRUCH'S OUTER LIMIT OF LAW

Radbruch's prewar jurisprudence and his post–World War II writings have both been read as positivist and antipositivist. That he has been interpreted in such radically opposing ways derives from the structural complexity of the basic elements of his philosophy of law. That complexity can already be glimpsed from the evidence of the famous core paragraph of "Statutory Lawlessness and Supra-Statutory Laws."

> The conflict between justice and legal certainty may well be resolved in this way: the positive law, secured by legislation and power, takes precedence even when its content is unjust and fails to benefit the people, unless the conflict between statute and justice reaches such an intolerable degree that the statute, as a "flawed law," must yield to justice. It is impossible to draw a sharper line between cases of statutory lawlessness and statutes that are valid despite their flaws. One line of distinction, however, can be drawn with utmost clarity: where there is not even an attempt at justice, where equality, the core of justice, is deliberately betrayed in the issuance of positive law, then the statute is not merely "flawed law," it lacks completely the very nature of law. For law, including positive law, cannot be otherwise defined than as a system and an institution whose very meaning is to serve justice. Measured by this standard, whole portions of National Socialist law never attained the dignity of valid law.[7]

The complexity of Radbruch's theory derives from his idea that law itself has three constitutive elements: (political) purposiveness, justice, and legal certainty. Legal certainty is the domain of positivity, the empirical actuality of law. Even here, Radbruch insists that the domain of legal certainty—"positive law, secured by legislation and power"—takes precedence, practically and morally, we might say. Legal certainty requires that even when the laws are unjust, like a nonprogressive tax system, or, despite their claim to represent the general good, laws that only benefit the powerful or the wealthy, should be taken as a legally valid. Both occurrences are so pervasive and routine that were we to strike down a legal system on their basis alone, none would be left standing. It is assumed, for reasons we shall return to, that there is a good to legal order that is independent of both substantive justice and determinate social purpose.

Nonetheless, Radbruch argues, a complete separation between law and morality is unintelligible: beyond the broad structural fact that the very idea of having a legal system is for the sake of justice—"law is the reality the meaning of which is to serve justice"[8]—there is something in the very idea of law demanding that once a certain threshold is passed, once the "conflict between statute and justice reaches such an intolerable degree," then the statute must "yield" to justice, where so yielding provides the category of not merely "flawed law"—law failing the requirements of justice generally—but "invalid law"—law no longer deserving the title of law. Radbruch understands this moment not as law yielding to morality as something external to it but, rather, as a moment in which the justice component of law trumps the legal-certainty component such that we must regard the statute in question as invalid, as law whose claim to authority and obedience has been *internally* subverted. At least this is necessary if the normative authority of law is going to be separable from the sheer force of command. Having an appropriate legislative source can never be a sufficient criterion of lawfulness—or rather, that restriction is what the exorbitance of patently morally evil laws seems to demand.

Why should we believe this thesis? We recognize the intelligibility and necessity of the idea of the extreme of "flawed law" if we can make out the case for statutory lawlessness: some statutes are so systematically flawed from the point of view of justice they can no longer be counted as an item of law at all. Justice functions as the outer limit of lawfulness. If this claim can be made, then it will follow that law, including positive law, cannot "be otherwise defined than as a system and an institution whose very meaning is to serve justice." In brief, Radbruch's argument for statutory lawlessness is coextensive with his claim that *justice is a structural element of the concept of law*. Radbruch arrives at his formulation as a consequence of wanting to demonstrate, at least, that positivism's "a law is a law" if unqualified would undermine judges' capacity to challenge unjust laws since it makes the idea of statutory lawlessness a contradiction in terms; positivist conceptions of law, Radbruch assumes, entail that judges are abandoned to whatever laws have been enacted, and thus lack any resources *internal to the law itself* with which to confront blatantly unjust laws.

In attempting to locate the outer limit of lawfulness, Radbruch opts for the formal principle of justice, the minimum core idea of the rule of law of "equal treatment of equals."[9] (The principle that "like cases should be treated alike and differences cases treated differently," in giving procedural heft to the difference between sameness and difference, is close to a formal principle of reason.) What he is considering is transparent, namely, Nazi laws that treated Germans and Jews differently; he continues, "Legal character is also lacking in all the statutes that treated human beings as subhuman and denied them rights, and it is lacking too, in the caveats that, governed solely by the momentary necessities of intimidation, disregarded the varying gravity of offenses and threatened the same punishment, often death, for the slightest as well as the most serious crimes."[10] All these are indeed instances of flouting the principle of treating like cases alike. The problem is not that we are not tempted by the thought that statutes of this kind should not count as law; it is, rather, that their disavowal of the principle itself is not at issue. After all, the principle of equal treatment is broken *whenever* race, sex, class, party, and the like, are made legally disqualifying in some way. The issue is not whether laws embodying such disqualifications are unjust; it is whether their *degree* of injustice is so exorbitant that they thereby lose their title to lawfulness. Failing the equal treatment principle is not the same as an "intolerable" cleavage between statute and justice, and it cannot be such for Radbruch precisely because he insists that degrees of injustice matter, and that there must be conceptual space within our understanding of law for a notion of valid but unjust laws.

This is not to deny the thesis that extreme injustice is no law; it is to claim that searching out an *outer limit* of lawfulness is the wrong place for defeating positivist conceptions of law and capturing law's ethical impulse, for three reasons. First, because extreme injustice is necessarily indeterminate between an item that no longer deserves the title of law, and laws that are, as H. L. A. Hart expresses it, "too evil to be obeyed."[11] The very idea of an outer limit places morals at the boundary of lawfulness, at which point there seems little to choose between saying that a statute does not deserve to be called law or to say the statute morally deserves to be disobeyed. Second, if one accepts that the title of being *lawful* is only rarely categorically classificatory, that we rather tend to think of degrees of lawfulness, including considering whole legal systems as tainted, defective, more or less corrupt, barely legitimate, and so on, then extreme cases, outer limits, are, again, going to make us look in the wrong direction; we need to be able to speak of the kinds and degrees of flawed law even more than we require the concept of statutory lawlessness; given the force of the first argument against the outer limit thesis, it follows that statutory lawlessness should be an extreme of defective law rather than considering flawed law an emanation of the absolute limit. Third, focusing on the instance of extreme injustice must betray Radbruch's own lingering intuition that the rule of law, legal certainty, itself contains the orienting ethical idea of lawfulness.

I want to suggest, however briefly, that these tensions in Radbruch's position are systematic, rooted in the neo-Kantian disposition of his *Legal Philosophy*. Gaining a little clarity about these systematic issues will aid the argument further down the line. In 1932 Radbruch argued that the three structural elements of the concept of law—justice, purposiveness, and legal certainty—were equiprimordial: "The three aspects of the idea of law are of equal value, and in the case of conflict there is no decision between them but by the individual conscience" (*LP*, 118); by 1946 he found it necessary to rank the aspects, giving a nod to justice as the outer limit. The necessity for generating a rank value-ordering of the three aspects was to defeat not only *Legal Philosophy's* equality of values arguments, but even more important, its own presumption that a judge had a role-bound "professional duty . . . to validate the law's claim to validity, to sacrifice his own sense of right to the authoritative command of the law, to ask only what is legal and not if it is also just" (*LP*, 119).[12] This argument, if carried forward, would have legitimated Nazi jurists in rationally and morally following the dictates of unjust law; Radbruch had good reasons for wanting a revision in his theory. Yet, if the argument for a rank ordering amounts to no more than an argument that justice should be a structural aspect of law in general, then we are deposited back in the situation of the three value aspects being equal and the decision between them left to the extralegal determinations of conscience. Once conscience is the pivot, then claiming that it is a jurisprudential question rather than a direct moral one is hard to make emphatic.

In an effort to undermine the positivist exigencies of Nazi law, Radbruch's later essays attempt a response to the logical anarchy among the three governing ideals of law proposed in *Legal Philosophy*. Yet, since the later essays are operating with the same three elements, each having precisely the same features as they possessed previously, it is unclear how the introduction of a rank ordering is possible. Further, if one agrees that the application of the ideal of justice requires supplementation in order to be effective, then one might even urge that it is precisely the laws that one feels morally compelled to disobey that should be designated by the idea of statutory lawlessness—thus subsuming the antipositivist locution within the positivist separation of spheres.

If one agrees that law fundamentally concerns the precepts determining good living together (*LP*, 81), and further that there is something correct about Radbruch's three-part schema, that the law is answerable to and yet constitutively determined by irreducibly competing ideals, then we require some explanation as to how it can be that the logical anarchy of the three elements can so radically bring ruin to the orienting ideal of our good living together; how can the end and terms of law so ruinously come apart? One simple hypothesis here is that Radbruch's methodical dualism between fact and value leads him to interpret legal certainty in wholly factual—positivist—terms as power and effectiveness, yielding a baroque notion of the validity of the factual: "The law is valid not *because* it can be carried through effectively; rather, it is valid *if* it can be carried through effectively, *because* it is only then that it can afford legal certainty" (*LP*, 118). Radbruch's conception of legal certainty, despite itself, contains nothing that might distinguish the "peace" (118) it is meant to afford from sheer terror. If legal certainty is not only challengeable by justice and purpose but also lacking in the wherewithal to distinguish certainty from arbitrariness, then Radbruch's version of legal certainty is radically inadequate in its own terms.

Now recall that it was legal certainty that was at the center of the immanent utopian ideal of the rule of law and we have an even sharper puzzle: what sense can be made of legal certainty representing indifferently a utopian ideal and a terroristic threat? I take the simple explanation of this to be that Radbruch has severely stripped the idea of legal certainty of any idealizing, normative elements through which we might recognize the kind of certainty provided *as lawful* and not merely powerful, as a certainty belonging to the notion of law itself. The positivism of his concept of legal certainty deprives that certainty of the qualification of lawfulness, such that precepts having the structure and form of law—in being, in effect—might yield a certainty providing confidence, security, and trust. Law's positivity must itself possess a "legal" character, where that character belongs to empirical actuality and is not solely a creature of an ideality—justice or purpose—external to it. What Radbruch's account of legal certainty lacks (or lacks in his central accounts of it) is an appropriate conception of the rule of law, that is, of the kind of rule that law alone provides. Because of his methodical fact/value dualism, he transposes into the notion of justice—*both* substantive justice, the just distribution of power, rights, welfare, and so on, and the demands of formal justice, the kinds of formal considerations that belong to a legal regime as such.

FULLER'S INNER MORALITY OF LAW

"If laws, even bad laws, have a claim to our respect, then law must represent some general direction of human effort that we can understand and describe, and that we can approve in principle even at the moment when it seems to us to miss its mark."[13] Although Lon Fuller is responsible for inserting Radbruch's antipositivist legal theory into English-speaking jurisprudence, making it a pivot in his debate with Hart, Fuller too was skeptical about the proposal of making extreme injustice an outer limit to legality that would thereby secure law's relation to morality. Fuller's conception of the rule of law as providing an "inner morality" of law plants law's authority and dignity in the very place where Radbruch locates its utopian ambition, namely, in the domain of legal certainty. Rather than conceiving of legal certainty as an achievement of stability through force alone, Fuller contends that the stable framework of interaction that legal certainty provides is an ethos, a form of ethical life that receives it shape from the rule of law itself. But this claim would be suspicious in the extreme if the rule of law were presented in terms of lofty moral ideals, joining law and morality through subsuming the law directly under morality or justice conceived in thick moral terms.

Fuller's philosophical tour de force is to "establish a necessary connection between law and justice, on the ground that the precepts of formal legality [that are the fundaments of the rule of law [are] necessary conditions for the existence of law."[14] Fuller proposes eight wholly formal criteria for lawfulness that are not themselves transparently moral in character but nonetheless, he thinks, are ingredients in the goodness of law; so the idea of an "inner morality" of law turns on how these eight formal, even grammatical characteristics of lawfulness secrete an ideality that makes fidelity to law morally compelling. The eight criteria follow.

Generality: legal rules are general—addressing types of activities and social roles, never individuals, which supports the principle that like cases are to be treated alike, and thereby that the law applies to all equally (no one is above the law).

Publicity: laws are to be promulgated widely and publicly so that all those affected by them will know of them; laws should not be kept secret from those affected. Secrecy is antithetical to legality as such.

Prospectivity: laws should govern future actions, and retrospective laws should be avoided except in extreme instances. Retrospective laws would be versions of secret laws since like them the agent could not have planned his or her actions differently, and further, since retrospective laws cover what has already been done, then even if stated in general terms, they carry the unmistakable taint of particularity.

Clarity: laws should be comprehensible to those they affect, or, where that is not possible, comprehensible to those with legal expertise who can represent those affected (entailing the subrequirement of the need for sufficient access to legal representation when necessary).

Noncontradiction: legal norms should be consistent with one another in a sufficient manner to allow individuals to satisfy all legal obligations imposed on them.

Practicability: a version of the "ought implies can" principle, requiring that legal obligations be within the ordinary powers of citizens to satisfy them.

Constancy: a principle opposing the idea of continuous and radical transformations in the law; laws should remain stable and continuous through time in a manner sufficient to allow those affected to know them and plan their actions accordingly. Constancy naturally clusters with the demands for prospectivity, consistency, and practicability since, in practice, lack of constancy will abridge the purpose served by the other three.

Congruence: laws should be effectuated, and there should be a continuous relation between the laws that are officially promulgated and the administration of the law.

As presented here, these eight criteria are starkly formal in character, none containing substantive moral content. This formality is central to the power of

Fuller's argument: justice and legality are to be conceptually connected through the form of law alone.

Even on the basis of their bare statement and without further elaboration, it is clear that Fuller's eight precepts of legality are the beginning of a resolution to the difficulties besetting Radbruch's theory. Let us say that *the eight precepts for legality are the fundamental requirements for legal certainty*: we cannot conceive of a legal system that would deliver the stability, the trustworthiness, and the claim to legal validity—which jointly are the conditions necessary to invite fidelity to the law—without conforming to these eight principles. While the bulk of what he wants to say about justice is packed into the principle of generality, even Radbruch's conceptions of force and effectivity are here provided with a normative profile in terms of constancy and congruence. Legal certainty always did mean to point to the actuality of the rule of law; what Fuller's precepts demonstrate is that legal positivity, the actuality of the law, is itself normatively constituted. The Kantian image of metaphysically discrete domains of facts and values as "closed circles" (*LP*, 53) incapable of thoroughgoing interpenetration and fusion is overcome if *to be a law* or, better, *to be a (recognizable) legal system* is itself in part constituted by conformity to formal principles; the positivity of law is suffused with principle through form alone.

There is fair agreement now that the appropriate unit for consideration of legality is not the individual statute but a legal system as a whole since each of the formal principles intend to pick out a threshold along a continuum of degrees of more or less: a legal system is not disqualified as delivering legal certainty if there are some laws that are never enforced (jaywalking), or where some laws change regularly (yearly changes in the tax code are acceptable, if irksome, while monthly changes would not be), or if some retrospection is found to be necessary in order to correct a previous wrong. It also is not disqualified if publicity remains narrowly relative to who is affected by a law or even more narrowly to those who represent those affected, or where clarity for some laws is narrowly construed as relative to a small segment of legal professionals, and the like. As Fuller's fable of the hapless Rex—in which Rex insistently flouts each of the principles in turn—is meant to illustrate; even an enlightened, well-intentioned, and benevolent legislator will fail to provide anything recognizable as a legal system if any one of the precepts is systematically and routinely flouted: all secret laws or incomprehensible laws or laws that change week to week or are never enforced or are physically impossible to satisfy or contradict one another or are legislated only after the act in question has been done or apply to only arbitrarily selected individuals. In each of these cases the law would be incapable of being followed;

individuals would not be able to regulate their conduct in accordance with law because either the law was not available, or impossible to follow, or utterly arbitrary in its application or meaningless because it is not a reliable indicator of government action. Together with further requirements for the successful implementation of the rule of law—a competent judiciary, access to legal representation, separation of powers, and, as we shall see, a series of procedural and due process requirements (e.g., habeas corpus[15])—a legal system will possess more or less validity, be more or less corrupt, more or less effective, more or less just; and at the extremes we will want to withhold the title of "legal system" altogether: not every system of rule and control is a legal system.[16]

The high formality of the principles themselves and the persuasiveness of Fuller's argument that flagrant disregard for any one of these requirements over an extended period of time would undermine legal validity and the conditions that make fidelity to a legal system possible has led even some leading positivist legal theorists to accept Fuller's precepts.[17] While this acceptance is testimony to the power of Fuller's argument, because Fuller's ambition in generating a conception of the "inner morality" of law was to overturn legal positivism, then a stronger conception of the principles is called for. To begin with we need an account of the connection between a narrow view of the principles as providing the minimum necessary conditions for legality, which captures their appeal to even positivist jurisprudence, and Fuller's own robust interpretation of them as constituting the "inner morality" of law.[18]

Fuller's precepts are neither essential to human action generally nor even to cooperative action: we often aim at unachievable perfection; hold competing values that cannot be jointly realized; sometimes discover that secrecy is the morally generous gesture; realize that opacity in the context of the arts can be an affirmative value; eschew routine and stability because we find being sensitive to changing conditions, individually or as a group, requires a willingness to be spontaneous rather planning ahead; and tailor our actions to the individual before us because to treat her as "like" relevant others would be to mistreat her. Despite their broad and patent formality, the eight precepts do seem specific to legal systems, which acknowledges that the "good" of a legal system is distinct from the morally good itself (whatever it is). What are the *stakes* of a legal system that makes the flagrant failure of any of those eight principles reason for disqualification?

In contrast with a managerial system directed toward achieving particular ends, Fuller argues that law "is basically a matter of providing the citizenry with a sound and stable framework for their interactions with one another, the role of government being that of standing as a guardian of the integrity of the system."[19] The primary emphasis in consideration of law is not about rule or governmentality or political processes; in the first instance, to think about law is consider the characteristics necessary for a framework and infrastructure—without any particular purposes of its own—that is suitable for a large and diverse community to interact with one another in pursuit of their routine and everyday affairs; that is, legality refers to a particular form of collective life that we lead with a large and diverse cohort of anonymous others whom we understand to have categorical desires, contingent preferences, and orienting values that are different from our own, where our shared life together is one in which these diverse desires, preferences, and values are capable of being acted upon. Something like this thought is percolating behind Radbruch's espousal of legal certainty with his claim that legal value points to precepts good for living together. Law is about a form of living together that arises when we can no longer rely on tradition (customary practices) or a unifying collective purpose or set of purposes, or the pertinences of affect and context suitable for practical engagement in a narrow setting or the absolute authority of a recognized ruler in order to solve the problems of action coordination, moral disagreement, and the sheer multiplicity of ends we must mutually accommodate. In brief, a modern legal system provides an escape from arbitrariness under conditions of value pluralism, social complexity, and social change that enables individualized life plans and pursuits of desire.

A legal system is further distinguished from a managerial system (or a system of training and habituation in which conformity and obedience are essential) by addressing its demands to the deliberative capacities of individuals construed as self-determining and responsible agents.[20] All the business about publicity, prospectivity, clarity, and the like only makes sense if we conceive of laws as items that agents are to deliberatively take into account in interacting with others here and now, and in planning their future course of action. (Notice how these particular principles converge to underwrite the principle *nulla poema sine lege*—no penalty without law.) But this entails, Fuller argues, that "there is a kind of reciprocity between government and citizen with respect to the observance of rules";[21] in addressing citizens in this manner, the government is simultaneously binding itself to those rules and the procedures for determining what rules should be instituted and how it is to occur. In addressing citizens as deliberative agents, governments generate a structure of *vertical reciprocity* in which they become answerable to citizens if they fail to abide by the rules of law; without answerability to citizens, the address to them as deliberative agents would be hollow. But within a system of law, citizens are responsible for judging the worthiness of the rules addressed to them.[22] From this perspective, democracy can be interpreted as the fulfillment of law's deliberative address, as the authorized authority of law rather than, say, the workings of an imposing collective will. Law is the resultant of the ongoing dialogue between legislator and citizen.

Return to the initial question of freedom from arbitrariness that legal certainty is to provide; this can now be refined to say that where "the rule of law is observed in a community, i.e., where law rules, it provides a substantial measure of protection in two dimensions: protection of the governed against arbitrary power of those who govern (vertical) and protection of members of the society against the arbitrary exercise of power by their fellows (horizontal)."[23] Fuller's principles provide, precisely, legal certainty; but, as Radbruch rightly states, legal certainty remains distinct from concrete legislative and political purposes—the rule of law is about legal form, and even more radically distinct from substantive conceptions of justice; a fully just society or a society in which the full raft of international human rights were law would be something more and other than a legally certain one. Law, in this sense, is a morality for grown-ups: it, again, assumes that those affected will have desires, ends, and moral commitments that are diverse; that there will be not only bad laws, but routinely there will be laws that some who are affected take to be immoral and unjust but still, somehow, are deserving of respect because they are the law. Laws can be legally valid without being morally true, and we do not need to judge our fellow citizens' motives for conforming their behavior to law—being law-abiding is sufficient, and virtue unnecessary. Unlike ideal morality, a system of law leaves room for the alienated and the disaffected to cooperate in whatever way they deem appropriate so long as they are, in fact, law-abiding (and when they are not, sanctioning can kick in); but, the determinations of the rule of law itself are of a kind to invite moral allegiance when they are widely and consistently implemented, that is, the idea of the rule of law *invites* (summons) moral allegiance and responsiveness.

This is, one might argue, the great achievement of Fuller's theory: from one angle, legality appears wholly in the guise of an instrumental good, allegiance to which can be as narrow as fear of punishment; while from an opposing angle it can appear as a moral summons to an adult form of mutually respectful living together, where even government acts in a manner that is respectful of citizen's individuality, autonomy, and conception of self-worth. Nonetheless, there would appear to remain an essential gap between the inner morality of the rule of law and morality proper, a gap that is, one might argue, sufficient for the purposes of bending even the rule of law back in a positivist direction since for *each* citizen there will be a gap between legal validity and moral truth; but if for each citizen there is a separation between law and morality, then essentially the law is first positive before it is moral. Said somewhat differently, it is the persistence of the Radbruchian tripartite schema in Fuller that continues to generate a gap between morality proper—the justice and substantive (moral) purposes of law—and legal certainty as constituted by the rule of law, making the latter continue to appear as mere form, as depicting a collective social arrangement that insists upon a certain gap between itself and morality in its substantive sense, and which hence can be designated for all intents and purposes as value-neutral. The Radbruchian tripartite schema enables the perception of not only Radbruch's own thought, early and late, as being positivist despite his insistence to the contrary but also further permits Fuller's principles to be adopted by positivism.

LEGAL PERSECUTION: THE RED HERRING RETURNS

There is an evident clash between interpreting Fuller's eight rule of law principles as the ethics of a deflationary utopia—"a government of law is like our daily bread, like water to drink and air to breathe"—as opposed to taking them as providing the conditions for the operation of a complex, value-neutral instrument, the Swiss army knife of human institutions, with many purposes but no generic purpose.[24] I term this clash *the problem of the persistence of positivism* in the analysis of the rule of law. Positivism persists in jurisprudence with more title than elsewhere because (i) laws are human creations, posits, enacted rules, that, in the first instance and in the final instance, have whatever force they do because humans are willing to have their conduct ordered by them; (ii) laws are components of social practices that can be observed and analyzed like any other stretch of social reality; (iii) however else they are understood, laws are also instruments that solve a diversity of social problems, including moral problems, entailing that at least some part of their value is instrumental; (iv) strong readings of i–iii take them to entail that law is morally value-neutral. The final inference is certainly overly hasty. My analysis of the persistence problem begins from the continuance of the Radbruchian tripartite schema whereby the legal certainty provided by the rule of law remains distinct from substantive conceptions of justice and concrete political purposes. Legal positivists attempt to leverage the weak morality of the rule of law into outright value-neutrality by arguing that logically and conceptually the rule of law is compatible not only with flawed law, bad law, and laws with which we morally disapprove but also compatible with even outright evil practices dressed in legal form.

> Raz: "A non-democratic legal system, based on the denial of human rights, on extensive poverty, on racial segregation, sexual inequalities, and religious persecution may, in principle, conform to the requirements of the rule of law better than any of the legal systems of the more enlightened Western democracies."[25]
>
> Hart: "Proof that the principles by which we evaluate and condemn laws are rationally discoverable . . . leaves untouched the fact that there are laws which may have any degree of iniquity or stupidity and still be laws. And conversely there are rules that have every moral qualification to be laws and yet are not laws."[26]

Hart's and Raz's claims strike me as true but irrelevant. As we have already seen Radbruch argue, no account of formal justice and formal equality on its own is sufficient to determine *who* belongs within the class of justice-deserving individuals and who does not; the scope of "all" in any formation of "all individuals are to be treated equally" has always been and must always be determined historically, with each widening and inclusion of a heretofore excluded group the consequence of moral and political struggle. That a formally excluded class of persons comes to be included within the scope of justice-deserving regard is a matter of *moral truth*—the individuals belonging to class X possess the same intrinsic moral (and therefore civic) worth as the individuals belonging to class Y, and therefore deserve the same treatment—*not moral principles*.[27] Moral principles, norms, and values do not themselves determine who or what falls within their scope. Hence, the argument that a law, norm, principle, or value is compatible with great iniquity is no less true of the rule of law than it is of Kant's moral law: Kant's own emphatic racism only comes to contradict the categorical imperative once the moral equality of the races is acknowledged—because there are no races—and the meaning of that acknowledgment taken as entailing a strong version of the equal treatment principle; neither of those two claims automatically belongs to the categorical imperative itself.[28] No one, however, supposes that because the *actual* scope of Kant's moral law requires further appraisals and empirical determinations for its application that the categorical imperative is itself value-neutral, or of only instrumental value.

Throughout modern history, presumptively universalist *moralities* have treated some humans as less than fully equal and fully human—those others are human, but too emotional or ignorant or uneducable or dependent to be fully morally responsible for their own lives or to participate fully in civic life; they are human, but perpetual children in need of governance and guidance from above. Women, we should recall, did not have the right to vote in France until 1944, and in Switzerland not until 1971; marital rape laws were still in effect in the United States in the 1980s. Moral values and principles require substantive moral beliefs about others before they can become empirically effective. The rule of law is in this regard no different than any other morality; substantive universalism and equality are always a concrete moral-political achievement based on substantive moral beliefs about others rather than a feature of moral values and principles themselves. Hence, the inference from cases of the rule of law being compatible with gross iniquity says nothing about whether the rule of law is moral in itself or value-neutral.

Although never elaborated upon in sufficient detail, Fuller insists that the moral stakes of the rule of law turn on their capacity to acknowledge, protect, and nurture human dignity. Every departure from the law's inner morality is an affront to man's dignity as a responsible agent. To judge his actions by unpublished or retrospective laws, or to order him to do an act that is impossible, is to convey to him your indifference to his powers of self-determination.[29]

In my initial pass at the inner morality of law, I underlined how law as determining what is good for acting together assumed both a horizontal and vertical reciprocity among agents: laws provide the broad framework through which we can in our everyday affairs treat one another as self-determining agents, which in turn presumes, vertically, that the law must itself treat all those affected as self-determining agents. To regard agents in this way is to respect their dignity.

Raz agrees with this claim: "observance of the rule of law is necessary if the law is to respect human dignity. Respecting human dignity entails treating humans as persons capable of planning and plotting their future."[30] After usefully profiling offenses to dignity as falling into three classes—insults (humiliation), enslavement, and manipulation (brainwashing)—and pressing, once more, a version of the iniquity argument "The law may . . . institute slavery without violating the rule of law,"[31] Raz attempts to drive a wedge between law and morality by claiming that the essential virtue of the rule of law is its preventing *legal* abuses; that is, the rule of law corrects forms of abuse that are internal to having a legal regime, and hence the idea of a legal regime is antecedent to the rule of law. This is both stipulative and implausible. As Jeremy Waldron pointedly argues, "the Rule of Law aims to correct abuses of power by insisting on a particular mode of the exercise of political power: governance through law"; and this, he continues, is thought to better protect us from abuse, better protect our dignity, than managerial governance or rule by decree, for example.[32]

BECCARIA'S REFORMATION: NOTES FOR A GENEALOGY OF THE RULE OF LAW

Although Raz is conceptually wrong, he is historically correct: the modern idea of the rule of law took hold in the eighteenth century precisely in response to massive abuses that were then endemic to the law. Those abuses collectively defined "arbitrariness"; hence, if the rule of law is for the sake of overcoming arbitrariness and preserving and protecting human dignity, then a survey of the eighteenth-century context of its emergence is required.[33]

Judicial and penal torture were essential ingredients in all continental European legal regimes from the eleventh century until their remarkable abolition in the latter part of the eighteenth century and early part of the nineteenth century. In ways that might now seem implausible, torture was *not* regarded as the paradigm of human cruelty, the worse thing one person might do to another; on the contrary, the entire Roman-canon criminal law system revolved around torture—first as a pivotal element in the law of evidence and, second, as a component of the penal system. In the Roman-canon legal system that began emerging in the twelfth century, crimes punishable by the death penalty, or by severe mutilation or maiming, required either the testimony of two eyewitnesses or a confession. This was a hard standard to satisfy—murderers tend not to commit the vile deeds before eyewitnesses, nor do they readily confess them; hence, torture was used as a supplement in order to prompt a confession.

The intelligibility of penal torture had a different source: it depended on the general configuration of the relation between the sovereign authority of the monarch and the body of the victim that was displayed in penal torture—which was as common in England (the "Bloody Code" that made death by hanging and associated tortures the punishment for over two hundred different crimes, many minor) as on the continent. In a world in which there was as yet no police, no routine mechanisms of law enforcement, punitive public executions were certainly meant to terrify and deter. But these characteristics had a specific contour in monarchies in which the authority of the law and the authority of the sovereign person were united. In breaking the law, the criminal is attacking the very person of the sovereign, attacking her or his authority. Public executions thus had a juridical-political function of reconstituting the momentarily injured sovereignty; it "restores sovereignty by manifesting it as it most spectacular. . . . Its aim is not so much to re-establish a balance as to bring into play, at its extreme point, the dissymmetry between the subject who has dared to violate the law and the all-powerful sovereign who displays his strength."[34] What the tortured body spectacularly demonstrates is the power of the sovereign, that is, both the authority or validity or legitimacy of the sovereign's laws and the force of those laws.

In the course of the eighteenth century, the sovereign law of torture entered into crisis because the fundamental form of its affirmation and vindication, penal torture, came increasingly to be considered brutalizing and violating, as cruel and vicious.[35] Foucault carefully documents how the collapsing sovereign system came to be viewed as arbitrary and irrational, where this change of perception is what lay behind the view that sovereign torture was a violent attack on the individual, as something personal and therefore not lawful, as arbitrary and therefore illegal. The hollowness of sovereign authority was perceived as pervasive in the system as a whole by the reformers, from "too much power in the lower jurisdictions . . . [who] could carry out arbitrary sentences without adequate supervision," to "too much power in the hands of judges who were able to content themselves with futile evidence," to, finally, "too much power exercised by the king, who could suspend courts of justice, alter their decisions, remove magistrates from office, or exile them. . . . This dysfunction of power was related to a central excess: what might be called the monarchical 'super-power,' which identified the right to punish with the personal power of the sovereign."[36] I understand the shift in the perception of torture from celebration to horror as generating a *contradiction* in the very idea of the sovereign law of torture: the event that was to demonstrate the authority of the sovereign, the meaning of sovereignty, and the meaning of law, demonstrated, at the very least, an abuse of authority and, even more, an arbitrariness in the application of law that effectively reduced legal authority to brute power. This is the arbitrariness that the rule of law is designed to curb. The abolition of, first, judicial torture and then penal torture that tore through Europe in less than a century was not solely about the abolishing of a practice that had come to be pervasively viewed as the paradigm of cruelty and brutality; to abolish torture was to alter the relation of the citizen, and the bodies of citizens, to the state; it was to adopt an opposing conception of legality—*it was to embrace the rule of law as the determinate negation of the sovereign law of torture*.

Cesare Beccaria's *On Crimes and Punishments*, first published in 1764, with its short but fierce arguments against "the barbarous tortures that have been elaborated with prodigal and useless severity, to punish crimes either unproven or illusory."[37] Beccaria's work was almost immediately translated in twenty-two

European languages, including Dutch, Polish, and Spanish; it went through twenty-eight Italian editions and nine French ones before 1800 (often accompanied by a laudatory commentary by Voltaire); it was translated into English in 1767 (Jeremy Bentham becoming Beccaria's "apostle"), with multiple editions in both Britain and the United States (Jefferson copied long passages from it into his commonplace book; his proposals for revising the Virginia criminal code were drawn directly from Beccaria). It played a direct role in law reforms initiated by Catherine II, Frederick the Great of Prussia, and those carried out in France. Comprehending why Beccaria's work was so influential is impossible if one directly focuses on his famous detailed arguments against torture (chapter 16), or even his novel arguments against the death penalty (chapter 28), the first systematic philosophical and jurisprudential critique of it of which I am aware.

The all-too-familiar and now accepted ideas that Beccaria presents are just standard rule of law and procedural due process requirements: separation of powers, judicial constraint, clear laws publicly communicated, trial by a jury of peers, public trials, and so on. What gives these thoughts their power in the context in which they are presented is that they emerge as *determinate negations* of the sovereign law of torture. Beccaria argues that each rule of law and procedural due process provision, as well as the general constraints for a just system of punishments, *is a necessary condition* to escape from the arbitrariness and cruelty of the sovereign law of torture. For example, in his critique of judicial (interrogational) torture, although Beccaria underlines all the ancient ideas about why pain is not conducive to truth telling, and that a system of interrogation through torture presents massive jeopardy to the sensitive innocent and maximal benefit to the guilty brute, the core of his argument is the adoption of the principle of "innocent until proven guilty": "No man may be called guilty before the judge has reached his verdict; nor may society withdraw its protection from him until it has been determined that he has broken the terms of the compact by which that protection was extended to him" (39). The principle that a person is innocent until proven guilty is precisely what is denied by legal torture for purposes other than punishment. Judicial torture takes possession of the body of the accused anterior to the proceedings that are for the sake of determining innocence or guilt. This is contradictory, however, only if it is assumed that criminal justice is for the sake of protecting the freedom and well-being of citizens through the establishment of the rule of law. One might say that the presumptive innocence of the accused follows from individuals' *moral independence* from the criminal justice system, whose existence depends on their voluntary adherence—conceptually and morally the state must be conceived of as a voluntary association. Only by being found guilty of, effectively, breaking his contractual promise does the citizen lose more than the portion of freedom originally surrendered in consenting to the social compact; any earlier interference in his liberty and well-being usurps his freedom, his legal personality, and thus his dignity.

Beccaria elaborates upon this collapsing sovereign logic thus: "the laws torture you because you are guilty, because you may be guilty, or because I want you to be guilty" (43). Although Beccaria will lodge a series of empirical criticisms against the use of torture—showing its fundamental uselessness with respect to the purposes for which it is employed—his fundamental critique of judicial torture is not for humanitarian reasons (although its cruelty matters) but because its judicial uses for anything other than punishment run contrary to the very idea of the rule of law. To employ the means of punishment prior to the establishment of guilt involves government employing a power that no one has given to it, it denies that the individual charged has standing and rights, and it transforms legality into the rule of the greater force, reintroducing the very arbitrariness that having a legal system was meant to overturn. Nothing could be worse for an individual than to lose the very freedom for the sake of which he agreed to the social contract in the first place. Hence, not only must an individual be presumed innocent until proven guilty but also, Beccaria insists, nothing less than a moral "certainty" is adequate for the sake of establishing guilt (34)—guilty, we now say, beyond a reasonable doubt.

The kind of argument offered in defense of the principle of "innocent until proven guilty" could be developed for each of Fuller's eight principles since the converse of each was indeed a feature of the sovereign law of torture—this, in effect, is just what Beccaria does. The ambition is to make the law legislatively just, transparent in its meaning and in its operation, and judgment of individual cases fair, constrained, and, again, transparent. In the language of contemporary jurisprudence, Beccaria is engineering a double transformation of the rule of law: from a "thin" to a "thick" conception of the rule of law in accordance with "substantive" principle, so making the "thick" conception itself substantive. The thin conception of the rule of law is intended to provide a wedge separating law from personal command: coercive government powers can be legitimately exercised only if they are the product of recognized legislative practice. Legitimate legislative processes beget legitimate legal products. It was this positivist conception of the rule of law that Beccaria was protesting against since the right to make law does not entail the making of right law; even if laws derive from a legitimating source, those laws may be not only unjust and unfair but even lacking in those syntactical and formal features requisite for lawfulness in general. The idea of a "thick," formal, and procedural rule of law stipulates the Fuller and Beccaria principles—broadly: generality, prospectivity, clarity, and neutrality—together with the requisite procedural and due process analogues. For Beccaria, however, we adopt these formal and procedural thick rules of law and due process requirements not for formal reasons (that they can be viewed as formal constraints on legality is no part of Beccaria's argument) but, above all, in order that the conditions for our protection from civil violence—the provision of a system of criminal justice—do not become a form of legal, state violence as exemplified by arbitrary laws, arbitrarily applied, backed by judicial and penal torture. Hence, for Beccaria formal and procedural rule of law considerations embody substantive ethical conceptions of human freedom and dignity. Or better, *the entire purpose of rule of law considerations is to generate a moral standing of the citizen-subject in relation to the law*; legality is a self-limiting construction of a living together where the citizen-subject is the limit that must not be transgressed upon until and unless he or she is shown to have transgressed the limit represented by another subject. The citizen-subject as the limit and condition of legality is just what Fuller saw as the foundational "inner morality" of his eight precepts.

The provision of that substantive basis is always elliptical in *On Crimes* because Beccaria so emphatically eschews the use of natural law and natural rights considerations; their adoption, he argues, is always and necessarily historically provincial and thus, whatever the intention, conventional once more—just "our" provincial conception of what natural law requires or what natural rights we possess. In place of natural law and natural rights, Beccaria discretely places before us, as the rhetorical and moral center of his argument, the broken bodies of the tortured and the long history of morally horrific legal state violence. If we could not agree that *that* is wrong, then no further moral or legal agreements are possible. Even Beccaria's deployment of the ideals of moral freedom and equality as premises for his argument takes its force as a determinate negation of palpable forms of social domination, state violence, unfreedom—of various ways in which we are enslaved—and inequality. Beccaria's elaboration and imaging of formal and procedural rule of law arrangements as possessing and generating a substantive ethical idea is the transfiguration of a massive, enduring, and finally all-too-visible history of legal state violence into an image of justice and public well-being. Beccaria's rule of law doctrine, we might say, *erects an image of a dignified civil body out of the remnants of its repeated sovereign mutilation through a process of determinate negation*: what must a system of laws, criminal procedures, and practices of punishment be that would prohibit all the excesses, vices, arbitrariness, and cruelty of the system of sovereign torture? What idea of *lawfulness* can be offered as an alternative to the idea of sovereign law? As we answer these questions via the adoption of formal and procedural rule of law requirements, what begins to emerge is a conception of the autonomous and dignified human subject whose body is his or her own and thus should never be violated by the hand of the state. Hence, formal and procedural rule of law as the generative mechanism for a conception of human dignity arises, in its first announcement, as nothing other than the determinate negation of sovereign torture or, what is the same, as a remembrance of suffering. By its restraint, the rule of law remembers past suffering as that which should never be repeated.

NOTES

1. Gustav Radbruch, "Statutory Lawlessness and Supra-Statutory Law," trans. Bonnie Litschewski Paulson and Stanley L. Paulson, *Oxford Journal of Legal Studies* 26, no. 1 (2006): 1–11.

2. John Locke, *The Second Treatise of Government*, ed. Peter Laslett (Cambridge: Cambridge University Press, 1991), chapter 4, "Slavery," section 22.

3. Judith Shklar, "Political Theory and the Rule of Law," in *Political Thought and Political Thinkers*, ed. Stanley Hoffmann (Chicago: University of Chicago Press, 1998), 36.

4. F. A. Hayek, *The Road to Serfdom* (London: Routledge, 1944), 55; second italics are mine). For a fair-minded evaluation of the policy implications of the rule of law as the necessary condition for a modern, capitalist economy, see the Carnegie Endowment–sponsored evaluations, edited by Thomas Carothers, *Promoting the Rule of Law Abroad: In Search of Knowledge* (Washington, D.C.: Carnegie Endowment for International Peace, 2006).

5. Hayek, *Road to Serfdom*, 59. A few sentences later, Hayek unproblematically assimilates the socialist objection to merely "formal justice" to the Nazi objection to that idea. For Hayek's most replete defense of the rule of law, see his *The Constitution of Liberty* (London: Routledge, 1960), part 2.

6. For a documenting of and response to the "equality," "difference," and "democracy" critiques of the rule of law from the perspective of socialism, see Christine Sypnowich, "Utopia and the Rule of Law," in *Recrafting the Rule of Law: The Limits of Legal Order*, ed. David Dyzenhaus (Oxford: Hart, 1999), 178–95. Sypnowich presents

an interesting defense of the rule of law with respect to the issue of socialist freedom in *The Concept of Socialist Law* (Oxford: Clarendon, 1990), 59–83.

7. Radbruch, "Statutory Lawlessness," 7.

8. Gustav Radbruch, *Legal Philosophy*, trans. Kurt Wilk, in *The Legal Philosophy of Lask, Radbruch, and Dabin* (Cambridge, Mass.: Harvard University Press, 1950), 75; hereafter cited in the text as *LP*.

9. Radbruch, "Statutory Lawlessness," 8. We might sense that the gap between antipositivism and positivism is less than meets the eye when we notice that H. L. A. Hart, "Positivism and the Separation of Law and Morals," *Harvard Law Review* 71, no. 4 (February 1958): 623–24, is equally emphatic that the "*one* essential element of the concept of justice is the principle of treating like cases alike. This is justice in the administration of law [that is, procedural justice], not justice of the law."

10. Radbruch, "Statutory Lawlessness," 8.

11. Hart, "Positivism and Separation," 620. Hart's critique of Radbruch is that beginning with the separation of law and morals does not entail an inability to make moral criticisms of law; moral criticism of the law is preferable to attempting to say of some statute that it is not law. One need not agree with Hart's preference in order to accept that simply *on their own* extremely unjust statutes say nothing about whether morality is integral to legality.

12. In 1932 this struck Radbruch as a way to correct the prejudicial practice of the German courts for habitually failing to indict right-wing political murders (354 murders resulting in only one life sentence), and routinely sentencing left-wing murderers to death (22 murders punished by 10 death penalties and 3 life sentences). See Stanley L. Paulson, "Lon L. Fuller, Gustav Radbruch, and the 'Positivist' Theses," *Law and Philosophy* 13, no. 3 (August 1994): 354.

13. Lon Fuller, "Positivism and Fidelity to Law—A Reply to Professor Hart," *Harvard Law Review* 71, no. 4 (1958): 632.

14. T. R. S. Allan, *Constitutional Justice: A Liberal Theory of the Rule of Law* (Oxford: Oxford University Press, 2001), 61. Allan's book offers a sweeping and detailed defense of Fuller's theory.

15. A fine handling of habeas corpus in the light of Fuller's precepts can be found in Larry May, "International Criminal Law and the Inner Morality of Law," in *The Hart-Fuller Debate in the Twenty-First Century*, ed. Peter Cane, 79–96 (Oxford: Hart, 2010).

16. Agreeing here with Jeremy Waldron's critique of "casual positivism" in his "The Concept and the Rule of Law," *Georgia Law Review* 43, no. 1 (Fall 2008): 13–19. The emphases of Waldron's argument are broadly convergent with the ambition of this essay.

17. Mathew H. Kramer, *Objectivity and the Rule of Law* (Cambridge: Cambridge University Press, 2007), 101–86; Scott J. Shapiro, *Legality* (Cambridge, Mass.: Harvard University Press, 2011), 388–400.

18. Kramer, *Objectivity*, 28, argues that the eight principles "do not have any inherent moral bearings," although they "acquire" moral bearings from the character of any regime in which they exist, and in particular acquire deep moral substance in liberal-democratic societies.

19. Lon L. Fuller, *The Morality of Law*, rev. ed. (New Haven, Conn.: Yale University Press, 1969), 210. This quote is from "A Reply to Critics," which concludes this revised edition.

20. Ibid., 162.

21. Ibid., 39.

22. The theme of the law's address to the deliberative capacity of agents is developed in potent ways by Gerald J. Postema, "Implicit Law," *Law and Philosophy* 13, no. 3 (August 1994): 361–87.

23. Gerald J. Postema, "Positivism and the Separation of Realists from Their Skepticism: Normative Guidance, the Rule of Law and Legal Reasoning," in Cane, *Hart-Fuller Debate*, 275–76.

24. While the knife image is Raz's, I cannot now recall the origin of the Swiss army elaboration.

25. Joseph Raz, "The Rule of Law and Its Virtue," in *The Authority of Law: Essays on Law and Morality* (Oxford: Oxford University Press, 1979), 211.

26. Hart, "Positivism and Separation," 626. On 624 Hart points to our recent past: "This is so because a legal system that satisfied these minimum requirement might apply, with the most pedantic impartiality as between those affected, laws which were hideously oppressive, and might deny to a vast rightless population the minimum benefits of protection from violence and theft. The stink of such societies is, after all, still in our nostrils."

27. See J. M. Bernstein, *Recovering Ethical Life* (London: Routledge, 1994), 191–96.

28. Robert Bernasconi, "Who Invented the Concept of Race?: Kant's Role in the Enlightenment Construction of Race," in *Race*, ed. Robert Bernasconi, 11–36 (Oxford: Blackwell, 2001).

29. Fuller, *Morality of Law*, 162.

30. Raz, "Rule of Law," 221.

31. Ibid.

32. Waldron, "Concept," 11.

33. This section excerpts the argument of chapter 1 of my *Torture and Dignity: An Essay on Moral Injury* (Chicago: University of Chicago Press, 2015).

34. Michael Foucault, *Discipline and Punish: The Birth of the Prison*, trans. Alan Sheridan (New York: Vintage Books, 1979), 48.

35. For historical refinements to this analysis, see Pieter Spierenburg, *The Spectacle of Suffering* (Cambridge: Cambridge University Press, 1984), and his useful survey,

"Punishment, Power, and History: Foucault and Elias," *Social Science History* 28, no. 4 (Winter 2004): 607–36.

36. Foucault, *Discipline and Punish*, 79–80.

37. Cesare Beccaria, *On Crimes and Punishments and Other Writings*, trans. Richard Davies, Virginia Cox, and Richard Bellamy (Cambridge: Cambridge University Press, 1995), 8. All page references in the text in this section are to this edition.

11

SEXUAL DIFFERENCE

Joan Copjec

A NUMBERS GAME

In the mid-1970s a global warming began to melt the icy resistance of feminists to psychoanalysis. Yet only a decade later signs of another climate change in the relations between feminism and psychoanalysis were already apparent. Teresa de Lauretis, in her groundbreaking book, *Technologies of Gender*, articulated the slogan under which the reverse winds would effectively uncouple the two discourses, breaking apart their short-lived alliance: "A feminist theory of gender [she argued] points to a conception of the subject as multiple, rather than divided."[1] Suddenly "the end goal of the feminist revolution"—at least as Shulamith Firestone had defined it: "not just the elimination of male privilege, *but of the sex distinction itself*"—seemed finally within reach.[2] For, from the mid-1980s on, the psychoanalytic category of sexual difference was deemed suspect and largely forsaken in favor of the *neutered* category of gender. Yes, *neutered*, I will insist on this; for it was specifically the *sex* of *sexual difference* that dropped out when this fundamental psychoanalytic term was replaced by *gender*. Gender theory should thus be viewed as having performed one major feat: it removed sexuality from sexual difference. While gender theorists continued to speak of sexual *practices*, they ceased to inquire into what constituted the sexual; no longer the subject of theoretical inquiry, sex thus reverted to being what it is in common parlance: a secondary characteristic (when applied to the subject) or (when applied to acts) limited to a highly restricted—and naughty—subset. In short, gender theory reduces sex by turning it into a predicate and confining it to a specific domain of life. Some of us, however, rebelled against this feminist rebellion. What follow are some of the reasons why:

1. The turn away from the Freudian theory of sexuality and sexual difference meant that many important questions it posed would also come to seem outdated, evaporated of their urgency. Take, for example, the antiquated criticism of Freud's "pan-sexualism." This charge, that Freud overrated the importance of sex, found it everywhere, the ubiquitous cause of everything, is stunning in its obtuseness. Noting, correctly, that Freud was intent on thinking sex and cause together, his accusers neglected to consider that this reconceptualization of the two in light of each other would leave neither untouched, but would, on the contrary, alter our commonsense notions of both. It never occurred to these detractors that if sex has a way of showing up everywhere, this is because it has no proper domain. Sex cannot be located either in the biological or cultural domain, nor does it have a separate domain of its own; rather, it is manifested exclusively in parasitic, negative phenomena: lapses and interruptions where there occurs a discontinuity or jamming of what is known as the causal chain—that chain which, like a noose, tethers us to something that falls outside it. If this negative definition of sex sounds like a definition of the unconscious, this is because the reality of the unconscious *is* sexual.

2. The flight into the multiple, conceived as discrete instances, had of course several other adverse consequences for the theory of sexuality. If sexual difference became problematic for gender theory this is because the former was presumed to be heterosexist. It divided subjects into two species and implied a necessary and/or natural relation between them. Why—gender theory asks—must there be *only two* sexes, rather than an infinite number of them? I think of this as the Oprah Winfrey distribution of sex: "You get a sex and you get a sex and you get a sex," in which sex is distributed to each and can be owned like a car or some other piece of property. But property, Proudhon taught us, is theft and so we would not be going too far if we accused gender theorists of stealing sex from us by converting it into gender. To say that the subject is sexuated is to say that she is not *enclosed within* herself but intimately *close to* herself. Sex expropriates the subject from herself, desequesters her interiority by linking it to the common, that is to say, to jouissance.

Jouissance? Here is what Lacan says about it in the *Encore* seminar: jouissance is a "negative instance" that opposes itself to division, distribution, or reattribution. The word is derived from an old legal term, "usufruct," which grants one the use of one's means, permits one to enjoy them, but not to acquire legal title to them nor use them up.[3] In order to prevent, then, any further squandering of this common dimension, which we as subjects enjoy, let us look more closely at some of gender theory's basic assumptions.

First question: Is it automatically the case that many are superior to two? Many are *more numerous*, granted, but one balks at this precipitous multiplication, which merely pushes aside questions that need to be asked. Doesn't the proliferation of kinds of subjects (whereby each is her own kind) represent a retreat of thought rather than an advance? An analogy: Freud conceived the drives as fundamentally divided in two, though he was never quite satisfied with the way he defined their duality; his enthusiastic contemporaries, however, pitched in to "improve" on his theory by multiplying the drives such that every action in which a subject might engage was explained by the existence of a separate drive. But it was quickly evident that the question of what caused these actions was not answered by this *ad hoc* proliferation of drives; it was simply deferred. The proliferation of genders repeats the same mistake; it multiplies rather than thinks. Why multiple *rather than* divided; why not multiple *because* divided? The former alternative shirks from thinking difference and simply adds another one to a previous one, indefinitely: 1 + 1 + 1 . . . and so on to infinity. A problem remains: the ones are wholes unto themselves and the pluses are signs that relation has been expelled from them.

Second question: From where do all these individual ones come? I frame this question out of deference to the one that inaugurates an important line of argument in *The Ego and the Id*: "Where are conscious ideas prior to their becoming conscious?"[4] Rather than closing down the question, the answer—in the unconscious—opens a series of definitions of the unconscious and culminates in the unexpected assertion that "not all that is *Ucs.* is repressed."[5] That is, by posing his initial question, Freud is led to a momentous conclusion: there must be something more elementary than external perceptions, and more elementary, too, than the ego that emerges or differentiates itself from that prior instance. Undifferentiated and pre-individual, there must exist a reservoir of libido—of excitation or tension—that is never drained by the differentiations of the ego that start from it. Prior to the ego, this elemental instance cannot be repressed and thus can never "return" or express itself, as repressed unconscious material is wont to do.

My argument is this: Freud here implicitly eschews nominalism and declares himself a realist. Nominalists hold that there is no unity other than numerical unity, that whatever makes a subject this particular subject makes her so per se;

they rigorously deny the existence of universals, which they regard as mere fabrications of mind, and insist that all there is is individual, concrete existence. Freud argues, contrarily, that there is "something" not concrete, differentiated, individual, or actual from which individual existence comes. He names this prior instance "id"—borrowing from Groddeck not only the German term (which is impersonal and general, as in "it rains" or "one assumes") but also the conviction that the "ego behaves essentially *passively*" toward it, implying that the ego is able to undergo infinite modulation as long as it remains open to it/id.[6] It is precisely this "latent," impersonal or common dimension—which, as Freud himself notes, in being neither (actual) being nor nothing, in short, in being without a domain, is intolerable to philosophers—that is missing from gender theory, which is essentially nominalist in its assumptions. To phrase this all a bit differently, gender theory is indissociable from its insistence that gender and other differences simply *are*, they exist, without acknowledging any inexistent (or latent) part. The "latency of sexuality," I want to argue, refers not simply to a temporal lag in the onset of sexuality but, more radically, to its status as nonbeing.

THE ONE

It is impossible not to sympathize, to a point, with the flight into the multiple, with the desire to be rid of every overarching One in which differences would be included and reduced to local and minor variations of a class that unifies them. We are right to resist labels and markers of identity that would freeze us in essentialized forms of being or array us under abstract categories that have no real but only a conceptual existence. The problem is that the rejection of the universal, or the One, *tout court*, deprives us of the ability to think politically, that is, to think change and relation. Lacan therefore declares explicitly what is implicit in Freud, psychoanalysis's advocacy of realism, in plainly political terms. If we choose realism, Lacan states, it is not "in the sense one was a realist in the Middle Ages, that is in the sense of a realism of universals," but because we refuse to "renounce dialectical materialism," which nominalism obliges us to do."[7] Now, if Lacan is able to link realism to dialectical materialism, it can only be through his notion of the real, that is, the radical impasse or cut that rends the symbolic, thus destroying the possibility of its constituting a harmonious whole. The One is divorced from the medieval universal and married to the cut that is its condition.[8] We find the One just there where we meet with an irreconcilability, there where an older notion of the universal definitively falters.

ONCE MORE

One of the events igniting Anglo-American and French feminist interest in psychoanalysis in the 1970s was surely Lacan's *Encore* seminar; and yet the enthusiastic reception of this seminar was mostly a false start. This is because the formulation for which it became famous, "There is no sexual relation," was immediately trivialized, rendered unworthy of the attention it received. Accepted as an effort to expose the fact that sexual relations are inevitably freighted with compromise and disappointment and ultimately doomed to failure, this negative formulation was embraced as an incontrovertible, pessimistic truth and its admission of failure celebrated as sober political wisdom. In truth, this statement never stood any chance of being understood inasmuch as it was taken in isolation from its neglected and much less easily co-optable companion: "There is (something, or a bit, of) One [*Y a d' l'Un*]."[9] This prenumerical One is the same latent, impersonal One we have been attempting to bring into focus.

It is quite clear in Lacan's seminar that this "something of One" does not encompass or constrain the subjects who enter into relation through its mediation; it is not an overarching or transcendent term that guarantees their harmonious union. The negation of the "there is" establishes precisely the impossibility of any such term; it disambiguates the sexual drive from instinct, from the latter's preprogrammed relation to a specific object of satisfaction. Drive means in large part that there is no preordained object toward which sexual subjects strive. Yet this very lack, which makes inevitable a certain disharmony and dissatisfaction, is accompanied in Lacan's seminar by the "something of One" that makes up for or supplements the lack, which is not to say that it removes it. *Suppléance*, a term of eighteenth-century French rhetoric, is a synonym for catachresis, which designates the substitution not of one term for another but a term for a nonexisting one. Lacan radicalizes this idea of pure metaphor, making *suppléance* name the operation that substitutes a little gain (that is to say: jouissance) for an absolute loss. The little gain retains, however, the negative value of the loss. Lacan defines "jouissance," recall, as a "negative instance" not only because it cannot be titled to us but also because it is not something we want.

Before we can return to the question of sexual difference, it is critical that we pursue the red thread of our argument a bit further, that is, the thread that ties Freud's fundamental insights on sexuality and sexual relations to the materialist theory of social relations propounded by Marx. As noted earlier, Freud was accused of talking too much about sexuality, of finding it everywhere. He is responsible, we could say, for discovering the promiscuity of sex, that is, for defining the nature of sex, and not a certain abuse of it, as promiscuous. We should be careful, however, to read this promiscuity not as an indiscriminate mingling but, rather, as a disrupting. That sexuality disrupts, divides, displaces is too often forgotten. Freud had reason to be concerned about the facile acceptance of his theory, which rendered it anodyne by stripping it of its "negative instances." It would be instructive, in this light, to read "On the History of the Psycho-Analytic Movement"—in which Freud, in high dudgeon, ridicules some of the sterilizing adaptations of his concepts—alongside Foucault's *The History of Sexuality*. Set side by side, the latter might appear to be doing some of Freud's work for him by demonstrating how the rapid dispersion of psychoanalysis led to a betrayal and distortion of its concepts—were it not for the fact that Foucault failed to recognize the betrayal. That Victorian society was not reticent about sex, but talked endlessly about it does not mean that sex became suddenly ubiquitous—or, again, promiscuous—in Freud's profound sense. For all the endless discoursing about sex was pressed into the service of making it over into the ideal point of the subject's cohesion, the elusive core of her identity. That this is a distortion of Freud's notion of sex does not dawn on Foucault, who launches into a critique of Freud's "repressive hypothesis" on the grounds that it sets up an invitation to transgressions that eventuate in the propping up of the very law they would transgress and tether us to the endless searching and safeguarding or our individual and group identities. But sex in the Freudian sense is not a matter of prohibition, of law and transgression; it is a matter of impossibility, of radical impasse. A matter of *cannot* rather than *must not*.

"Some obstacle is necessary," Freud wrote, "in order to heighten libido."[10] Foucault would argue that the stated relation between obstacle and libido ends up creating the "perpetual spirals of power," wherein "the pleasure that comes from exercising a power" and "the pleasure that kindles at having to evade this power" circle around and incite each other, rather than (as psychoanalysis assumed) erect impassable boundaries between themselves.[11] Eager to put an end to negative notions of power, Foucault converts the "negative instance" of the obstacle into a kind of lure. Prohibition kindles desire for evasion, and sexual excitement attaches itself to the exercise of power. And yet the "circular incitements" of this relation, the charming harmony of their two-step, can hardly disguise the dreary monotony of the bad infinity they represent. Sex, which Foucault regards as a "mirage," perpetually recedes from grasp, which advantages power by perpetually expanding its territory.[12] Limits are liquidated, there is always one more step to be taken, one more turn of the spiral, but nothing really changes.

To understand sex, we have to take seriously the obstacle that Freud defines as "necessary" for libido's emergence. This implies that sexuality is a phenomenon not of the "one more" but of its exhaustion; it is a phenomenon of the "no more" or: of the limit. It was to hold onto the necessity of this obstacle, to prevent its confusion with the notion of a violable prohibition, that Lacan invented the concept of the real as impossible, through which he not only preserved Freud's theory of sexuality but also its connection to dialectical materialism. Or perhaps it would be better to say (since the simple term "dialectical materialism" can cover a multitude of interpretive errors) that Lacan underlines the way in which Freud's theory of sexuality contributed to an appreciation of the fundamental antagonism, or irreconcilable difference, which sustains sociality. To be brief, the real is the limit both of the subject and the social and the point where they "gear into" each other.

I described above the obstacle to which Freud refers as a "negative instance," not, however, to suggest an equivalency between this obstacle or limit and the "negative instance" of jouissance but to mark the intimacy of their relation. How we arrive at this limit is theoretically obscure. On the one hand, it clearly comes from without; we meet it by accident. On the other, drive renders the subject accident-prone; it pushes us toward the limit of the real, to the point we described as the "no more." What does this mean? Our designation of it as a point of exhaustion, along with Freud's decision to call it "death drive," tempts us to conceive the limit as a terminal point. We have noticed, however, that in *The Ego and the Id*, the limit appears not as the terminal point of death but as an instance of pure priority. The limit is clearly the origin, located, however, not chronologically but within the subject. Now, if we push back all the way to the beginning, to the origin of the causal chain from which the subject emerges, what do we find? Nothing.

Well, more or less. We find no far shore, no outside where might reside a final cause that could operate within us remotely to guide our actions. But what we do find, instead, is a "breaking off of our roots," a splitting or displacement through which we become elusive to ourselves.[13] This breaking off, splitting, displacement *is* the origin of the subject, which lies precisely here in ego's abandonment of its pretense of autonomy in favor of the re-adoption of its relation of radical passivity, of passionate openness to the anonymous instance of id. The encounter with the negative instance of the obstacle, the impossible, presents us with the finality of the absence of a final cause. This swells the tide of jouissance, described by Lacan as a "negative instance" because it emerges as a "heightened" pleasure only at this point of impasse; it is otherwise vigorously shunned. If the paradoxical one that we were hoping to elucidate seems to have been lost in this account, it is because we associate the real and jouissance with the shattering or splitting of the subject's unity. Yet the paradoxical one at issue for us is not the one of this unity shattered by the traumatic encounter but, on the contrary, the one constituted by the shattering. For the shattering does not divide the subject into two distinct parts but into the differentiated ego and an undifferentiated surplus, id, which can be neither subjectivized (that is, assumed by ego) nor objectivized (and thus completely separated from it). If there is "some One," it is that of the *intimate relation* that links the subject indissolubly to its own otherness.

To say that the subject is sexed by definition is to reference this intimate relation as the condition of subjectivity. Fixated, however, on the "repressive hypothesis" of Freud, and thus on the permeable limit between the repressed unconscious and the conscious, Foucault remains oblivious to the Freudian logic of the nonrepressed unconscious and the absolute, impermeable limit that separates id from ego. Because it is the latter limit that is at stake in the Freudian definition of sexuality, the argument of Foucault, based as it is on the former, strikes out at a paper tiger, a "mirage" of his own making.

Lest misunderstandings or questions remain regarding this impassable limit and the one that is constituted by it, I will return to Freud once again in order to track the way he proceeds to disabuse a colleague of his mistaken notion of "oneness." The colleague, and friend, is Romain Rolland, who has written in defense of an "oceanic feeling," a "feeling of an indissoluble bond, of being one with the world as a whole."[14] *Civilization and Its Discontents* begins with Freud's quarrel with this notion. In a first step, Freud disputes Rolland's ascription of this idea to feeling, insisting that it strikes him, rather, as being "of the nature of an *intellectual perception*." The notion of oceanic oneness, Freud asserts, strikes us instead as an *abstraction* inasmuch as it carries, like all abstractions, no conviction. Much as Kant disqualifies respect for the moral law as a "higher (non-pathological) feeling," dismissing it as a mere "analogue" of feeling, so Freud disqualifies "oceanic oneness" from the realm of feeling, even though—he admits—the idea of oneness may be accompanied by some "feeling-tone."[15] Rolland's abstract idea fails to necessitate the existence of anything; it has no reality in the empirical world. Freud in short views "oceanic feeling" as a generality, an abstract universal, and as such rules it out.

This dismissal—which appears to be a straightforward nominalist rejection—does not, however, end the discussion, but leads to the articulation of another option in which the outline of a realist position is visible. After expressing near revulsion at the idea of an "oceanic feeling," Freud reverses course by returning to his own theory to find how his friend's mistaken idea might have arisen. That is, there is something about One that Freud cannot dismiss and it is this he tries next to salvage. He begins by admitting that while we often think of ourselves as "autonomous and unitary, marked off distinctly from everything else," his own theory of the ego shows why complete separation of ourselves from the world is not possible. His argument comes straight from *The Ego and the Id*: the ego is attached or semiattached to the id and it is for this reason, he tells us, that "we cannot fall out of the world." It is the relation of the ego to the id—before it is the relation of the ego to external objects—on which Freud stakes his psychoanalytic claim that no individual can mark herself off distinctly from everything else.

The ego, however, acts as a kind of façade blocking evidence of its relation to the id, which remains for the most part hidden, an "unconscious mental entity." An event is necessary—Freud chooses the event of love to illustrate his point—for the relation to become manifest. A quick reading would lose the point, so let us proceed carefully. While the ego "seems to maintain clear and sharp lines of demarcation" from the outside world, "at the height of being in love the boundary between the ego and the object threatens to melt away." Freud describes an experience of fusion that is not to be trusted, since it goes against "all the evidence of [the] senses." The implication is that Rolland's idea of "oceanic feeling" arises from a similar disregard for the senses. Focused entirely on the relation of the individual (or the ego, in psychoanalytic terms) to outside objects, Rolland blinds himself to the relation between the ego and the id, which relation is ultimately responsible for the way we draw the boundaries between ourselves and the external world. By attending to the ego-id relation, we arrive at a different understanding of what happens in love; no longer an illusory phenomenon of fusion, of a "melting of boundaries," love now becomes visible as a real encounter. Rather than an experience of a "melting of boundaries," love is an encounter with an absolute limit. Ego is brought to its limit because it encounters not some unknown that it can come to know or grasp in a next step but something unknowable, ungraspable. This "swells the tide of libido," or awakens ego to its passive relation to id; that is to say, a splitting occurs in which the subject becomes alien to herself, displaced or expropriated from herself. If we bear in mind that Freud is not merely rejecting the "oceanic feeling" of Rolland's account, but attempting to salvage something from it, some "one" that would be suitable to psychoanalytic thought, then we are able to see that this expropriation is precisely the way in which one is constituted, albeit as paradoxical, as "superior to unity."[16] How could the heterogeneous instances, ego and the id, ever constitute a unity, ever be anything other than separate? In love, this separation is not abolished but altered; it becomes proximity, an affecting nearness by which ego feels amplified: more than one with itself because capable of being other than itself. For, through this intimate relation, ego loses its rigidity and is able to redraw the boundaries between itself and the external world. There where ego experiences its intimate passivity toward id, there it remakes its relation to others.

THE OTHER SEX

Only at this point can we return, finally, to the topic of sexual difference, which is a question that emerges rather late in Freud and not as a matter of the biological/anatomical differences between men and women, but as a difference within the field of sexuality. The theory of sexuality (of the way the subject lives the relation between meaning and jouissance) comes first, has to be thought first, before the question of sexual difference is raised. To not make this clear at the beginning is to increase the chances of missing this further point: the two of sexual difference is not a duality; it is pre-dual. That is, the tension that constitutes sexual difference is not pushed all the way to contradiction.

Let us thus consider another point in his theory where Freud refused to give up entirely on the one, preferring to hold to it firmly, despite the fury with which feminists—not exclusively, but mainly—greeted his refusal. I am thinking of the period in the 1920s when heated debates erupted over Freud's theory of castration, which is in his view the event from which the splitting or sexuation of the subject results. What many in the fledgling field of psychoanalysis—including Ernest Jones, Helene Deutsch, Melanie Klein, and Karen Horney, among others—found unpalatable was the universality of castration, its indifference to the anatomy of the subjects it was supposed to bring into being. If castration aims at the phallus and the little girl has none, so the reasoning went, then the theory does not do her justice and must be modified to take account of her anatomical and biological differences from the boy. Juliet Mitchell summarized these early debates in the following way: "The opposition to Freud saw the concept of the castration complex as derogatory to women. . . . Women, so to speak, had to have something of their own. The issue *subtly* shifts from what distinguishes the sexes to what has each sex got of value that belongs to it alone. In this context, and in absence of the determining role of the castration complex, it is inevitable that there is a return to the very biological explanation from which Freud deliberately took his departure."[17]

The first thing to note is that this early opposition to the Freudian theory of sexuality was aimed specifically at what one could call his monocentric conception of sexuality, his thesis that sex and sexual difference could only be thought on the basis of the one. There is only one libido, Freud insisted time and again, and it is male. Abandoning this counterintuitive thesis like the plague it was, his opponents ended up reducing sexual difference to the prelinguistic, brute difference between the sexual organs of boys and girls, a difference to which psychoanalysis seemed doggedly indifferent. The second thing to note is that the shift from sexual difference to gender that took place in the 1980s resulted in a symmetrical error. The elimination of sexual difference in favor of a study of the social technologies of gender construction left biology behind altogether and produced paper subjects without any verdure, without bodies, or, more precisely, *without sexual organs* (that is, organs in the psychoanalytic rather than the biological sense). Allow me to restate my argument thus far: Freud located sexuality neither in the biological nor in the cultural domain but posed it as a deviation effecting both, that which separated each domain from itself; he did not, however, go so far as to assign sexuality a domain of its own. One can clearly see that in the feminist resistances to Freud, in the 1920s and again in the 1980s, something was lost when sexuality ceased to be linked to the deviation affecting both biology and culture and thus to that supplement that Lacan in his *Encore* seminar baptizes *enjoying substance:* jouissance.[18] What remains when this supplement or surplus is discounted in both cases is a purely abstract contradiction in which one of the terms—either biology or culture—cancels out, takes over, the other. Sexuality gets completely absorbed by one term or another and is effectively lost. Paraphrasing Badiou one could say that Freud would be the first to admit that there is only biology and culture, *except* there is also surplus enjoyment. This is, in fact, the explicit argument of the *Encore* seminar.

This argument paves the way for a response to another feminist complaint: the fact that Freud arrived at the question of feminine sexuality, and thus sexual difference, quite late in his thinking is held against him as if femininity were merely an afterthought, an add-on introduced as exception to the universal notion of the subject he himself constructed. Here's Freud: "Throughout history people have knocked their heads against the riddle of the nature of femininity. . . . Nor will *you* have escaped worrying over this problem—those of you who are men; to those of you who are women this will not apply—you are yourselves the problem."[19] Admittedly, this sounds as if "people throughout history," that is, men, were being placed on one side, and women, the exception, on the other, the outside, but this impression is dissipated by what follows. For, in this late lecture on "Femininity," Freud confronts the question of femininity squarely *without retracting his old position*: nowhere in the essay does he claim there is a libido other than the one he has always insisted upon and nowhere is he prepared to locate anything one might call "femininity." In fact the essay reads like a litany of places where feminine sexuality *cannot* be found. And yet Freud dares to name the essay after that very "thing" to whose absence he is at pains to draw our attention. Examining every possibility—genes, chromosomes, behaviors, and connotations—he fails to turn up any sure indicator of femininity and yet none of these failures is sufficient, it seems, to prevent him from writing about it—precisely as a problem that continues to elude him.

One must not lose sight of the psychoanalytic fact we tried earlier to establish: it is not only feminine but also masculine sexuality that is nowhere locatable; sexuality *as such* lacks a domain. The sexual is not another domain beyond being; it insures, rather, that man is the being whose being fails fully to be, whose being defaults. Why not leave it at that? Why insist on a double default of being? Why go further by positing another sex, one that is, moreover, shrouded in darkness, a dark continent or dark spot that insists only in the troubling of our minds? If sexuality is a phenomenon of the subject's displacement, its failure to coincide with itself, and this swerve is essential to the very definition of the subject, we could say that it is common to all subjects, without exception. Sex is one in that sense, an inescapable dimension of every subject, without exception. But if it were simply, unproblematically one, *a* one or *the* one, one of two problems would arise. Were it *a* One, the possibility of another One would remain open, which would mean that sexuality would no longer be that which is common to all subjects. If it were *the* One, all subjects would be included in it, but this would mean that sexuality no longer split but instead contained or circumscribed the subject. The domain of sexuality must therefore itself be divided, split from itself, or incomplete in its givenness. And femininity must not be on the side of the exception but that which declines the exception; not on the side of the All, but of the not-All. Womanliness cannot be that which escapes or stands outside (male) sexuality, but that which in preventing male sexuality from being fully given maintains it as such. To sum it all up: sexuality has to name not just the impasse of the subject's being, but its own impasse, its own inconsistency as well.

THE RETURN TO TWO

The two of sexual difference needs to be thought precisely in these terms. Not as two separate and opposed ones, not as "that binary partition one . . . spontaneously thinks of [as] 'sexual difference,'" but as "predual," as "more originary than the dyad" to which doxa always seems to reduce sexual difference.

More originary than the dyad is the cut, the split, which is not a split into two "determinities [*Bestimmtheiten*]," or into two determinate ones, nor even an intervention or cut in an originary One.[20] For, in the end the One is, as we have repeatedly said, not so much that which is split, as that which is formed from a splitting. Thus formed, the One is paradoxical, it is from the start a severed One, detached from any unifying One and appearing only between the terms it separates rather encloses.

Derrida's argument in "*Geschlecht*: Sexual Difference, Ontological Difference," from which I have just been selectively quoting, is that Heidegger chose the seemingly *neutral* term *Dasein* for that form of being that places its own being in question, chose *Dasein* rather than man [*Mensch*], not in order to disavow the ontological status of sexual difference but to distinguish it from the commonplace understanding of it as a dyadic structure. This would make Heidegger's position parallel to that of Freud, who adamantly maintained—against feminist protests—the paradoxical oneness of libido. This also draws Heidegger's position close to that of Lacan, who besides conceptualizing woman as not-all, also spoke of feminine sexuality only in the future conditional. It would be misguided, I believe, to take the relation of femininity to futurity as the opening of a horizon on which one day there might appear another sexuality on a par with or superior to masculinity. The futurity of femininity is not merely something that may arrive, but something that in its not-yet-arriving, its futurity, insists, acts now to unground any ground that might be attributed to sexuality as such.

Finally, as long as Heidegger has been entered into the conversation, I will end by noting that Lacan once proffered the term "being-toward-sex," clearly referencing Heidegger's term "being-toward-death," in order presumably to displace the latter. The coinage of the new term goes beyond a simple terminological substitution by seeming to call for a rethinking of the arguments that led up to the original term. Where Heidegger links anxiety to the encounter with death, for example, Lacan insists that we see anxiety as, instead, an encounter with jouissance. As Alenka Zupančič notes, it would be an error to conclude that the naming of sex rather than death as the limit of the subject paints a rosier picture of that limit, given the psychoanalytic associations of sex with death.[21] A reduction of the difference between the philosopher and the psychoanalyst to a matter of their respective levels of pessimism or optimism not only trivializes that difference but expends, once again, with the need for thinking through what is meant by the psychoanalytic claim that being is sexuated. The phrase "being-toward-sex" challenges the proposition that sexual difference is, in fact, an ontological difference. The status of the unconscious, of which the sexual is the reality, is not ontological, but that which calls being into question and causes it to fail. We would rather say that the status of sexual difference is transcendental. Perhaps the most significant agenda behind Lacan's gently mocking phrase is the forging of a new understanding of the common, one that in preserving the asymmetry of the different ways it is approached preserves the common itself, that is, preserves it full stop. As radical impasse. Irreducible antagonism.

NOTES

1. Teresa de Lauretis, *Technologies of Gender: Essays in Theory, Film, and Fiction* (Bloomington: Indiana University Press, 1987), x.

2. Shulamith Firestone, *The Dialectic of Sex* (New York: Bantam, 1972), 10–11.

3. Jacques Lacan, *Encore: The Seminar, Book XX*, ed. Jacques-Alain Miller, trans. Bruce Fink (New York: Norton, 1998), 3.

4. Sigmund Freud, *The Ego and the Id*, in *The Complete Psychological Works of Sigmund Freud*, vol. 19, trans. James Strachey (London: Hogarth Press and the Institute of Psycho-Analysis, 1961), 18; hereafter cited as SE (Standard Edition) with volume and page numbers.

5. Ibid., 19:23.

6. Ibid, 19:14.

7. Lacan, *Le seminaire, livre XVI: D'un autre à l'Autre* (Paris: Seuil, 2006), 28.

8. See Gilles Deleuze, *Difference and Repetition*, trans. Paul Patton (New York: Columbia University Press, 1995), in which Deleuze similarly embraces and distances himself from Duns Scotus's realist position.

9. Lacan, *Encore*, 6.

10. Sigmund Freud, "On the Universal Tendency to Debasement in the Sphere of Love" (SE 11:187).

11. Michel Foucault, *The History of Sexuality*, vol. 1, *An Introduction*, trans. Robert Hurley (New York: Pantheon, 1978), 45.

12. Ibid., 157.

13. Jacques Lacan, *The Other Side of Psychoanalysis: The Seminar, Book XVII*, ed. Jacques-Alain Miller, trans. Russell Grigg (New York: Norton, 2007), 144. Lacan is illuminating here the notion of "unconscious affect" in Freud and thus the argument in *The Ego and the Id* where Freud distinguished the repressed unconscious, to which ideas may be consigned, and the nonrepressed unconscious, where the id dwells.

14. Sigmund Freud, *Civilization and Its Discontents* (SE 21:64–66); all references to this work are from these first three pages.

15. I borrow from Gilles Deleuze's analysis of Kant's *Third Critique*, which seems a propos in ways I cannot begin to detail here. Gilles Deleuze, *Kant's Critical Philos-*

ophy, trans. Hugh Tomlinson and Barbara Habberjam (Minneapolis: University of Minnesota Press, 1984), 46.

16. Christian Jambet coins this perfectly suitable phrase in "The Paradoxical One," trans. Michael Stanish, in *Umbr(a)* (2009): 145, special issue on "Islam and Psychoanalysis"; Jambet's essay does not deal with the Lacanian notion of the "some One," but with an idea in Ismaili philosophy.

17. Juliet Mitchell, "Introduction I," in *Feminine Sexuality: Jacques Lacan and the École Freudienne*, ed. Juliet Mitchell and Jacqueline Rose (New York: Norton, 1982), 20.

18. Lacan, *Encore*, 23.

19. Sigmund Freud, "Femininity," *New Introductory Lectures on Psychoanalysis* (SE 22:1113).

20. Jacques Derrida, "*Geschlecht*: Sexual Difference, Ontological Difference," in *A Derrida Reader,* ed. Peggy Kamuf (New York: Columbia University Press, 1991). All quotations are from 386–87.

21. In *Why Psychoanalysis?: Three Interventions* (Uppsala: NSU Press, 2008), Alenka Zupančič draws our attention to Lacan's single use of the term, dated October 22, 1967.

12

TRANSLATION

Jacques Lezra

Once adopted into the production process of capital, the means of labour passes through different metamorphoses, whose culmination is the machine, or rather, an automatic system . . . set in motion by an automaton, a moving power that moves itself; this automaton consisting of numerous mechanical and intellectual organs, so that the workers themselves are cast merely as its conscious linkages (*die Arbeiter selbst nur als bewußte Glieder desselben bestimmt sind*). . . . In no way does the machine appear as the individual worker's means of labour.

—Karl Marx, *Grundrisse*

Dear Dr. Seitz: In April of 1964 you formed an Automatic Language Processing Advisory Committee at the request of Dr. Leland Haworth, Director of the National Science Foundation, to advise the Department of Defense, the Central Intelligence Agency, and the National Science Foundation on research and development in the general field of mechanical translation of foreign languages. We quickly found that you were correct in stating that there are many strongly held but often conflicting opinions about the promise of machine translation and about what the most fruitful steps are that should be taken now.

—"Language and Machines: Computers in Translation and Linguistics," A Report by the Automatic Language Processing Advisory Committee Division of Behavioral Sciences (ALPAC Report), National Academy of Sciences (1966)

A question that is of considerable interest is the optimum combination of man and machine. It has come to be generally recognized that machine translation with intensive human pre- and post-editing is hardly worthwhile since this method is largely concerned with remedying the defects of the machine. A far more satisfactory concept is that of companionship. An efficient translating machine that can operate whenever required, can continue when its human partner is fatigued, can instruct its partner without the wearisome labor of consulting dictionaries and grammars, and can retire quietly into the background when the human partner desires to exercise his powers unaided qualifies in considerable measure as a good companion.

—R. H. Richens, "Preprogramming for Mechanical Translation"

There are urgent reasons for reworking "translation" as a "political concept." What's tricky is to know what sort of translation one is setting out to rework, in part because treatments of translation—its theories as well as its practices—largely turn on a disabling, if (or because) authoritative, distinction between instrumental and noninstrumental uses of language. Translations may thus be relevant or not; technical or poetical; practical or literary; idealizing or materialist. They may be domesticating or foreignizing; the field of translation may orient itself about translatability or untranslatability.[1] Can we set that archaic distinction aside? What contemporary concepts will step in to organize the complex, discontinuous, antagonistic semantic fields designated by the term "translation"? In what way will these contemporary concepts of translation be political? How is what we call "politics" transformed—translated—when "translation" becomes a political concept (and joins terms we might more readily be willing to call "political": a *people*, a *tongue*, *representation*, *interest*)? In this brief essay I will sketch the outlines of the prevailing, but conceptually trivial, sense of translation we might be tempted to press into service as a political concept. I'll then describe a different sense of translation, with different futures as a political concept, that flows from the rise of so-called machine translation and which may already organize, and if not already may soon come to organize, the semantic field covered by the term "translation." Finally, with the help of different sorts of machines entirely, or different sorts of mechanical entities, I'll hope to show how these two senses of "translation" should be thought in relation to one another, and then reworked into our understanding of the practices of translation we encounter today.

It is no secret that the group of phenomena that we call "globalization" today takes shape around the differential flow of peoples, labor, commodities, and capital among different regions, along axes that line up north to south but also east to west, and which might be charted politically on a slightly different map, in which domains of protectionist legislation, specific labor practices, relations to colonial tradition or access to natural resources are the organizing devices rather than national borders or strictly geographical ones. Translation, the conveying of information between natural languages, is a political concept in this sense: it is at the same time one of the instruments that make possible certain of the flows, and it is itself what one might call a second-order commodity-practice whose value is established in relation to the flow of capital and of first-order, material commodities. I am using the rather special term "commodity-practice" where others would probably use the expression "immaterial labor," so as to decouple, sharply for the sake of brevity, the notion of value from the scheme of "material labor" on which it classically depends.[2] "In no way does the machine appear as the individual worker's means of labor," says Marx in the "Machine fragment" from *Grundrisse*. This is the tendency I would like to stress: in no way does "translation" appear today as a worker's "means of labor."

Something like this articulation of commercial production and translation has of course obtained for a very long time indeed. Translation and mercantilism emerge hand in hand well before the modern concepts of "market," "commodity," and "value" are agreed upon, and well before translation joins its other hands to religious evangelization and to colonial administrative practices. The situation today inflects that longer, geocultural picture with the particularities of labor-export manufacturing, a highly articulated global transportation and communication system, and a system of global credit and finance that makes both possible. If I want to locate my widget-making assembly line in Nicaragua or my iPad factory in China, where labor laws are lax, environmental regulations negligible, and the cost of labor sits at about one-fifteenth of what it might be in the European Union or in the United States, then I'll need to understand Spanish or Mandarin, or hire a translator who does, in order to transact business; the value of the practice of translation is indexed among other things to the worth of that business, and not only to the supply of speakers of Spanish or Mandarin who can serve as translators, or to the supply of laborers who speak only those languages, and who must be convinced in them to work on my assembly lines.

The governing fantasy of this sort of translation is the fantasy of strict or rigid designation, a widget and an iPad being rigidly designated or, minimally, designable in all natural languages. We understand this fantasy of strictness or rigidity in two complementary though quite different senses. I say to my Nicaraguan partner, "Let's make widgets," and for him or her to understand me, my partner must first understand that what I am saying is, in fact, intentional and communicative speech, an expression with some sense to it and not just gibberish. In this bare, stipulative sense, it is necessary that my partner grant that in my phrase there is sense, and that this sense is sufficiently independent of my expression and of the words themselves, that the sense of whatever it is that I'm saying, for instance, "Let's make widgets," is transferable to Spanish. This bare double stipulation—that we are engaging in communicative, intentional expression, and that what is being expressed can be severed from whatever it is that expresses it—is necessarily true if there is to be translation, or so we believe. It is at any rate a condition for my seeking the services of a translator, whom I would not require if no communicative situation of this sort were stipulated or envisioned. (We could put it like this: for there to be translation, we have to agree, in some shared language, that there *are* natural languages, always more than one.)

This version of the widget story has an important kinship to the stories that underwrite *some* theologies of translation, Pauline ones specifically: the severability, the circumcision, of letter from spirit is underwritten by, and in turn comes to underwrite, a tradition severing expression from content that may date to Socrates.

The second way in which we should understand the strict or rigid designation of the term "widget" is related to this theological strain, but derives most closely from Saul Kripke's early work in what comes to be called modal semantics, where some linguistic unit, a name or a demonstrative, is said to be a rigid designator "if in every possible world it designates the same object."[3] In the world of the global factory, we are in the presence of a highly simplified version of "identity across possible worlds"; perhaps, even, we are in the presence of the type or archetype of such identity across possible worlds. This is our ecology: the world of Mandarin or Spanish, the world of English, an object common to both, and two names, one in English, one in Mandarin or in Spanish, designating that object.

But it could even be slightly different. Let's say that there are no widgets in Nicaragua, and that there's no name for a widget in Spanish. My translator will produce the object that I have handed him or her, show it to my partner, and describe its uses. My translator will then say in Spanish something like "In English, this is called a widget, and Jacques proposes that we should make them." "Widget" in the target language now means "the object called 'widget' in English." A description of the object might follow, its uses enumerated, and so on. An ostensive act—showing the object—is linked to an act of naming or, rather, to one explicit act that serves to designate the object, and to an implicit act of ostension, the metalinguistic designation "in English." At this point, and perhaps to my distress, my Nicaraguan partner might possibly strike off on her own and do business with a Portuguese company, also perhaps lacking the word and object called in English a widget and in Spanish "the object called 'widget' in English." She employs a Spanish-Portuguese translator, who will call the object he holds, in Portuguese, "the object called 'the object called widget in English' in Spanish," and perhaps describe in Portuguese its uses, even its color and possible benefits, attending to the different uses that an object of that description might have in Portugal. (Where circumstances of culture, geography, climate, or circumstance might dictate different uses for a widget than might seem appropriate, or even conceivable, in different circumstances, conditions, times, and so on.) The whole eventual global edifice stands on two bases: on the regressive, metropolitan stipulation that in English the object is called a widget; and on the supposed commonality, the zero degree of linguistic expression, in which ostension and designation are linked *before translation* and *as the condition for* translation, in English, in Spanish, in Portuguese, in Mandarin, and on and on. (Explicit ostension, as regards the object I seek to designate; implicit or metalinguistic ostension, as regards my designating the language or the designation-practices in which I make that explicit designation.) In the political economy of "possible worlds"-philosophy what is designated by the notion of "possibility" is the universal of an index for value, and of a naked anteriority in which such indexing may rigidly occur, the "real" time of the designated entity, of the potential commodity before, and as the condition of, its stepping into the market. Here, "possible" means "bearing ostensibly a value that is translatable across possible markets." Whatever the term "widget" may be in Mandarin, and even if there is no term in Spanish or in Portuguese for the object my translator is holding, there is some sense, and beyond that sense some real thing, to which the English "widget" refers, and the Mandarin or Spanish for "widget" refers rigidly to that referential or baptismal moment, as does each subsequent translation.

A visual analogue may help here. Recall the "stone which Euripides calls a magnet" (*ὥσπερ ἐν τῇ λίθῳ ἣν Εὐριπίδης μὲν Μαγνῆτιν ὠνόμασεν*), used by Socrates in Plato's *Ion* (533d) to describe the inspiring power of the Muse. The magnet "not only attracts iron rings but also puts power in the rings so that they also have power to do the same thing the stone does and attract other rings. Sometimes quite a long chain of iron rings hangs suspended from one another; but they're all suspended by the power derived from that stone" (*πᾶσι δὲ τούτοις ἐξ ἐκείνης τῆς λίθου ἡ δύναμις ἀνήρτηται*).[4] But the "real" things designated in the possible worlds scenario, or in the global possible markets scenario, need not be real in the sense of "really existing in the world right now or at one time": we do not mean that what widget designates is real in the way that the magnet that imparts the charge to the chain's rings must be real, or must, to impart the charge, have been materially real, the charge imagined now as the subsisting trace of that initial *touch*.[5] We do not mean that this or that thing must have a value in a market before it can acquire a different one in another market; we mean only that it *might* have a value because the concept of valuation or the mechanism of valuing pertains in this or that thing's home ecology, even if that thing itself isn't immediately understood in that ecology as being the sort of thing that has value. And we mean this because the stipulative phrase "this or that thing" (or something like this phrase), however different the "thing" it designates may be in one or another world, works to designate in all possible worlds. (Designation conventions are, if not identical across all possible worlds, at least sufficiently *analogous* to be translatable across all possible worlds: this is a fact of all possible worlds, even if the conventions of each world differ. Modal semantics stands upon the stipulation that "possible world" designates a possible world in all possible worlds, that is, that the convention of designation is itself *rigid.*)

We say that "the king of France" designates something that is real but does not necessarily exist, or that a "widget" designates something that *could* have a value. Now we mean by "real" a complex of things—we mean that it is not analytically impossible that there be such a thing as a king of France (a king of France is not a round square); we mean that there have been kings in France historically; we mean that we can imagine a world in which there is a king in France, even though there is none in this world, the one we share; we mean that we rely, in making an argument concerning the special reality of widgets, upon a mediating allusion to Bertrand Russell's arguments regarding denoting, which I use here to baptize or magnetize my widgets with a further, philosophically regal surplus value.[6] We also mean that a widget is something that *could* have a value, whether of this sort or of that, in this market or another. When it comes to widgets themselves, there is even some lexical support for this seeming casuistry. Generally, when we use the word "widget," and if we are speaking before 2002 or so, the date when electronic programs called "widgets" entered the lexicon, then we are referring to what the *Oxford English Dictionary* defines as the "indefinite name for a gadget or mechanical contrivance, especially a small manufactured item."[7] *Before* 2002, a widget is a real, but indefinite, place-holding term for any manufactured gadget, but it is not a "really existing" gadget that I can hold in my hand and pass to my Nicaraguan translator. Absent a real thing (though not necessarily a really subsisting thing or a material thing) designated by the English, the Spanish, and the Mandarin, it would be meaningless to speak of translating the term "widget" into Spanish or Mandarin, or indeed to speak of translatability in general. Absent this reality principle, this principle of "identity across possible worlds," or more properly this principle of the sufficient analogy of "identity" and the sufficient analogy of "designation" across all possible worlds, we would be unable to compare the worth of this or that commodity across frontiers—including the second-order commodity-practice of "translation."

I have been speaking so far about directly instrumental translation practices of technical documents, business contracts, restaurant menus, travel schedules, and so on, including the transference or transport of this bit of information, for instance, the information that "Jacques wants to produce widgets," which is accidentally expressed in one or another natural language, English in this case, into a different natural language. Now let us consider those practices—of literary translation principally—in which the supposed worth of the aesthetic dimension of the original language and of the translation is part of the value accruing to each. Here the relation between the bit of information and the "natural language" in which it is expressed or into which it is cast is not imagined to be accidental, though it may not rise to the Aristotelian level of an "essential" or undisseverable relation, in which case translation would simply not be possible. Very little else about my widget scenario changes, however. A communicability agreement seems to be stipulated strictly. In place of a real, though not necessarily existent, object underlying the rigid designation of the term "widget" or the term "translation," I now imagine a real, though not necessarily existent, concept called "aesthetic value," which is rigidly predicable of my expressions, whatever they may be. That bare predicate is then undisseverably, rigidly, characteristically applied to the specific translation of my expression or my poem, from English to whatever other natural language I may envision, whether I am reciting a poem that begins "Let's make widgets," or one that sings, "Love is not love / Which alters when it alteration finds."

We might comfortably imagine the long history of translation, the practices as well as the theory or conceptualization of translation, in terms of these two poles or foci, which are also paradigms for valuing one translation over another, even for deciding what counts or does not count as a translation. We might remark that at different times and under different economic, political, and cultural pressures, the comparative value of the instrumental form of translation on one side, and of the aesthetically inflected sort on the other, will fluctuate in relation to one another and to different criteria. We might believe ourselves to be working on the ground of a three-way analogy or ratio—a natural language is to a term in that language, say, "widget" or "translation," *as* the ecologies in which it is to be valued and marketed are to a real object; the movement from one natural language to another in which "widget" or "translation" is to be expressed is like the movement from one ecology or one market in which a widget or a translation is to be valued, to another. In this imagining and remarking we establish the genealogy of the concept and practices of translation and we globalize the ecology and the market in which these concepts and practices obtain. We reassure ourselves in doing so that, after all, we are, still and always, the expression of the word despite ourselves, the animal or *zoon logon ekhon* who in the course of forgetting its archaic relation to the word becomes the rational or marketing animal.[8] And in this remarking and imagining we remain, always and necessarily, at sea in the modern political economy of possible markets.

In all this remarking and imagining, however, we will be overlooking two related matters. We will be overlooking, in the first place, something that appears in some respects entirely new: the epochal shift introduced in the standing map of practices and theories of translation by the advent, in and following the Cold War, of machine translation.[9] No longer do *workers* translate; the task of the translator is no longer primarily a human, even a humanistic task. The paradigm of Babel, turning in the ellipse formed by the two foci of instrumental and aesthetic translation, underwriting but also expressing a distinction between technical and intellectual labor, a conception of the human as *homo laborans* or *homo faber*, has given way to what one might reasonably call the Babel Fish paradigm. Or the Babel Fish epoch, the age of a double displacement: on one hand, the displacement of what might allow *Logos*, the flashing-forth and gathering-in of Being as unconcealment, Heidegger would say, to flash forth in otherwise technical expressions like "natural language," "linguistic difference," "information," or "semantic distinction or drift."[10] But on the other hand—and this is what would make the story something other than the account of the advent of a technological world-picture—is the simultaneous displacement of the characteristically inessential, mystified dimension of linguistic expression that, in Heidegger's telling, steps in where *Logos* is forgotten. The Babel Fish epoch marks the displacement *both* of whatever in language attends to what Heidegger calls "the being that was originally opened up in gathering," *and* of whatever in language becomes "mere hearsay"; becomes the work of *glossa*; becomes the mechanical organ of the tongue; of whatever in language represents the "loosening" of "truth"; that is, the displacement also of language becomes the expression of a machine, "the act of speaking, the activation of the organs of speech, mouth, lips, tongue."[11] The Babel Fish epoch takes from us our tongues, the act of speaking, expression inasmuch as it pertains to the articulating machine we call our body; indeed, but it *also* takes from us whatever relations to more authentic, primary, archaic terms the long history of metaphysics has sought to employ to designate what is not merely expressible, and yet makes the human animal properly and distinctively human.

The Babel Fish epoch: a different keying of value to time and to labor than obtained before the advent of machine translation—a different indexing of labor to human action, intention, body,[12] and, as a result, a different concept of the human altogether. Witness, for instance, the fate of the metaphor that governs the conceptualization of machine translation in 1956—the cozy figure of the collaboration between the human translator and his machine aide: "An efficient translating machine [is] a good companion," writes R. H. Richens. But when Franz Joseph Och, the lead developer of Google Translator, was asked in 2010 by the *Los Angeles Times* about the "training of the translator," it was not companionship between human and machine translators that was envisioned. Instead, it was the combination of statistical-machine-translating algorithm, database, and search engine that the word "translator" referred to, and the three forms of labor the question rather foggily envisioned—the "training of the translator," the "searching," and the "translating"—were to be understood as instances of the same process, a process camped out in anachronistic metaphors as the most primitive form of extractive manual labor, mining, carried out by entirely nonhuman means. This is Och, in answer to the question "When you train the translator, you've got to get so-called parallel data sets, where every document occurs in at least two languages. Where do you get all of those translations from?" Och says, "When we started, there were standard test sets provided by the Linguistic Data Consortium, which provides data for research and academic institutes. Then there are places like the United Nations, which have all their documents translated into the six official languages of the United Nations. And there's a vast pool of documents available there in the database, which has been very useful because the translation quality has been very good. But then otherwise, it's kind of 'the Web.'. . . Our algorithms basically mine everything that's out there."

To this the interviewer remarks, "So it's sort of analogous to the way Google's Web crawler spiders Web pages?" And Och answers, "It's similar. While the Web crawler is mining the whole Web and indexing it, then for the translation crawler is the subset of documents that include translations [*sic*]. The challenge is to find which texts are translated into another language—and where to find the corresponding translation."[13]

Note the outrageously anachronistic use of the term "mining"; the wonderful and symptomatic verbalization of the noun "spider." Remark the awkward anacoluthon in Och's answer. We are watching the interview's language strain to express a state of affairs for which there is not yet a lexicon or a syntax. Something, and it is neither *Logos* nor *glossa,* flashes. We are, it appears, in the event.

Of course, when we tell the story in *this* way we are surrendering to a different sort of temptation. We imagine that an event has occurred or is occurring, and we stand in its shadow or at its advent, we moderns, like bold Cortez upon a peak, or Zarathustra at the opening to his cave, or like Captain Kirk on the deck of the *Starship Enterprise.* Nothing about this new, adventitious time is or will be translatable into its forerunner; our world has changed; the linguistic function of "referring" differs, and what we refer to does as well, semantically and syntactically—a spider now "spiders," an algorithm mines, and the search for "a corresponding translation" to a string of words is carried out neither instrumentally nor aesthetically, but mechanically. When we say "language," or "translation," different things, unimaginably different things, are designated rather than when the same words were used *before* Alan Turing, and *before* the Cold War.

The temptation, then, is twofold. In the first place, we are tempted to imagine the advent of machine translation in the breathless light of the messianic—or its proxies, the robotic, the inhuman. "The Android version of Google Translate allows the user to speak to the application, and have his or her words translated," says the *Los Angeles Times* interviewer. "Is it," he continues, "just one short step from here to real time, speech-to-speech translation, a la 'Star Trek's' universal translator?" And Och answers, "To really do the integrated speech-to-speech translation, where you can have a phone call with someone and it would [be] interpreted live? I believe that based on the technology that we have, and the improvement rate we have in the core quality of M[achine] T[ranslation] and speech recognition, that it should be possible to do that in the not-too-distant future."[14] The garishness of this science-fiction scenario tends to obscure the second, related mistake, which is to imagine that the advent of machine translation does indeed mark an epochal break with the Babelian paradigm, whose humanist heroics and elliptical circuit, defined by and mapping the fluctuation of value invested in the foci of technical and aesthetic labor, would seem untranslatable into the emerging lexicon and syntax of machine translation. Each, we like to think, is cut from the other by a historical caesura every bit as sharp, as unbridgeable and untranslatable, as any we might find in the christological imaginary.

But is this indeed so? Might there be other ways of rethinking translation, the concept, the history and the present state of translation?

Which brings me to the second thing we will have overlooked in all this imagining and remarking. Let us say that machine translation has always and already inhabited the Babelian paradigm. You can imagine already the consequences this might have for the various maps in which we've settled what we call "translation"—the map of the market, of evangelization, of the long-cherished definitions of the human animal as *homo faber*, or as the animal that produces art. You can imagine what it might mean for the long linking of value to material production to claim that an inhuman commodity-practice has always and already spidered away in the texture of what seems to be most proper to human animals, to *zoon logon ekhon*. We can imagine these consequences of claiming that machine translation has always spidered away at natural languages, at an angle to the twin foci of instrument and aesthetic enjoyment that I've graphed—we can imagine the consequences of the claim, but what would it mean to claim such a thing? Not, of course, offering some sort of time-traveling marriage of Google with Heraclitus, the mere reverse of the science-fiction scenario I have been evoking, peopled with Androids and *Star Trek* translating devices. What we mean by a "machine" will have to change; what we mean by "translation" too; "history" as well—not to the point where the *modern* "machine" cannot serve us as a translation of the older one, but also in a way that does not stand or fall upon the fantasies of designation, of possible-world economies, that I have been outlining. To claim that machine translation has always and already inhabited, worked, or spidered away at natural languages would mean claiming that the difficulties the concept of translation entails work, silently or clamorously, or occur, not just across societies and at different historical moments, but structurally in natural languages and in the space of single, determining descriptions of the processes of translation.

To say that difficulties of this sort occur structurally in natural languages, and that they crop up across historical moments and locations, would not *seem* terribly different from the rigid fantasies of designation and of value-indexing attached to the "possible worlds" of the global market and of the commodity-practice of translation. But it is. Let us say that in place of widgets, in place of the commodity I hope to produce with my Nicaraguan partner, my translator and I are discussing the related commodity that my translator is hoping to produce for my consumption, the second-order commodity or commodity-practice that is his or her translation. We are not talking about an object either of us can hold or produce as one would a widget (presuming for the moment that a "widget" is a really subsisting, material object): what we are discussing, roughly speaking, is the object we call "a natural language," or two such languages, and the relation between them. We are discussing the uses to which that relation is to be put, the costs associated with moving between them, the value of the product my translator delivers, and so on. The Mandarin or Spanish translator and I will have to agree that we are engaging in some sort of intentional, communicative expression, and we will have to have a minimally similar understanding of what it means to "translate" when I set about hiring him or her. Here, where the object under discussion is not a widget but the means of designating a widget in two different languages, that is, where the object designated is what we call "translation," the threat of a poisonous regress is unavoidable. This poisonous regress distinguishes this level of discussion concerning this sort of object-which-is-not-an-object, called a "natural language," from the discussion my translator and I might have regarding a widget, however the reality of such an object is to be imagined. And note: poisonous though it may be, this threat of regress is also, crucially, the source of unassimilable values and designation-effects, values and effects immeasurable according to the ecologies of *either* language and of *either* market, original or target. When we say that some word or expression in Mandarin or in Spanish is a translation of the English "widget," and that this holds true in all possible worlds because of the logical requirement imposed by the notion that we are indeed "translating" between languages, then we seem to be required to stipulate that designation conventions are, if not identical, then sufficiently similar among natural languages that "widget" may be said to designate in much the same way in the original language as in the target—independently of what, in fact, is designated by "widget" and its translation in Spanish or Mandarin. What obtains for the concept of designation convention is also true for the concept of translation, and in general for metalinguistic terms that natural languages use to designate themselves, and which may indeed be said not just to designate, but to translate the natural language into the condition of being a discursive *object* (composed of statements, a lexicon, conventions of usage, syntax, and so on) named or designated by a metadiscursive statement, or a name, *in that same natural language*.

As you might suppose, what's happening here—whatever process I am designating when I describe this objectification of a language from within that language, this metaphorization of the language by means of itself—this process is neither simply instrumental nor aesthetic. As to its strictness or rigidity across possible worlds, you will get a sense of how tricky the situation can become when you note that metalinguistic terms are not always and exclusively metalinguistic in a given context (metalinguistic statements, like performative utterances, are always, an early Derrida might put it, parasitized by context); when you note that certain "object" terms can and often are used tropically with a metalinguistic function; and that the rules for deciding when a term is being used in one way or another are themselves conventional, partial, changing, and contentious, when not contradictory, and when they are not also the consequence of such metalinguistic uses.

Let us call the widget that produces intralinguistic translation- and designation-effects of this sort "machine translation," the spider in the linguistic cup *before* Turing and *before* the Cold War. This widget produces the flickering, undecidable movement between statements' (or names' or terms' or metaphors') linguistic and metalinguistic status. It works between statements and what they designate; it spiders away to tip a particular thing designated into the ensemble of designation conventions, lexicon, and syntax that makes up the natural language within which that designation takes a place. It is internal to the metalinguistic statement or term, its designation, and the object it designates. What does this sort of machine translation look like?

I will give you an example taken from the canon of phrases regarding translation, repeated mechanically since Quince, one of the "rude mechanicals" of *A Midsummer Night's Dream,* first uttered it some four centuries ago, in an infamously haunted forest, treading heavily among fairies, monarchs, and translated lovers. We are the audience at Shakespeare's most subjunctive play, his most extravagant exploration of the fantasy of possible worlds, the most radical staging of philosophical modality in the theatrical canon. (Prose is another matter.) Shakespeare peppers his text with the most severe marker of unconditionality, the word "never"—used in the play over thirty times, more often than in any other comedy (with the exception, oddly, of *Much Ado about Nothing*). "Never"—yes, but set against the most basic and pervasive form of counterfactual wondering. What if the woodland held a fairy court? Is a world possible in which a weaver can become an ass and stay a Bottom; where domestic dilemmas of Athenian politics are solved extramurally by sprites, mechanicals, actors; where senses become disjoined and garbled, voices can be seen, and faces heard ("I see a voice: now will I to the chink, / To spy an I can hear my Thisby's face," says Bottom's Pyramus (5.1.192–93))? The theater, of course, is always structurally counterfactual, a staging of modality—but this is Shakespeare's most alarming, seductive, and rigorous enacting or *translating* of that staging.

And so, when Quince says to Bottom's Pyramus in *A Midsummer Night's Dream*, "Bless thee, Bottom! bless thee! thou art translated" (3.1.119), the poor ass-headed weaver, Nick Bottom, hears, we presume, that he is "transformed" as well as "translated," even though he does not realize just how translated, or in what ways transformed, he is (and this perhaps should be a sign to his audience that Bottom is, at bottom, already and always an ass, although and because he is unable to recognize himself as one).[15] This, after all, is the double sense Shakespeare's audience has learned to expect in *Midsummer Night's Dream,* Helena having told Hermia, "Were the world mine, Demetrius being bated, / The rest I'd give to be to you translated" (1.1.190–91). Quince's famous line follows, as if glossing or translating it, Snout's much less famous exclamation, to the same effect: "O Bottom, thou art changed! what do I see on thee?" (3.1.114–15). Shakespeare's audience might well have heard the same synonymy of "change" or "transformation" in "translation," though they, unlike Bottom, would have also heard the linguistic "translation" of "change" into "translation" and of "Bottom" into "ass," and they might well have registered the additional metalinguistic value of Quince's word "translated," which also designates and describes what has happened between the partially synonymous expressions "O Bottom, thou art changed!" and "Bless thee, Bottom! bless thee! thou art translated," as it also designates and describes what has happened between the terms "Bottom" and "ass." (Analogues? Translations of each other?) For a contemporary public, a public at the Public Theater in New York in 2012, for example, the archaic sense of "translated" as "changed or metamorphosed" would be largely lost, as would the old sense of a "Bottom" as a "skein" or ball of thread, or a nucleus on which thread or cord could be wound, in order to produce the warp of a fabric. Today's public would render "translation" "conformable to *our* manners," as Cicero might say, "*verbis ad nostram consuetudinem aptis,*" and hear, minimally, the flicker of an interlinguistic pun opening from the scabrous play on ass-bottom onto the wonderful resonances between the transformed Bottom's human speech and a donkey's braying.[16]

To us today, as to Shakespeare's audience but *not* to Bottom himself, or not *yet* to Bottom himself, or not in a way that the play registers *as* the character's "knowing" this, to us and to Shakespeare's audience Bottom's words from this point forward sound in both registers, in English and in Ass, though of course without our being in any way able to say what, precisely, Bottom's words or near neighs designate *in* Ass. (Rather, to the extent that we understand Bottom's words we find that we may be able to understand, not just English alone but Ass as well—with the consequent, rather demoralizing realization about our own intelligence.) As for what it is that Titania hears when she's roused from sleep by the sounds of Bottom's singing, before she sees him even, plucked from her midsummer night's dreams by an "angel" who "wakes [her] from [her] flowery bed"—this remains forever foreclosed to us. We, and Shakespeare's Elizabethan audience, hear the mechanical sing, and some of us hear also the extraordinary metalinguistic surplus-value that "translation" adds to "change," and Ass to Bottom—but who among us is "[moved] perforce / On the first view," or on first hearing the weaver, "to say, to swear, I love thee" (3.1.137–41) to an ass? His ass head having scared away the other "mechanicals," Bottom sings to scare away his fright just after his translation, "The finch, the sparrow and the lark, / The plain-song cuckoo grey, / Whose note full many a man doth mark, / And dares not answer nay" (3.1.130–33).

We hear Bottom's "nay" not once but twice, here and in answer to Titania's professions of love: "Nay, I can gleek upon occasion" (3.1.146–47). But what do we hear? Onomatopoeically, some sort of utterance in Ass, of course—a "neigh," what man "dare not answer," an expression of a man's asininity, what one might call an example or a *use* of the language Ass. (A man "dare not" "neigh," because he understands a "neigh," whatever it may designate in Ass, to be uttered *in Ass,* and to designate collectively the natural language I am calling, rudely and mechanically, Ass. To answer "nay" is to "neigh," or to be an ass: the "neigh-ness" of "neigh" removes "nay" from the language human animals can use without losing their humanity, in whole or—like Bottom—in part.) But "nay" also lines up, syntactically, in the parallel shape the little ditty takes, with the "plain-song" of the cuckoo, an adjectivized noun phrase first characterizing the cuckoo (the bird that sings in plain-song) and then becoming, tremblingly, the antecedent, with that cuckoo itself, of the cuckoo's "note." A man's nay is not just *what* he dare not answer: for example, I'd like to say nay, or no, to the note that the cuckoo-cuckold calls to me, but I dare not answer nay to that call because in my heart I believe or fear myself to be a cuckold, to be a cuckoo, that is, I fear myself to be the bird that calls its own name and calls me by that name, a name that names *and* describes me. A man's nay is not just *what* he dare not answer, it is the name of the language in which he *dare not* answer: *either* the "plain-song . . . note" of cuckoo, which makes him out, as the utterer of notes in the language onomatopoeically named "cuckoo," to be a cuckold himself; *or* the plain-song note of "neigh" or "nay," which designates him an ass for denying, *in Ass,* that he is, indeed, a donkey and cuckold to boot. It's hardly a coincidence that Titania refers to Bottom's speech in the same way Bottom does to the cuckoo's "note": "I pray thee, gentle mortal, sing again, / Mine ear is much enamored of thy note" (3.1.137–41).

Here much of Shakespeare's humor stands upon the uncontrollable translation between discursive *use* and metadiscursive *mention*, between languages—the English language of weavers and other mechanicals, the languages of asses and cuckoos, of fairies and spirits like Puck—and metalinguistic terms designating languages, English, Ass, Cuckoo, "neigh," note, plainsong, or language uses. Extraordinarily *threatening* humor, however, and not just for the poor man, unmanned at finding himself unable to say nay to being cuckolded—unable to say nay for fear of losing his tongue and speaking "neigh" in ass, and thus, silent, assenting to the plainsong of the cuckoo, which not only calls to but also *names him:* "Cuckoo," cuckold, it calls to him. If Nick Bottom's man answers yes, he has agreed to the cuckoo's designation and to the bird's description of himself, and the man thus answers *in Cuckoo,* with his name. ("Cuckoo!" says the bird. "Yes?," answers Bottom, or any other man—"Yes, that's me, I am Cuckoo, a cuckoo, inasmuch as I understand your call, in the language that calls me and to me that and calls itself 'Cuckoo,' inasmuch as I understand that your call designates me. And it is in that language that I answer you, cuckoo to cuckoo or Cuckoo to cuckoo, my 'Yes?' in English serving to confirm that yes, I am (a) Cuckoo, that my English is also the natural language called Cuckoo, spoken by cuckolds and cuckoo birds alike.) If he answers "nay," he answers in ass, and reveals that he is an ass for not knowing that he is, at heart, a cuckold, who should have answered, also or instead, in cuckoo. Bottom must, perforce, keep silent—and what sort of theater is it that enjoins silence upon its characters, that calls upon them to "love, and be silent," for example, as Cordelia calls upon herself to do? (*Lear* 1.1.62). The designation of a language *as* a language, that rigid condition on which translation among possible worlds stands or falls, frays: is "neigh" a word in ass or in English? (Is a "word" in ass even a word? Is it not, rather, a neigh?) Is "neigh" a word in *both*, as Bottom seems to be both human and ass? Does "cuckoo" designate the language, the bird-speaker, the husband, the ass-man? Among the first things to fail: the identity of the designation "natural language," parasitized by the language of birds, donkeys, to say nothing of fairies.

So threatening, so possibly *tragic*, is this little comic scene, that even the most loving, the most charmed audience, Titania herself, cannot bear to listen to Bottom's speech, to his frenetic riffing on the senses of her retinue's proper names, Cobweb, Peaseblossom, and Mustardseed, names suddenly translated into ass, as it were, by Bottom, demoted from proper names to descriptions of different mechanical or natural functions much as the name "cuckoo" passes from the bird that utters the plainsong note in Cuckoo, to designate the object it calls to and who marks himself in it. *So* disturbing is what the queen of the fairies hears in her beloved Bottom's voice, a voice she praised absurdly not a hundred lines above, a voice whose angelic notes she wished to hear again and again; *so* shaken is fair Titania that (whether out of fear some like fate will befall her own name or perhaps out of fear or awareness that her "love" for Bottom will indeed produce at least one more "cuckoo": Oberon himself, cuckolded by the ass-headed weaver) the fairy queen orders Cobweb, Peaseblossom, and Mustardseed to "Tie up my lover's tongue, bring him silently" (3.1.201). Titania, deprived of the sweet neighs of her lover's voice, thus confirms for herself, in compensation, that it is she who gets to determine what functions her servants have, and not their names, and not the translating voice of a mere mechanical ass—and that she will be able to cuckold Oberon with an ass without having the fairy king's shame designated and neighed about openly, in Cuckoo, in Ass or in English.

So disturbing is this mad scene that the crowned king of Shakespeare's translators, August Wilhelm Schlegel, that fairy king on whom the plays, and this one in particular, exercised a charm with far-reaching consequences in European modernity, finds it impossible to translate Bottom's translation literally. About the transformation scene, Schlegel writes, in the *Lectures on Dramatic Art*, that "the extremes of fanciful and vulgar are united when the enchanted Titania awakes and falls in love with a coarse mechanic with an ass's head, who represents, or rather disfigures, the part of a tragical lover. The droll wonder of Bottom's transformation is merely the translation of a metaphor in its literal sense" ["Das scherzhafte Wunder der Verwandlung Bottoms ist eigentlich nur die Uebersetzung einer Metapher in ihren buchstäblichen Sinn"].[17] The translation of a metaphor. This is promisingly abyssal, easily reversed into the metaphor of a translation, a translation of a translation and a metaphor of and for a metaphor, and these nice reversals immediately throw into question the notion that the ass-head's "literal sense," *buchstäblichen Sinn,* can be determined rigidly. In Schlegel's words, we appear to be, in other words, very much in Shakespeare's threatening lexicon and wood, where the antic widget of intralinguistic translation between discursive and metadiscursive statements threatens to lead to silence, or to tragedy. But when Schlegel *translates* the scene, he tends to silence this strange and threatening aspect of Shakespeare's text. Snout's "Changed" is rendered, unexceptionably, *verwandelt* ("O Zettel! du bist verwandelt!"), but the not-quite-synonymous, because immediately and dangerously metalinguistic, "translated" with which Quince translates "changed" is translated not through *übersetzung*, as the *Lectures on Dramatic Art* would seem to urge, but through the slightly different *transferiert:*

> Zettel. Warum laufen sie weg? Dies ist eine Schelmerei von ihnen, um mich fürchten zu machen.
> (Schnauz kommt zurück.)
> Schnauz. O Zettel! du bist verwandelt! Was seh ich an dir?
> Zettel. Was du siehst? Du siehst deinen eigenen Eselskopf. Nicht?
> (Schnauz ab. Squenz kommt zurück.)
> Squenz. Gott behüte dich, Zettel! Gott behüte dich! du bist transferiert.
> (Ab.)
> Zettel. Ich merke ihre Schelmerei: sie wollen einen Esel aus mir machen

Transferieren does mean, Grimm tells us, "*verteutschen*," an archaic form of *verdeutschen*, "*in ein andere sprache setzen*," and it's used, for instance by Luther, to designate "translation."[18] But Grimm tells us that such metaphoric—translated—meanings are distinctly secondary to *ein ding von ein ort zum andern tragen,* in the literal sense, "to carry a thing over from one place to another."

And as if to confirm that this translation, willy-nilly, ties up Bottom's tongue, ass and Bottom become *Esel* and *Zettel*. Each of these transformations is amusing in its way, the ass-*Esel* perhaps echoing in Titania's word about the music that she hears, the word "angel," *Engel;* and *Zettel,* which Schlegel gets from Wieland's earlier translation, losing much of its physicality, its association with stupidity and doltishness, its synonymy with *Esel,* but gaining a peculiar compensatory metatheatricality, a *Zettel* being, not just a piece of paper or a chit, but also a playbook or a script. The metalinguistic function of our weaver's "nay," opened by the linguistic sense of the word "translation" in English, is absent from the German—Bottom's little cuckoo song now goes: "Der Kuckuck, der der Grasmück / So gern ins Nestchen heckt / Und lacht darob mit arger Tück / Und manchen Ehmann neckt." The German for "neighing" is *wiehern*—so although "necken" may *sound* like neighing to speakers of English and to Schlegel's readers and audience, the word's function of naming its onomatopoeic function is lost, as is, of course, the play on negation and expression we saw in the English "nay."

All of this goes far to paint Schlegel as a latter-day Titania, a translator who ties the tongue of Shakespeare's play and seeks to keep at bay the English play's riotous transformation of statements, syntax, lexicon, and names into functional elements taking as their designation and object the ensemble of statements, syntax, lexicon, and names from which they derive—and back. Schlegel appears to silence Bottom-Zettel as Titania does, Bottom's tongue chained to the chit of paper or to the playbook, speech become writing, the play become a playbook, the translation machine become a sort of transcription machine. But this is not quite right, or not sufficient to this strange translation scene, where instrument and aesthetic enjoyment meet Shakespeare's rude mechanicals. Schlegel, and before him Wieland, captures marvelously something that is almost silent in Shakespeare's text, but which the German gives us loudly: it gives us the connection of "change" and "translation" to the practical and repetitive crafts of the mechanicals—precisely under the aspect of the machine. For a *Zettel* or *Zettelmaschine* is also the name of the weaver's and the carpet-maker's so-called "warping machine," the cylinder or framework on which the thread or the cord is turned so as to make it into the warp for the woof to cross, themselves the support and structure of the textile.[19] This translation of Bottom's mechanical "bottom" into a full-fledged machine, we might say, is the widget of machine translation that Schlegel's version of *A Midsummer Night's Dream* discloses for us—and discloses precisely where the translation fails to translate Shakespeare's own translation machine. This *disclosing* of the translation machine, however, is not to be conceived as the appearing of a historical invariant, a general equivalent, or a universal index of value that would apply across markets, like the word of archaic being in language, *Logos* in its lying-before-to-be-collected, *Logos* flashing forth in *glossa*. In Shakespeare a translation machine moves the hand of the weaver, the eye and ear of the fairy queen, and the ear and the eye of the audience, bottom to Bottom, "nay" to "neigh," cuckoo to Cuckoo, word to the eye machine and to the ear machine. There, as in the early industrial lexicon, the translation machine translates the material supports of linguistic expression, warp to the woof of expression—but always conditioned by the surplus enjoyment, and the conceptual risk, posed by its being produced or scrambled: "I see a voice: now will I to the chink, / To spy an I can hear my Thisby's face." It is a different matter in our days than it is in Cicero's, in Heidegger's, or today, where I have been giving it the strange and indeterminate name of a "widget."

To return in conclusion to my charge, to thinking translation as a political concept in the age of credit capital and machine translation. To tell the history of the differences I've been charting—the history of the literalizations of the translating machine and of machine translation—is to tell the history of postwar, postcolonial capitalism over again in a peculiar, even queer way. This history allows us to give a longer arc than has previously been possible to the seemingly postmodern phenomenon of the dematerialization of labor; this history allows us to rethink and distress, transversally, on a bias, the informing foci of the labor-value ellipse, instrument, and aesthetic enjoyment; it allows us to account for labor time differently, by bringing into our accounting the inhuman spidering work of translating machines at different times; it allows us to think differently the nature of laboring machines. But most important, reworking the nature of political thought and association through the concept of translation conceived in this way allows us to disengage the language of the "possible"—in the modal, philosophical sense and in the revolutionary sense—from the silencing binds in which the postcolonial export-labor imaginary has tied it, as Titania's laborers once bound Bottom's tongue.

NOTES

1. For a review of recent theories of translation in a historical context, see Susan Bassnett-McGuire, *Translation Studies* (New York: Routledge, 2002). The most forceful articulation of the "domesticating-foreignizing" distinction is to be found in Lawrence Venuti's *The Translator's Invisibility: A History of Translation* (London: Routledge, 1995). Lydia He Liu's edited volume *Tokens of Exchange: The Problem*

of Translation in Global Circulations (Durham, N.C.: Duke University Press, 2000), along with Emily Apter's *The Translation Zone: A New Comparative Literature* (Princeton, N.J.: Princeton University Press, 2005), provide the most comprehensive contemporary approaches to the relation between globalization and translation—from a conceptual rather than a practical perspective. See particularly Liu's "The Question of Meaning-Value in the Political Economy of the Sign," 13–41, for a very clear reconsideration of the rather muddy analogy between meaning and value to be found in weak readings of Baudrillard's early works. My own earlier work on the philosophy of translation seems to me to settle too quickly on a polar or focal structure I would now like to distress—the distinction between "idealist" and "materialist" philosophies of translation. See Jacques Lezra, "The Indecisive Muse: Ethics in Translation and the Idea of History," *Comparative Literature* 60, no. 4 (2008): 301–30.

2. On the structuring of the "pure expenditure of time and money" in post-Fordist economies, see Maurizio Lazzarato, *Lavoro immateriale: Forme di vita e produzione di soggettivita* (Verona: Ombre Corte, 1997), and *Videofilosofia: Percezione e lavoro nel postfordismo* (Rome: Manifestolibri, 1996).

3. Saul Kripke, *Naming and Necessity* (Cambridge, Mass.: Harvard University Press, 1980), 48. The literature regarding possible worlds, including possible worlds semantics, modal semantics, and so-called Kripke semantics, is vast. A milestone, and among the most controversial works in the field, remains David Lewis's *On the Plurality of Worlds* (Oxford: Blackwell, 1986). I take Lewis's necessarily guarded allowance for the operation, "perhaps," of "immanent universals exercising their characteristic privilege of repeated occurrence" (2) to be a way of securing the principle of translatability across possible worlds that I describe here. The literature on possible world semantics includes important contributions not only from the perspective of the philosophy of language, but also from psychoanalysts and political philosophers (see Slavoj Žižek, *The Sublime Object of Ideology* [London: Verso, 1989]; Judith Butler, *Bodies that Matter* [New York: Routledge, 1993], 187–223; Ernesto Laclau, *On Populist Reason* [London: Verso, 2005], 101–17); and critical theologians (Hent de Vries, *Philosophy and the Turn to Religion* [Baltimore: Johns Hopkins University Press, 1999], 147–58). Only two aspects of the argument need concern us here: the bare indexicality of the scenario (the eventual, and necessary, *description* to another, my translator and then my partner, of the widget's uses, qualities, value, and so on, stands on an act of ostension understood as such); and the universalizability of this primary act of ostension (it is the ground on which the possibility of translation stands). In the meta-world of possible worlds, a world is only a world when acts of ostension secure the designation of things in that world, whether they are subsisting or nonsubsisting things.

4. Plato, *Ion* 533d, in *The Dialogues of Plato*, vol. 3, *Ion; Hippias minor; Laches; Protagoras*, trans. Reginald E. Allen (New Haven, Conn.: Yale University Press, 1996), 13. The Greek is from the online edition provided by Project Perseus, accessed

March 9, 2012, http://www.perseus.tufts.edu/hopper/text?doc=plat.+ion+530a. See Adriana Cavarero, *For More than One Voice: Toward a Philosophy of Vocal Expression* (Stanford, Calif.: Stanford University Press, 2005), 85–89, who reads Socrates's story as an allegory of the loss of particular voice from *Logos*.

5. The values of the term "real" in this sort of claim, as in Lewis's early arguments for "modal realism," are rather hard to parse. Securing the ontological priority of objects is not the same, exactly, as granting them the quality of "reality." Here—though not at all elsewhere—I am in agreement with the work of Graham Harman—for instance, his *Tool-Being: Heidegger and the Metaphysics of Objects* (Peru, Ill.: Open Court, 2002).

6. I am drawing my example of the "present king of France" from Russell's "On Denoting," where it is used to show that phrases denote formally rather than according to the existence or nonexistence of what it is they are supposed to denote. Bertrand Russell, "On Denoting," *Mind*, n.s. 14, no. 56 (October 1905): 479–93.

7. *OED*, "widget," n., 2nd ed., 1989; online version December 2011, accessed March 13, 2012, http://www.oed.com/view/Entry/228908; first published in *A Supplement to the OED IV*, 1986. The updated (after 2003) entry adds: "(a) A visual component of a graphical user interface (and the code associated with it), which allows a user to perform a particular function (e.g., a scroll bar, dialogue box, menu, etc.). (b) A small software application."

8. Heidegger not infrequently cites Aristotle's definition or description, in Greek, of man as *zoon logon ekhon,* in order *then* to translate that into Latin as *animale rationale,* and to argue that this translation from *Logos* to *ratio* is the mark of a characteristic and definitive metaphysical forgetting. The phrase *zoon logon ekhon* occurs nowhere, exactly thus, in Aristotle—so Heidegger's seeming citation is in fact already something more like a gloss or a translation. To cite the phrase, then, and to attribute it to Aristotle is to obscure a specific sort of work—a sort of thought. *Zoon logon ekhon* may not figure as such in Aristotle, but its constituent terms and their relations do appear, in different spots. We may say that Heidegger assembles the definition from other places in Aristotle's corpus where nearly synonymous expressions do occur: he gathers them together from the point of view of what lay before him, recognizing the kinships of the terms from the point of view of what the definition will come to be. Heidegger "translates" Aristotle when appearing to cite him, and this "translating" expresses Heidegger's gleaning of the traces of man's disposition toward the word from within the word, from a corpus in which the expression of that disposition lay scattered. Elsewhere Heidegger will call this assembling-gathering by the name of "thought." Here, as in Heidegger's treatment of the translation of Aristotle's term *energeia,* it is only slightly more modestly called "translation." See Martin Heidegger, "The Anaximander Fragment," in *Early Greek Thinking,* trans. David Farrell Krell and Frank A. Capuzzi (1975; repr., San Francisco: Harper and Row, 1984).

9. The history of the development of machine translation (MT) is a complicated and rich one; the term is the most recent of a series, and is not guaranteed to last. An excellent review of the history of MT—and a useful definition—may be found in W. John Hutchins and Harold L. Somers, *An Introduction to Machine Translation* (London: Academic Press, 1992): "The term Machine Translation (MT) is the now traditional and standard name for computerised systems responsible for the production of translations from one natural language into another, with or without human assistance." Calling it a Cold War phenomenon does not seem to me controversial. The first major studies of MT in the United States were all funded by the U.S. Department of Defense and the Central Intelligence Agency (CIA), who were interested among other things in finding ways of translating, quickly and accurately, documents in Russian.

10. In Martin Heidegger, "Logos," we find this famous concluding thought-image: "Once, however, in the beginning of Western thinking, the essence of language flashed in the light of Being—once, when Heraclitus thought the *logos* as his guiding word, so as to think in this word the Being of beings" (in *Early Greek Thinking,* 78).

11. Martin Heidegger, *Introduction to Metaphysics*, trans. Gregory Fried and Richard Polt (New Haven, Conn.: Yale University Press, 2000), 198; see also Martin Heidegger, *On the Way to Language*, trans. Peter D. Hertz (1971; repr., New York: Harper and Row, 1982), 96: "If we take language directly in the sense of something that is present, we encounter it as the act of speaking, the activation of the organs of speech, mouth, lips, tongue. Language manifests itself in speaking, as a phenomenon that occurs in man. . . . Language is the tongue."

12. Among the most promising developments of this line of thought are to be found in treatments of so-called immaterial labor by the Italian sociological and philosophical school since Antonio Negri's *Marx beyond Marx* (originally published in Italian in 1979 as *Marx oltre Marx: Quaderno di lavoro sui Grundrisse*; French and English translations published in 1984). See Negri's remarks about Marx's "Machine fragments" in *Marx beyond Marx,* ed. Jim Fleming, trans. Harry Cleaver et al. (New York: Autonomedia, 1991), 139–50; and Paolo Virno, "The Ambivalence of Disenchantment," in *Radical Thought in Italy: A Potential Politics,* ed. Michael Hardt and Paolo Virno (Minneapolis: University of Minnesota Press, 1996), 21–24, especially his comments regarding the "general intellect" in Marx, the "epistemic models that structure social communication [and] incorporate the intellectual activity of mass culture, no longer reducible to 'simple labor,' to the pure expenditure of time and money. There converge in the productive power of the general intellect artificial languages, theorems of formal logic . . . and images of the world."

13. David Sarno, "Franz Josef Och, Google's Translation Über-Scientist, Talks about Google Translate," *Los Angeles Times*, March 11, 2010, accessed March 3, 2012, http://latimesblogs.latimes.com/technology/2010/03/the-web-site-translategooglecom-was

-done-in–2001-we-were-just—licensing–3rd-party-machine-translation-technologies -tha.html.

14. Ibid.

15. William Shakespeare, *A Midsummer Night's Dream,* in *The Riverside Shakespeare: The Complete Works*, 2nd ed., ed. G. Blakemore Evans et al. (Boston: Houghton Mifflin, 1997); hereafter cited by act, scene, and line in the text. The reading of this famous scene that most closely resembles mine is in John Sallis's *On Translation* (Bloomington: Indiana University Press, 2002), 25–31; see also 94. Sallis's excellent, brief analysis of Schlegel's translation of the scene stresses the paradoxical need to translate proper names—which might be considered, strictly speaking, untranslatable. He is concerned, as are most critics who write about the encounter between Schlegel and Shakespeare, with ways in which Schlegel "compensates" for the necessary "losses" (94) in his translation—and to this extent Sallis is very much at work within the economic register that organizes conventional theories of translation. A helpful review of the scene's intertexts is Madeleine Forey's "'Bless thee, Bottom, bless thee! Thou Art Translated!': Ovid, Golding, and *A Midsummer Night's Dream*," *Modern Language Review* 93, no. 2 (April 1998): 321–29. More pertinent in a sense is Margaret Tudeau-Clayton's "Scenes of Translation in Jonson and Shakespeare: 'Poetaster, Hamlet,' and 'A Midsummer Night's Dream,'" *Translation and Literature* 11, no. 1 (Spring 2002): 1–23. Tudeau-Clayton uses Shakespeare's play to suggest the limits of Lawrence Venuti's notion that translations can be "domesticating" or "foreignizing."

16. Marcus Tullius Cicero, "De optimo genere oratorum," in *De inventione: De optimo genere oratorum. Topica*, trans. H. M. Hubbell (Cambridge, Mass.: Harvard University Press, 1960), 364.

17. August Wilhelm von Schlegel, *A Course of Lectures on Dramatic Art and Literature* (1815), trans. John Black and A. J. W. Morrisonn (London: George Bell and Sons, 1815), 329; the German is from A. W. V. Schegel, *Kritische Schriften und Briefe*, vol. 6, ed. Edgar Lohner (Stuttgart: Kohlhammer, 1962), 159.

18. Jacob Grimm and Wilhelm Grimm, *Deutsches Wörterbuch von Jacob und Wilhelm Grimm*, 16 Bde. in 32 Teilbänden (Leipzig, 1854–1961), accessed March 9, 2012, http://woerterbuchnetz.de/DWB.

19. Anston Bosman, "Shakespeare and Globalization," in *The New Cambridge Companion to Shakespeare,* ed. Stanley Wells and Margareta de Grazia (Cambridge: Cambridge University Press, 2010), notes the problem of Bottom's translation into German as well, though he does not work through the oddities of the moment. Note the persistence, in even so astute a critic, of Venuti's "domesticating" and "foreignizing" lexicon:

> An obvious problem is how to translate the name 'Bottom,' which evokes the character's profession by denoting a weaver's implement—the spool on which yarn was

wound—but also has bawdy connotations, even if different in the Renaissance from those picked up by modern ears. No translation could capture this *double-entendre.* Günther's word *Zettel* designates the warp in a woven fabric, but lacks bodily resonance. . . . Both choices [German and French translations of Bottom] yield losses and gains. They exemplify opposing strategies of translation: the German option domesticates the source in the target culture while the French marks the source as foreign. Most choices in translation fall between these extremes, and the diffusion of Shakespeare's texts depends on innumerable compromises made by editors and translators between the poles of alienation and acculturation. (293)

BIBLIOGRAPHY

Ackerman, Bruce. "Neo-Federalism?" In *Constitutionalism and Democracy*, ed. Jon Elster, 153–94. Cambridge: Cambridge University Press, 1988.

Agamben, Giorgio. "Le gouvernment de l'insecurité: Entretien avec Giorgio Agamben." *La Revue Internationale des Livres et des Idées* 4 (March/April 2008): 18–20.

——. *Homo Sacer: Sovereign Power and Bare Life.* Stanford, Calif.: Stanford University Press, 1998.

Agier, Michel. *Le couloir des exilés: Être étranger dans un monde commun.* Paris: Editions du Croquant, 2011.

Aidoo, Ama Ata. "For Whom Things Did Not Change." In *No Sweetness Here*, 8–29. New York: Feminist Press, 1995.

Allan, T. R. S. *Constitutional Justice: A Liberal Theory of the Rule of Law*. Oxford: Oxford University Press, 2001.

Althusius, Johannes. *Politica methodice digesta*. Translated by Frederick S. Carney. Indianapolis: Liberty Classics Edition, 1995.

Althusser, Louis. "Le marxisme aujourd'hui." In *Solitude de Machiavel et autres texts*, 292–310. Paris: Presses Universitaires de France, 1998; translated by James H. Kavanaugh as "Marxism Today" in *Philosophy and the Spontaneous Philosophy of the Scientists*. London: Verso, 1990.

Ambedkar, B. R. "Castes in India: Their Mechanism, Genesis and Development." In *The Essential Writings of B. R. Ambedkar*, edited by Valerian Rodrigues, 241–62. Oxford: Oxford University Press, 2004.

Ampelius, Lucius. *Liber memorialis.* Leipzig: B. G. Teubner, 1873. http://penelope.uchicago.edu/Thayer/E/Roman/Texts/Ampelius/home.html.

Anderson, Benedict. *Imagined Communities: Reflections on the Origin and Spread of Nationalism*. London: Verso, 1991.

Anderson, Claire. "The Genealogy of the Modern Subject: Indian Convicts in Mauritius, 1814–1853." In *Representing Convicts: New Perspectives on Convict Forced Labor Migration*, edited by Ian Duffield and James Bradley, 164–82. London: Leicester University Press, 1997.

Anidjar, Gil. "*Blutgewalt.*" *Oxford Literary Review* 31, no. 2 (2009): 153–74.

——. "Lines of Blood: Limpieza de Sangre as Political Theology." In *Blood in History and Blood Histories*, edited by Mariacarla Gadebusch Bondio, 119–36. Florence: Sismel—Edizioni del Galluzzo / Micrologus Library, 2005.

———. "We Have Never Been Jewish: An Essay in Asymmetric Hematology." In *Jewish Blood: Reality and Metaphor in History, Religion, and Culture*, edited by Mitchell Hart, 31–56. London: Routledge, 2009.

Anonymous. *Exercitation concerning Usurped Powers*. London, 1650.

Anonymous. *A Plea for Non-Scribers*. London, 1650.

Appian. *Civil Wars*. Translated by Horace White. Cambridge, Mass.: Harvard University Press, 2002.

Apter, Emily. *The Translation Zone: A New Comparative Literature*. Princeton, N.J.: Princeton University Press, 2005.

Arato, Andrew. *Civil Society, Constitution, and Legitimacy*. New York: Rowman and Littlefield, 2000.

———. "Forms of Constitution Making and Theories of Democracy." *Cardozo Law Review* 17, no. 2 (1995): 202–54.

Arendt, Hannah. *The Human Condition*. Chicago: University of Chicago Press, 1958.

———. *On Revolution*. New York: Viking Press, 1963.

———. *The Origins of Totalitarianism*. New York: Harcourt, Brace, 1979.

———. *The Portable Hannah Arendt*. Edited by Peter Baehr. New York: Penguin, 2000.

Aristotle. *Politics*. Translated by B. Jovett. Oxford: Clarendon Press, 1885.

Austin, John. L. "A Plea for Excuses." *Proceedings of the Aristotelian Society*, n.s. 57 (1956–57): 1–30. Accessed October 28, 2016. https://sites.ualberta.ca/~francisp/NewPhil448/AustinPlea56.pdf

Balibar, Étienne. *Violence and Civility*. Translated by G. M. Goshgarian. New York: Columbia University Press, 2015.

———. *Violence et civilité*. Paris: Editions Galilée, 2010.

Barclay, William. *De regno et regali potestate adversus Buchanum, Brutum, Boucherium et reliquios monarchomacos*. Paris: G. Chaudière, 1600.

Bazard, Saint-Amand et Olinde Rodrigues, *Exposition de la Doctrine Saint-Simonienne*. Première Année, 1829. Nouv. éd. publ. avec introd. et notes par C. Bouglé et Elie Halévy, Paris, Marcel Rivière, 1924.

Bassnett-McGuire, Susan. *Translation Studies*. New York: Routledge, 2002.

Bataille, Georges. *The Accursed Share: Consumption*. Vol. 1. Translated by Robert Hurley. New York: Zone Books, 1988.

Baud, Jean-Pierre "La nature juridique du sang." *Terrain—Revue d'ethnologie d'Ethnologie de l'Europe* 56 (2011): 95–105.

Baughman, Elizabeth. "The Scythian Archers: Policing Athens." In *Dēmos: Classical Athenian Democracy, The Stoa: A Consortium for Electronic Publication in the Humanities*, edited by C. Blackwell. http://www.stoa.org.

Beaud, Olivier. *Théorie de la fédération*. Paris: Presses Universitaires de France, 2007.

Beccaria, Cesare. *On Crimes and Punishments and Other Writings*. Translated by Richard Davies, Virginia Cox, and Richard Bellamy. Cambridge: Cambridge University Press, 1995.

Benveniste, Émile. *Le vocabulaire des institutions indo-européennes*. [Hebrew] Paris: Minuit, 1969.

Bergmann, S. H. *Introduction to Logic: The Theoretical Science of Order*. Jerusalem: Mossad Bialik, 1964.

Berlin, Isaiah. "Two Concepts of Liberty." In *Four Essays on Liberty.* Oxford: Oxford University Press, 1969.

Berman, Harold J. *Law and Revolution: The Formation of the Western Legal Tradition*. Cambridge, Mass.: Harvard University Press, 1983.

Bernasconi, Robert. "Who Invented the Concept of Race?: Kant's Role in the Enlightenment Construction of Race." In *Race*, edited by Robert Bernasconi, 11–36. Oxford: Blackwell, 2001.

Bernstein, J. M. *Recovering Ethical Life.* London: Routledge, 1994.

——. *Torture and Dignity: An Essay on Moral Injury*. Chicago: University of Chicago Press, 2015.

Bèze, Théodore de. "Rights of Magistrates" (1574). In *Constitutionalism and Resistance in the Sixteenth Century: Three Treatises*, translated and edited by Julian H. Franklin. New York: Pegasus, 1969.

Binoche, Bertrand, ed. *L'homme perfectible.* Paris: Editions du Champ Vallon, 2004.

Blackstone, Sir William. "Rights of Things—Title by Descent." In *Commentaries on the Laws of England*, edited by Hardcastle Browne. St. Paul, Minn.: West Publishing, 1897.

Böckenforde, Ernst-Wolfgang. "Die Verfassungsggebende Gewalt des Volkes-Ein Grenzbegriff des Verfassungsrechts." In *Staat, Verfassung, Democratie: Studien zur Verfassungstheorie und zum Verfassungsrecht*. Frankfurt am Main: Suhrkamp, 1991.

Bodin, Jean. *On Sovereignty*. Translated by Julian Franklin. Cambridge: Cambridge University Press, 1992.

——. *Six Books of the Commonwealth.* 1576.

Bosman, Anston. "Shakespeare and Globalization." In *The New Cambridge Companion to Shakespeare,* edited by Stanley Wells and Margareta de Grazia. Cambridge: Cambridge University Press, 2010.

Bourdieu, Pierre. *Choses dites.* Paris: Minuit, 1987.

Brossat, Alain. "Les dernières heures de la grande dramaturgie du sang?" *Drôle d'Époque* 19 (2006).

Brown, Norman O. *Life against Death: The Psychoanalytic Meaning of History*. Middletown, Conn.: Wesleyan University Press, 1985.

——. *Love's Body*. Berkeley: University of California Press, 1966.

Brubaker, Rogers. *Citizenship and Nationhood in France and Germany*. Cambridge, Mass.: Harvard University Press, 1992.

Brutus, Junius. *Vindiciae, contra tyrannos; or, Concerning the Legitimate Power of a*

Prince over the People, and of the People over a Prince. Edited by George Garnett. Cambridge: Cambridge University Press, 1994.

Buchanan, George. *A Dialogue on the Law of Kingship among the Scots*. Edinburgh: Saltire Society, 2006.

Burke, Edmund. *Reflections on the Revolution in France*. Edited by Frank M. Turner. New Haven, Conn.: Yale University Press, 2003.

Butler, Judith. *Bodies that Matter.* New York: Routledge, 1993.

Bynum, Caroline Walker. *Wonderful Blood: Theology and Practice in Late Medieval Northern Germany and Beyond*. Philadelphia: University of Pennsylvania Press, 2007.

Calhoun, John C. *Union and Liberty: The Political Philosophy of John C. Calhoun.* Edited by Ross M. Lence. Indianapolis: Liberty Funds, 2010.

Carothers, Thoma, ed. *Promoting the Rule of Law Abroad: In Search of Knowledge*. Washington, D.C.: Carnegie Endowment for International Peace, 2006.

Carré de Malberg, Raymond. *Contribution á la théorie générale de l'état.* Vol. 2. Paris: Librairie de la Société du Recueil Sirey, 1922.

——. *La loi, expression de la volonté générale*. Paris: Economica, 1984.

Castoriadis, Cornelius. *La cité et les lois—Ce qui fait la Grèce 2*. Paris: Seuil, 2008.

——. "The Logic of Magmas and the Question of Autonomy." In *The Castoriadis Reader*, edited by David Ames Curtis. Oxford: Blackwell, 1997.

——. *Philosophia kai Epistēmē*. Athens: Eurasia, 2003.

——. *Thucydide, la force et le droit*. Paris: Seuil, 2011.

——. "What Democracy?" In *Figures of the Thinkable*, translated by Helen Arnold, 122–24. Stanford: Stanford University Press, 2007.

——. *The Imaginary Institution of Society.* Translated by Kathleen Blamey. Cambridge, Mass.: MIT Press, 1987.

Cavarero, Adriana. *For More than One Voice: Toward a Philosophy of Vocal Expression*. Stanford, Calif.: Stanford University Press, 2005.

——. *Stately Bodies: Literature, Philosophy, and the Question of Gender*. Translated by Robert de Lucca and Deanna Shemek. Ann Arbor: University of Michigan Press, 2002.

Chamayou, Gregoire. *Les chasses à l'homme.* Paris: La Fabrique, 2010.

Champeaux, E. "*Jus sanguinis*: Trois façons de calculer la parenté au Moyen Âge." *Revue Historique de Droit Français et Étranger* (1933): 241–90.

Cheah, Pheng. *Spectral Nationality: Passages of Freedom from Kant to Postcolonial Literatures of Liberation*. New York: Columbia University Press, 2003.

Chroust, Anton-Hermann. "The Corporate Idea and the Body Politic in the Middle Ages." *Review of Politics* 9, no. 4 (1947): 430.

Cicero, Marcus Tullius. "De optimo genere oratorum." In *De inventione: De optimo genere oratorum. Topica*, translated by H. M. Hubbell. Cambridge, Mass.: Harvard University Press, 1960.

——. *De re publica*. Translated by Clinton Walker Keyes. Cambridge, Mass.: Harvard University Press, 1994.

Clark, J. C. D. *English Society, 1660–1832: Religion, Ideology and Politics during the Ancient Regime*. Cambridge: Cambridge University Press, 2000.

Cohen, Jean. *Globalization and Sovereignty: Rethinking Legality, Legitimacy and Constitutionalism*. Cambridge: Cambridge University Press, 2012.

Condorcet, Marquis de. *Condorcet: Selected Writings*. Edited by Keith Michael Baker. Indianapolis: Bobbs-Merrill, 1976.

——. "Sur la nécessité de faire ratifier la Constitution par les citoyens." In *Oeuvres de Condorcet,* vol. 9, 413–30. Paris: Firmin-Didot, 1847–49.

Cooper, Frederick. *Citizenship between Empire and Nation: Remaking France and French Africa, 1945–1960*. Princeton, N.J.: Princeton University Press, 2014.

Crossley, Ceri. "Using and Transforming the French Countryside: The 'Colonies Agricoles,' 1820–1850." *French Studies* 44, no. 1 (1991): 36–54.

Davis, Kathleen. *Periodization and Sovereignty: How Ideas of Feudalism and Secularization Govern the Politics of Time*. Philadelphia: University of Pennsylvania Press, 2008.

Dejours, Christophe, and Florence Bègue. *Suicides au travail*. Paris: Presses Universitaires de France, 2009.

Dekker, Jeroen. "Transforming the Nation and the Child: Philanthropy in the Netherlands, Belgium, France and England." In *Charity, Philanthropy and Reform: From the 1690s to l850,* edited by H. Cunningham and J. Innes, 130–47. New York: St. Martin's, 1998.

de Lauretis, Teresa. *Technologies of Gender: Essays in Theory, Film, and Fiction*. Bloomington: Indiana University Press, 1987.

Deleuze, Gilles. *Difference and Repetition*. Translated by Paul Patton. New York: Columbia University Press, 1995.

——. *Foucault.* Minneapolis: University of Minnesota Press, 1988.

——. *Kant's Critical Philosophy*, trans. Hugh Tomlinson and Barbara Habberjam. Minneapolis: University of Minnesota Press, 1984.

——. *The Logic of Sense*. New York: Columbia University Press, 1990.

Deleuze, Gilles, and Felix Guattari. *What Is Philosophy?* New York: Columbia University Press, 1994.

de Lubac, Henri. *Corpus mysticum: The Eucharist and the Church in the Middle Ages*. Translated by Gemma Simmonds, Richard Price, and Christopher Stephens. Notre Dame, Ind.: University of Notre Dame Press, 2006.

de Malberg, Raymond Carré. *Contribution á la théorie générale de l'état.* Vol 2. Paris: Librairie de la Société du Recueil Sirey, 1922.

——. *La loi, expression de la volonté générale.* Paris: Economica, 1984.

de Man, Paul. "The Resistance to Theory." *Yale French Studies* 63 (1982): 3–20.

Derrida, Jacques. *Archive Fever*. Chicago: University of Chicago Press, 1996.

———. "Declarations of Independence." *New Political Science* 15 (1986): 7–15.

———. "Force of Law: 'The Mystical Foundation of Authority.'" In *Deconstruction and the Possibility of Justice*, edited by Drucilla Cornell, 3–67. New York: Routledge, 1992.

———. "*Geschlecht*: Sexual Difference, Ontological Difference," In *A Derrida Reader*, edited by Peggy Kamuf. New York: Columbia University Press, 1991.

———. *Margins of Philosophy*. Translated by Alan Bass. Chicago: University of Chicago Press, 1982.

———. *The Politics of Friendship*. Translated by George Collins. New York: Verso, 1997.

de Tocqueville, Alexis. *Democracy in America*. Translated by Henry Reeve. New York: Vintage Books, 1990.

de Vries, Hent. *Philosophy and the Turn to Religion*. Baltimore: Johns Hopkins University Press, 1999.

Dickinson, Elizabeth. "GDP: A Brief History." *Foreign Policy*, 184 (2011): 37.

Dippel, Horst. "The Changing Idea of Popular Sovereignty in Early American Constitutionalism: Breaking Away from European Patterns." *Journal of the Early Republic* 16, no. 1 (1996): 21–45.

Drèze, Jean, and Amartya Sen. *An Uncertain Glory: India and Its Contradictions*. Princeton, N.J.: Princeton University Press, 2013.

Duverger, Maurice. "Légitimité des gouvernements de fait." *Revue du Droit Publique* (1948).

The Earth Institute. "Sustainability Essentials Training (SET) Program." Columbia University. Accessed September 3, 2016. http://earth.columbia.edu/sections/view/9.

Elazar, Daniel. *Exploring Federalism*. Tuscaloosa: University of Alabama Press, 1987.

Elliot, Jonathan. *Debates in the Several State Conventions on the Adoption of the Federal Constitution as Recommended by the General Convention at Philadelphia in 1787*. Vol 2. Edited by James McClellan. Cumberland, Md.: J. River Press, 1989.

Esposito, Roberto. *Communitas: The Origin and Destiny of Community*. Translated by Timothy Campbell. Stanford, Calif.: Stanford University Press, 2010.

Fassin, Didier. "Compassion and Repression: The Moral Economy of Immigration Policies in France." *Cultural Anthropology* 20, no. 3 (2005): 362–87.

Fazal, Tanisha. *State Death: The Politics and Geography of Conquest, Occupation, and Annexation*. Princeton, N.J.: Princeton University Press, 2007.

Federici, Silvia. *Caliban and the Witch: Women, the Body and Primitive Accumulation*. New York: Autonomedia, 2004.

Feldman, Eric A., and Ronald Bayer, eds. *Blood Feuds: AIDS, Blood, and the Politics of Medical Disaster*. New York: Oxford University Press, 1998.

Feuerbach, Ludwig. *The Essence of Christianity*. Translated by George Eliot. Amherst, Mass.: Prometheus Books, 1989.

Firestone, Shulamith. *The Dialectic of Sex*. New York: Bantam, 1972.

Forey, Madeleine. "'Bless thee, Bottom, bless thee! Thou Art Translated!': Ovid, Golding, and *A Midsummer Night's Dream*." *Modern Language Review* 93, no. 2 (April 1998): 321–29.

Forlivesi, Luc, Georges-François Pottier, and Sophie Chassat, eds. *Eduquer et punir: La colonie agricole et pénitentiaire de Mettray (1839–1937)*. Rennes, France: Presses Universitaires de Rennes, 2005.

Forsyth, Murray. "Thomas Hobbes and the Constituent Power of the People." *Political Studies* 29, no. 2 (1981): 191–203.

——. *Union of States*. New York: Holmes and Meier, 1981.

Foucault, Michel. *The Archaeology of Knowledge*. New York: Pantheon Books, 1972.

——. *Discipline and Punish: The Birth of the Prison*. Translated by Alan Sheridan. New York: Vintage Books, 1979.

——. *The History of Sexuality*. Vol. 1, *An Introduction*. Translated by Robert Hurley. New York: Pantheon, 1978; New York: Vintage Books, 1990.

——. *Language, Counter-Memory, Practice*. Ithaca, N.Y.: Cornell University Press, 1977.

——. *Sécurité, territoire, population: Cours au Collège de France, 1977–1978*. Paris: Gallimard, 2004.

——. "The Subject and Power." *Critical Inquiry* 8 (1982): 778.

——. "Table ronde du 20 mai 1978." In *Dits et écrits, tome IV*. Paris: Gallimard, 1994.

——. "What Is Enlightenment?" In *The Foucault Reader*, edited by Peter Rabinow, 32–50. New York: Pantheon, 1984.

Fox, Marvin. *Interpreting Maimonides: Studies in Methodology, Metaphysics, and Moral Philosophy*. Chicago: University of Chicago Press, 1990.

Frank, Jason. "Unauthorized Propositions: *The Federalist Papers* and Constituent Power." *Diacritics* 37, nos. 2–3 (2007): 103–20.

Franklin, Julian. *Constitutionalism and Resistance in the Sixteenth Century*. New York: Pegasus, 1969.

——. *Jean Bodin and the Rise of Absolutist Theory*. Cambridge: Cambridge University Press, 1973.

——. "Sovereignty and the Mixed Constitution: Bodin and His Critics." In *The Cambridge History of Political Thought, 1450–1700*, edited by J. H. Burns, 298–328. Cambridge: Cambridge University Press, 1991.

Fraser, Nancy, and Axel Honneth. *Redistribution or Recognition: A Political-Philosophical Exchange*. London: Verso, 2003.

Freud, Sigmund. *Civilization and Its Discontents*. In Freud, *Complete Psychological Works*, vol. 21.

——. *The Complete Psychological Works of Sigmund Freud*. 24 vols. Translated by James Strachey. London: Hogarth Press and the Institute of Psycho-Analysis, 1961.

———. *The Ego and the Id.* In Freud, *Complete Psychological Works*, vol. 19.

———. "Femininity." *New Introductory Lectures on Psychoanalysis.* In Freud, *Complete Psychological Works*, vol. 22.

———. "On the Universal Tendency to Debasement in the Sphere of Love." In Freud, *Complete Psychological Works*, vol. 11.

Friedrich, Carl. *Constitutional Government and Democracy: Theory and Practice in Europe and America*. Boston: Ginn, 1950.

Frow, John. "In the Penal Colony." *Journal of Australian Studies* (2000): 6.

Fuller, Lon L. *The Morality of Law*. Rev. ed. New Haven, Conn.: Yale University Press, 1969.

———. "Positivism and Fidelity to Law—A Reply to Professor Hart." *Harvard Law Review* 71, no. 4 (1958): 632.

Gager, Kristin Elizabeth. *Blood Ties and Fictive Ties: Adoption and Family Life in Early Modern France*. Princeton, N.J.: Princeton University Press, 1996.

Georges, Karl Ernst. *Ausführliches lateinisch-deutsches und deutsch-lateinisches Handwörterbuch aus den Quellen zusammengetragen und mit besonderer Bezugnahme auf Synonymik und Antiquitäten unter Berücksichtigung der besten Hülfsmittel.* Leipzig: Hahn, 1869.

Geroulanos, Stefanos. *An Atheism That Is Not Humanist Emerges in French Thought*. Stanford, Calif.: Stanford University Press, 2010.

Gewirth, Alan. *Marsilius of Padua: The Defender of Peace*. New York: Columbia University Press, 1951.

Gierke, Otto. *Natural Law and the Theory of Society, 1500–1800*. Boston: Beacon, 1957.

———. *Political Theories in the Middle Age*. Cambridge: Cambridge University Press, 1987.

Gil Harris, Jonathan. *Sick Economies: Drama, Mercantilism, and Disease in Shakespeare's England*. Philadelphia: University of Pennsylvania Press, 2004.

Gillespie, Michael Allen. *Ratifying the Constitution*. Lawrence: University Press of Kansas, 1992.

Goodman, Paul. *Of One Blood: Abolitionism and the Origins of Racial Equality*. Berkeley: University of California Press, 1998.

Gorski, Philip S. *The Disciplinary Revolution: Calvinism and the Rise of the State in Early Modern Europe*. Chicago: University of Chicago Press, 2003.

Gourgouris, Stathis "On Self-Alteration." *Parrhesia* 9 (2010): 1–17.

Grimm, Jacob, and Wilhelm Grimm. *Deutsches Wörterbuch von Jacob und Wilhelm Grimm*, 16 Bde. in 32 Teilbänden. Leipzig, 1854–1961. Accessed March 9, 1021. http://woerterbuchnetz.de/DWB.

Groebner, Valentin. *Liquid Assets, Dangerous Gifts: Presents and Politics at the End of the Middle Ages*. Translated by Pamela E. Selwyn. Philadelphia: University of Pennsylvania Press, 2002.

Guizot, François. "L'esprit d'insurrection est un esprit radicalement contraire à la liberté." *Discours à la Chambre des Députés*, December 29, 1830.

——. *Le moniteur universel*, August 20, 1842, 1807.

Hacking, Ian. *Historical Ontology.* Cambridge, Mass.: Harvard University Press, 2006.

——. *The Social Construction of What?* Cambridge, Mass.: Harvard University Press, 1999.

Hamilton, Bernard. Review of Tomaž Mastnak, *Crusading Peace: Christendom, the Muslim World, and Western Political Order. American Historical Review* 108, no. 4 (2003): 1204.

Haraway, Donna J. *Modest_Witness@Second_Millenium.FemaleMan©_Meets_Onco-Mouse™: Feminism and Technoscience*. New York: Routledge, 1997.

Hardt, Michael. "Affective Labor." *boundary 2* 26, no. 2 (1999): 89–100.

Hardt, Michael, and Antonio Negri. *Empire*. Cambridge, Mass.: Harvard University Press, 2000.

Harman, Graham. *Tool-Being: Heidegger and the Metaphysics of Objects*. Peru, Ill.: Open Court, 2002.

Hart, H. L. A. "Positivism and the Separation of Law and Morals." *Harvard Law Review* 71, no. 4 (February 1958): 593–629.

——. *The Concept of Law*. 3rd ed. Oxford: Oxford University Press, 2012.

Harvey, David. *A Companion to Marx's Capital.* Vol. 2. London: Verso, 2013.

Hauriou, Maurice. *Précis de droit constitutionnel.* Paris: Sirey, 1929.

Hayek, Friedrich von. *The Constitution of Liberty*. London: Routledge, 1960.

——. *The Road to Serfdom*. London: Routledge, 1944.

Hegel, G. W. F. *The Phenomenology of Spirit*. Translated by A. V. Miller. Oxford: Oxford University Press, 1977.

Heidegger, Martin. *Early Greek Thinking.* Translated by David Farrell Krell and Frank A. Capuzzi. 1975. Reprint, San Francisco: Harper and Row, 1984.

Hardt, Michael, and Antonio Negri. *Empire*. Cambridge, Mass.: Harvard University Press, 2000.

——. *Introduction to Metaphysics*. Translated by Gregory Fried and Richard Polt. New Haven, Conn.: Yale University Press, 2000.

——. *On the Way to Language*. Translated by Peter D. Hertz. 1971. Reprint, New York: Harper and Row, 1982.

Hobbes, Thomas. *Leviathan*. Edited by Richard Tuck. Cambridge: Cambridge University Press, 1996.

——. *On the Citizen*. Edited by Richard Tuck. Cambridge: Cambridge University Press, 1998.

Hobsbawm, Eric, and Terence Ranger, eds. *The Invention of Tradition*. Cambridge: Cambridge University Press, 1983.

Hotman, François. *Franco-Gallia; or, An Account of the Ancient Free State of France*. Cambridge: Cambridge University Press, 1972.

Hume, David. "Of Pride and Humility of Animals." In *Treatise of Human Nature*, vol. 2, bk. 2, sec. 12. Edinburgh, 1826.

Hutchins, W. John, and Harold L. Somers. *An Introduction to Machine Translation*. London: Academic Press, 1992.

Jambet, Christian. "The Paradoxical One." Translated by Michael Stanish. *Umbr(a)* (2009).

Jameson, John Alexander. *The Constitutional Convention: Its History, Powers, and Modes of Proceedings*. New York: Charles Scribner, 1867.

Jefferson, Thomas. *Jefferson: Political Writings*. Edited by Joyce Appleby. Cambridge: Cambridge University Press, 1999.

Justinian, *The Digest of Justinian*. Vol. 1. Translation by Alan Watson. 1985. Reprint, Philadelphia: University of Pennsylvania Press, 2009.

Kafka, Franz. *The Penal Colony*. New York: Schocken, 1948.

Kahn, Paul. *Putting Liberalism in Its Place*. Princeton, N.J.: Princeton University Press, 2005.

Kalyvas, Andreas. "The Basic Norm and Democracy in Hans Kelsen's Legal and Political Theory." *Philosophy and Social Criticism* 32, no. 5 (2006): 587–92.

——. "Popular Sovereignty, Democracy, the Constituent Power." *Constellations* 12, no. 2 (2005): 223–44.

Kantorowicz, Ernst H. *The King's Two Bodies: A Study in Mediaeval Political Theology*. Princeton, N.J.: Princeton University Press, 1997.

Kelsen, Hans. *General Theory of Norms*. Translated by Michael Hartney. Oxford: Oxford University Press, 1991.

——. *Pure Theory of Law*. Translated by Max Knight. Gloucester, Mass.: Peter Smith, 1989.

Kevles, Daniel J. *In the Name of Eugenics: Genetics and the Uses of Human Heredity*. Berkeley: University of California Press, 1985.

Klapisch-Zuber, Christiane. *L'ombre des ancêtres: Essai sur l'imaginaire médiéval de la parenté*. Paris: Fayard, 2000.

Klein, Claude. *Théorie et pratique de pouvoir constituant*. Paris: Presses Universitaires de France, 1996.

Kojève, Alexandre. *La notion de l'autorité*. Paris: Gallimard, 2004.

Kramer, Larry D. *The People Themselves: Popular Constitutionalism and Judicial Review*. Oxford: Oxford University Press, 2005.

Kramer, Mathew H. *Objectivity and the Rule of Law*. Cambridge: Cambridge University Press, 2007.

Kripke, Saul. *Naming and Necessity*. Cambridge, Mass.: Harvard University Press, 1980.

Kumm, Matthias. "Who Is the Final Arbiter of Constitutionality in Europe?" In *Ruling the World?: Constitutionalism, International Law and Global Governance*, edited by Jeffrey Dunoff and Joel Trachtman, 259–325. Cambridge: Cambridge University Press, 2009.

Justinian. *The Digest of Justinian*. Translated by Alan Watson. Philadelphia: University of Pennsylvania Press, 2009.

Lacan, Jacques. *Encore: The Seminar, Book XX*. Edited by Jacques-Alain Miller. Translated by Bruce Fink. New York: Norton, 1998.

——. *The Other Side of Psychoanalysis: The Seminar, Book XVII*. Edited by Jacques-Alain Miller. Translated by Russell Grigg. New York: Norton, 2007.

——. *Le seminaire, livre XVI: D'un autre à l'Autre*. Paris: Seuil, 2006.

Laclau, Ernesto. *On Populist Reason.* London: Verso, 2005.

Lafayette, Marquis de. *Mémoires, correspondance et manuscrits.* Vols. 1–4. Paris: Fournier Ainé, 1837–38.

Lambropoulos, Vassilis. "Stumbling over the 'Boundary Stone of Greek Philosophy.'" In *Justice in Particular: Festschrift in Honour of Professor P. J. Kozyris*, 193–210. Athens: Sakkoulas, 2007.

Laqueur, Thomas. *Making Sex: Body and Gender from the Greeks to Freud*. Cambridge, Mass.: Harvard University Press, 1990.

Laurence, Stephen, and Eric Margolis, eds. "Concepts and Cognitive Science." In *Concepts: Core Readings*, 3–81. Cambridge, Mass.: MIT Press, 1999.

Lawson, George. *Politica sacra et civilis*. Edited by Conal Condren. Cambridge: Cambridge University Press, 1992.

Lazzarato, Maurizio. *Lavoro immateriale: Forme di vita e produzione di soggettivita*. Verona: Ombre Corte, 1997.

——. *Videofilosofia: Percezione e lavoro nel postfordismo.* Rome: Manifestolibri, 1996.

Lefebvre-Teillard, Anne. "*Ius sanguinis*: L'émergence d'un principe (Éléments d'histoire de la nationalité française)." *Revue Critique de Droit International Privé* 82, no. 2 (1993): 223–50.

Lemire. Elise. *"Miscegenation": Making Race in America*. Philadelphia: University of Pennsylvania Press, 2002.

Lesaffer, Randall. "Peace Treaties from Lodi to Westphalia." In *Peace Treaties and International Law in European History from the Late Middle Ages to World War One*, edited by Randall Lesaffer, 9–44. Cambridge: Cambridge University Press, 2004.

Lévêque, Pierre, and Pierre Vidal-Naquet. *Cleisthenes, the Athenian: An Essay on the Representation of Space and Time in Greek Political Thought from the End of the Sixth Century to the Death of Plato*. Amherst, Mass.: Prometheus Books, 1997.

Lewis, David. *On the Plurality of Worlds*. Oxford: Blackwell, 1986.

Lezra, Jacques. "The Indecisive Muse: Ethics in Translation and the Idea of History." *Comparative Literature* 60, no. 4 (2008): 301–30.

Linke, Uli. *Blood and Nation: The European Aesthetics of Race*. Philadelphia: University of Pennsylvania Press, 1999.

Liu, Lydia He, ed. *Tokens of Exchange: The Problem of Translation in Global Circulations*. Durham, N.C.: Duke University Press, 2000.

Livy, *History of Rome*. Translated by B. O. Foster. Cambridge, Mass.: Harvard University Press, 1997.

Locke, John. *The Second Treatise of Government*. Edited by Peter Laslett. Cambridge: Cambridge University Press, 1991.

——. *"Two Treatises of Government" and "A Letter concerning Toleration."* Edited by Ian Shapiro. New Haven, Conn.: Yale University Press, 2003.

Loughlin, Martin. *The Idea of Public Law*. Oxford: Oxford University Press, 2004.

Loughlin, Martin, and Neil Walker, eds. *The Paradox of Constitutionalism: Constituent Power and Constitutional Form*. Oxford: Oxford University Press, 2007.

Lowry, S. Todd. "The Archaeology of the Circulation Concept in Economic Theory." *Journal of the History of Ideas* 35, no. 3 (July–September 1974): 429–44.

Luste Boulbina, Seloua. *Le singe de Kafka et autres propos sur la colonie*. Lyon: Parangon, 2008.

Madison, James. "Letter to Thomas Jefferson. February 4, 1790." In *Jefferson: Political Writings*, edited by Joyce Appleby, 608. Cambridge: Cambridge University Press, 1999.

Madison, James. "The Federalist." In Alexander Hamilton, John Jay, and James Madison, *The Federalist: A Commentary on the Constitution of the United States*. New York: The Modern Library, 1935.

Madley, Benjamin. "From Africa to Auschwitz: How German South West Africa Incubated Ideas and Methods Adopted and Developed by the Nazis in Germany." *European History Quarterly* 35, no. 3 (2005): 429–64.

Maine, Henry James Sumner. *Ancient Law: Its Connection to the History of Early Society*. Charleston, N.C.: BiblioBazaar, 2008.

Mantena, Karuna. *Alibis of Empire: Henry Maine and the Ends of Liberal Imperialism*. Princeton, N.J.: Princeton University Press, 2010.

Marsilius of Padua. *Defensor pacis*. Translated by Alan Gewirth. Toronto: University of Toronto Press, 1956.

Marx, Karl. *Capital: A Critique of Political Economy*. Vol. 1. Translated by Ben Fowkes. New York: Penguin, 1977.

——. *Capital: A Critique of Political Economy*. Vol. 3. Translated by David Fernbach. New York: Penguin, 1992.

——. "The Communist Manifesto." In *The Marx-Engels Reader*, edited by Robert Tucker. New York: W. W. Norton, 1978.

——. "Critique of Hegel's Doctrine of the State." In *Karl Marx: Early Writings*. Translated by Rodney Livingstone and Gregor Benton. New York: Penguin, 1975.

——. *Misère de la philosophie: Réponse à la philosophie de la misère de M. Proudhon*. 1847. Reprint, Paris: Éditions Sociales, 1961.

Mastnak, Tomaž. *Crusading Peace: Christendom, the Muslim World, and Western Political Order*. Berkeley: University of California Press, 2002.

May, Larry. "International Criminal Law and the Inner Morality of Law." In *The Hart-Fuller Debate in the Twenty-First Century*, edited by Peter Cane, 79–96. Oxford: Hart, 2010.

McIlwain, Charles Howard. *The Growth of Political Thought in the West: From the Greeks to the End of the Middle Ages*. New York: Macmillan, 1932.

Mehta, Uday. "Kinship and Friendship: Two Conceptions of Political Action." Paper presented at Society for the Humanities, Cornell University, 2003.

Meillassoux, Claude. *Maidens, Meal and Money: Capitalism and the Domestic Community*. Cambridge: Cambridge University Press, 1981.

———. *Mythes et limites de l'anthropologies: Le sang et les mots.* Lausanne, Switzerland: Editions Page Deux, 2001.

Michelman, Frank. *Brennan and Democracy*. Princeton, N.J.: Princeton University Press, 1999.

———. "Constitutional Authorship." In *Constitutionalism: Philosophical Foundations*, edited by Larry Alexander, 64–98. Cambridge: Cambridge University Press, 1998.

Mitchell, Juliet. "Introduction I." In *Feminine Sexuality: Jacques Lacan and the École Freudienne*, edited by Juliet Mitchell and Jacqueline Rose. New York: Norton, 1982.

Mkandawire, Thandika. *Africa: Beyond Recovery*. Legon, Ghana: Sub-Saharan Publishers, 2015.

Mommsen, Theodore. *Le droit public Romain.* Vol. 4. Paris: Thorin and Fils, 1884.

Montesquieu, Charles de Secondat, baron de. *The Spirit of the Laws*. Translated and edited by Anne M. Cohler, Basia Carolyn Miller, and Harold Samuel Stone. Cambridge: Cambridge University Press, 1989.

Morgan, Edmund S. *Inventing the People: The Rise of Popular Sovereignty in England and America*. New York: W. W. Norton, 1989.

Morris, Richard B. *The Forging of the Union, 1781–1789*. New York: Harper and Row, 1987.

Muthu, Sankar. *Enlightenment against Empire*. Princeton, N.J.: Princeton University Press, 2003.

Napoleon. *Correspondance de Napoléon Ier*. Vol. 3. Edited by Henri Plon and J. Doumaine. Paris: Plon, 1859.

Negri, Antonio. "From the Right to Resistance to Constituent Power." In *The Porcelain Workshop: For a New Grammar of Politics*, translated by Noura Wedell, 109–26. Los Angeles: Semiotext(e), 2008.

———. *Insurgencies: Constituent Power and the Modern State*. Minneapolis: University of Minnesota Press, 1999.

——. *Marx beyond Marx*. Edited by Jim Fleming. Translated by Harry Cleaver et al. New York: Autonomedia, 1991.

——. *Marx oltre Marx: Quaderno di lavoro sui Grundrisse*. Milan: Feltrinelli Libri 1982.

——. *The Porcelain Workshop: For a New Grammar of Politics*. Los Angeles: Semiotext(e), 2008.

——. "Political Subjects: On the Multitude and Constituent Power." In *Reflections on Empire*, translated by Ed Emery, 96–113. Cambridge: Polity, 2008.

Negri, Antonio, and Michael Hardt. "Sovereignty." In Antonio Negri, *Reflections on Empire*, translated by Ed Emery, 48–59. Cambridge: Polity, 2008.

Netanyahu, Benzion. "Américo Castro and His View of the Origins of the Pureza de Sangre." *Proceedings of the American Academy for Jewish Research* 46–47 (1979–1980): 397–457.

Nuovo, Victor. *Christianity, Antiquity, and Enlightenment: Interpretations of Locke*. Dordrecht, Netherlands: Springer, 2010.

Oswald, Martin. "Shares and Rights: 'Citizenship' Greek Style and American Style." In *Dēmokratia: A Conversation on Democracies, Ancient and Modern*, edited by Josiah Ober and Charles Hedrick, 49–61. Princeton, N.J.: Princeton University Press, 1996.

Paine, Thomas. *Thomas Paine: Collected Writings*. Edited by Eric Foner. New York: Library of America, 1995.

Palmer, R. R. *The Age of the Democratic Revolution: A Political History of Europe and America, 1760–1800*. Vol. 1. Princeton, N.J.: Princeton University Press, 1959.

Passerin d'Entrèves, Alexander. *The Medieval Contribution to Political Thought*. Oxford: Oxford University Press, 1939.

Paster, Gail Kern. *The Body Embarrassed: Drama and the Disciplines of Shame in Early Modern England*. Ithaca, N.Y.: Cornell University Press, 1993.

Paulson, Stanley L. "Lon L. Fuller, Gustav Radbruch, and the 'Positivist' Theses." *Law and Philosophy* 13, no. 3 (August 1994): 354.

Piketty, Thomas. *Capital in the Twenty-First Century*. Cambridge, Mass.: Harvard University Press, 2014.

Plato, *Ion*. In *The Dialogues of Plato*. Vol. 3, *Ion; Hippias minor; Laches; Protagoras*. Translated by Reginald E. Allen. New Haven, Conn.: Yale University Press, 1996. Also available at Project Perseus, http://www.perseus.tufts.edu/hopper/text?doc=plat.+ion+530a. Accessed March 9, 2012.

Pomata, Gianna. "Blood Ties and Semen Ties: Consanguinity and Agnation in Roman Law." In *Gender, Kinship, Power: A Comparative and Interdisciplinary History*, edited by Mary Jo Maynes et al., 43–64. New York: Routledge, 1996.

Porqueres i Gené, Enric. "Kinship Language and the Dynamics of Race." In *Race, Ethnicity and Nation: Perspectives from Kinship and Genetics*, edited by Peter Wade. New York: Berghahn Books, 2009.

Postema, Gerald J. "Implicit Law," *Law and Philosophy* 13, no. 3 (August 1994): 361–87.

———. "Positivism and the Separation of Realists from Their Skepticism: Normative Guidance, the Rule of Law and Legal Reasoning." In *The Hart-Fuller Debate in the Twenty-First Century*, edited by Peter Cane, 275–76. Oxford: Hart, 2010.

Preuss, Ulrich. "Constitutional Powermaking for the New Polity: Some Deliberations on the Relations between Constituent Power and the Constitution." In *Constitutionalism, Identity, Difference, and Legitimacy: Theoretical Perspectives*, edited by Michel Rosenfeld, 144–45. Durham, N.C.: Duke University Press, 1994.

———. *Constitutional Revolution*. Atlantic Highlands, N.J.: Humanities Press, 1995.

Rabinow, Paul. *French Modern*. Cambridge, Mass.: MIT Press, 1989.

Radbruch, Gustav. *Legal Philosophy*. Translated by Kurt Wilk. In *The Legal Philosophy of Lask, Radbruch, and Dabin*. Cambridge, Mass.: Harvard University Press, 1950.

———. "Statutory Lawlessness and Supra-Statutory Law." Translated by Bonnie Litschewski Paulson and Stanley L. Paulson. *Oxford Journal of Legal Studies* 26, no. 1 (2006): 11.

Rancière, Jacques. *On the Shores of Politics*. Translated by Liz Heron. London: Verso, 1995.

Ravitch, Norman. "Your People, My People; Your God, My God: French and American Troubles over Citizenship." *French Review* 70, no. 4 (March 1997): 515.

Rawls, John. "The Idea of Public Reason Revisited." In *Political Liberalism*. 435–90. New York: Columbia University Press, 1993.

Raz, Joseph. *The Authority of Law: Essays on Law and Morality*. Oxford: Oxford University Press, 1979.

Redfield, Peter. *Space in the Tropics: From Convicts to Rockets in French Guiana.* Berkeley: University of California Press, 2000.

Rodney, Walter. *How Europe Underdeveloped Africa*. London: Bogle-L'Ouverture, 1972.

Rogers, John. *The Matter of Revolution: Science, Poetry, and Politics in the Age of Milton*. Ithaca, N.Y.: Cornell University Press, 1996.

Rogin, Michael. *Fathers and Children: Andrew Jackson and the Subjugation of the American Indian*. New York: Vintage, 1976.

Ronell, Avital. *The Test Drive.* Chicago: University of Illinois Press, 2005.

Rosavanlon, Pierre. "Revolutionary Democracy." In *Democracy Past and Future*, edited by Sam Moyn, 79–97. New York: Columbia University Press, 2007.

Rossiter, Clinton. *1787: The Grand Convention*. New York: W. W. Norton, 1987.

Roumy, Frank. "La naissance de la notion canonique de consanguinitas et sa réception dans le droit civil." In *L'hérédité entre Moyen Âge et époque moderne*, edited by Maaike van der Lugt and Charles de Miramon, 41–66. Florence: Sismel—Edizioni del Galluzzo / Micrologus Library, 2008.

Rousseau, Jean-Jacques. "Discourse on the Origin and the Foundations of Inequality among Men." In Jean-Jacques Rousseau, *The Discourses and Other Early Political Writings*, edited by Victor Gourevitch, 111–231. Cambridge: Cambridge University Press, 1997.

Russell, Bertrand. "On Denoting." *Mind*, n.s. 14, no. 56 (October 1905): 479–93.

Sabean, David Warren. "From Clan to Kindred: Kinship and the Circulation of Property in Premodern and Modern Europe." In *Heredity Produced: At the Crossroads of Biology, Politics, and Culture, 1500–1870*, edited by Staffan Müller-Wille and Hans-Jörg Rheinberger, 37–60. Cambridge, Mass.: MIT Press, 2007.

Sahlins, Peter. *Unnaturally French: Foreign Citizens in the Old Regime and After*. Ithaca, N.Y.: Cornell University Press, 2004.

Salisbury, John of. *Policraticus*. Edited by Cary J. Nederman. Cambridge: Cambridge University Press, 1990.

Sallis, John. *On Translation*. Bloomington: Indiana University Press, 2002.

Sandywell, Barry. *Pre-Socratic Reflexivity: The Construction of Philosophical Discourse c. 600–450 BC*. London: Routledge, 1996.

Sankar Muthu, *Enlightenment against Empire*. Princeton, N.J.: Princeton University Press, 2003.

Sarno, David. "Franz Josef Och, Google's Translation Über-Scientist, Talks about Google Translate." *Los Angeles Times*, March 11, 2010. Accessed March 3, 2012. http://latimesblogs.latimes.com/technology/2010/03/the-web-site-translategooglecom-was-done-in-2001-we-were-just—licensing-3rd-party-machine-translation-technologies-tha.html.

Schauwers, Albert. "The 'Benevolent' Colonies of Johannes van den Bosch: Continuities in the Administration of Poverty in the Netherlands and Indonesia." *Comparative Studies in Society and History* 43, no. 2 (2001): 298–328.

Schlegel, August Wilhelm von. *A Course of Lectures on Dramatic Art and Literature*. Translated by John Black and A. J. W. Morrisonn. London: George Bell and Sons, 1815.

———. *Kritische Schriften und Briefe*. Vol. 6. Edited by Edgar Lohner. Stuttgart: Kohlhammer, 1962.

Schmitt, Carl. *Constitutional Theory*. Translated by Jeffrey Seitzer. Durham, N.C.: Duke University Press, 2008.

———. *Die Diktatur*. Berlin: Duncker and Humblot, 1994.

———. *Political Theology: Four Chapters on the Concept of Sovereignty*. Translated by George Schwab. Cambridge, Mass.: MIT Press, 1988; Chicago: University of Chicago Press, 2006.

———. *Über die drei Arten des rechtswissenschaftlichen Denkens*. Berlin: Duncker and Humboldt, 1993.

Schneider, David M. *American Kinship: A Cultural Account*. Chicago: University of Chicago Press, 1980.

——. *A Critique of the Study of Kinship*. Ann Arbor: University of Michigan Press, 1984.

Shakespeare, William. *The Merchant of Venice*. Edited by Jay L. Hallo. Oxford: Oxford University Press, 1994.

——. *A Midsummer Night's Dream.* In *The Riverside Shakespeare: The Complete Works,* 2nd ed., edited by G. Blakemore Evans et al., 251–83. Boston: Houghton Mifflin, 1997.

Shapiro, Scott J. *Legality*. Cambridge, Mass.: Harvard University Press, 2011.

Shell, Marc. *Children of the Earth: Literature, Politics, and Nationhood*. Oxford: Oxford University Press, 1993.

Shiller, Robert J. "Better Insurance against Inequality." *New York Times*, April 13, 2014, BU6.

Shklar, Judith. "Political Theory and the Rule of Law." In *Political Thought and Political Thinkers*, edited by Stanley Hoffmann. 21–37. Chicago: University of Chicago Press, 1998.

Sidney, Algernon. *Discourses concerning Government*. Edited by Thomas G. West. Indianapolis: Liberty Fund, 1996.

Sieyès, Emmanuel. *Qu'est-ce le Tiers État?* Edited by Roberto Zapperi. Geneva: Librairie Droz, 1970.

——. "Reconnaissance et exposition raisonnée des droits de l'homme et du citoyen." In *Orateurs de la révolution Française: Les constituants*, vol. 1, edited by François Furet and Ran Halévi. Paris: Bibliothèque de la Pléiade, 1989.

Skinner, Quentin. *Foundations of Modern Political Thought.* Vols. 1–2. Cambridge: Cambridge University Press, 1978.

——. *Rethinking the Foundations of Modern Political Thought*. Edited by Annabel Brett et al. Cambridge: Cambridge University Press, 2006.

Smith, Preserved. *A Short History of Christian Theophagy*. Chicago: Open Court, 1922.

Spierenburg, Pieter. "Punishment, Power, and History: Foucault and Elias." *Social Science History* 28, no. 4 (Winter 2004): 607–36.

——. *The Spectacle of Suffering*. Cambridge: Cambridge University Press, 1984.

Spinoza, Benedict de. "Correspondence." In *On the Improvement of the Understanding; The Ethics; Correspondence*, translated by R. H. M. Elwes, 273–427, New York: Dover, 1955.

——. *A Theologico-Political Treatise*. Translated by R. H. M. Elwes. New York: Dover, 1951.

Spivak, Gayatri Chakravorty. "A Penny for the Old Guy." *Cambridge Review of International Affairs* 27, no. 1 (2014): 184–98. Accessed May 28, 2014. http://www.tandfonline.com/doi/abs/10.1080/09557571.2014.877262#.U8afU_ldXTo.

——. "Scattered Speculations on the Question of Value." *Diacritics* 15, no. 4 (1985): 73–93.

Stahuljak, Zrinka. *Bloodless Genealogies of the French Middle Ages: Translation, Kinship, and Metaphor*. Gainesville: University Press of Florida, 2005.

Stalin, Joseph. *Marxism and the National Question*. Moscow: Progress, 1953.

Stoler, Ann Laura. *Along the Archival Grain: Epistemic Anxieties and Colonial Common Sense*. Princeton, N.J.: Princeton University Press, 2009.

———. "Colony and Camp: A Political Matrix." In *Durabilities of Imperial Duress.* Durham, N.C.: Duke University Press, 2016.

———. *Duress: Imperial Durabilities in Our Times*. Durham, N.C.: Duke University Press, 2016.

———. "On Degrees of Imperial Sovereignty." *Public Culture* 18, no. 1 (2006): 125–46.

———. *Race and the Education of Desire: Foucault's History of Sexuality and the Colonial Order of Things*. Durham, N.C.: Duke University Press, 1995.

Stourzh, Gerald. "Constitution: Changing Meanings of the Term from the Early Seventeenth to the Late Eighteenth Century." In *Conceptual Change and the Constitution*, edited by Terence Ball and J. G. A. Pocock, 43–44. Lawrence, Kan.: University Press of Kansas, 1988.

Sypnowich, Christine. *The Concept of Socialist Law*. Oxford: Clarendon, 1990.

———. "Utopia and the Rule of Law." In *Recrafting the Rule of Law: The Limits of Legal Order*, edited by David Dyzenhaus, 178–95. Oxford: Hart, 1999.

Terray, Emmanuel. *Combats avec Méduse*. Paris: Galilée, 2011.

———. *Marxism and "Primitive" Societies: Two Studies*. Translated by Mary Klopper. New York: Monthly Review Press, 1972.

Thottam, Jyoti. "Two Indias." *New York Times*, September 8, 2013, BR10.

Tilly, Charles. *The Formation of the National States in Western Europe*. Princeton, N.J.: Princeton University Press, 1975.

Tourdonnet, A., Le Comte de. *Essais sur l'éducation des enfants pauvrès des colonies agricoles d'éducation.* Vol. 2. Paris: P. Brunet, 1862.

Trentin, Bruno. *La cité du travail: La gauche et la crise du fordisme*. Paris: Fayard, 2012.

Tronti, Mario. "Il piano del capitale." In *Operai e Capitale*, 60–85. Torino: Einaudi, 1966. Passages from Tronti's major work translated into English are available on the web at https://operaismoinenglish.wordpress.com/category/mario-tronti/page/2.

Trouillot, M.-R. "Anthropology and the Savage Slot: The Poetics and Politics of Otherness." In *Recapturing Anthropology: Working in the Present*, edited by Richard G. Fox, 17–44. Santa Fe, N.M.: School of American Research Press, 1991.

Tudeau-Clayton, Margaret. "Scenes of Translation in Jonson and Shakespeare: 'Poetaster, Hamlet,' and 'A Midsummer Night's Dream.'" *Translation and Literature* 11, no. 1 (Spring 2002): 1–23.

Ullmann, Walter. *Principles of Government in the Middle Ages*. New York: Routledge, 2010.

United Nations. "The Rise of the South: Human Progress in a Diverse World." Human Development Report. New York: United Nations Development Program, 2013.

Venuti, Lawrence. *The Translator's Invisibility: A History of Translation*. London: Routledge, 1995.

Vérin, Hélène. *Entrepreneurs, entreprises: Histoire d'une idée*. Paris: Presses Universitaires de France, 1982.

Vernant, Jean-Pierre. *Myth and Thought among the Greeks*. London: Routledge, 1983.

——. *The Origins of Greek Thought*. Ithaca, N.Y.: Cornell University Press, 1984.

Virno, Paolo. "The Ambivalence of Disenchantment." In *Radical Thought in Italy: A Potential Politics,* edited by Michael Hardt and Paolo Virno, 13–36. Minneapolis: University of Minnesota Press, 1996.

Vlastos, Gregory. "Equality and Justice in Early Greek Cosmologies." In *Studies in Greek Philosophy,* vol. 1, *The Presocratics*, edited by Daniel W. Graham, 57–88. Princeton, N.J.: Princeton University Press, 1995.

——. "*Isonomia*." In *Studies in Greek Philosophy*, vol. 1, *The Presocratics*, edited by Daniel W. Graham, 89–111. Princeton, N.J.: Princeton University Press, 1995.

Volosinov, V. N. *Marxism and the Philosophy of Language*. Translated by Ladislav Mateijka and I. R. Titunik. Cambridge, Mass.: Harvard University Press, 1986.

Wade, Peter, ed. *Race, Ethnicity and Nation: Perspectives from Kinship and Genetics.* New York: Berghahn Books, 2009.

Waldby, Catherine, and Robert Mitchell. *Tissue Economies: Blood, Organs, and Cell Lines in Late Capitalism*. Durham, N.C.: Duke University Press, 2006.

Waldron, Jeremy. "The Concept and the Rule of Law." *Georgia Law Review* 43, no. 1 (Fall 2008): 13–19.

Wayper, Charles Leslie. *Political Thought*. New York: Philosophical Library, 1954.

Weinbaum, Alys Eve. *Wayward Reproductions: Genealogies of Race and Nation in Transatlantic Modern Thought*. Durham, N.C.: Duke University Press, 2004.

Whitman, James Q. *The Origins of Reasonable Doubt: Theological Roots of the Criminal Trial*. New Haven, Conn.: Yale University Press, 2008.

Wilder, Gary. *Freedom Time, Negritude, Decolonization, and the Future of the World.* Durham, N.C.: Duke University Press, 2015.

Williams, Bernard. "Internal and External Reasons." In *Moral Luck*. Cambridge: Cambridge University Press, 1981.

Wittgenstein, Ludwig. *Philosophical Investigations*. Translated by G. Anscombe. New York: Macmillan, 1958.

Wolin, Sheldon S. "Collective Identity and Constitutional Power." In *The Presence of the Past: Essays on the State and the Constitution*, 8–31. Baltimore: Johns Hopkins University Press, 1990.

——. "Norm and Form: The Constitutionalizing of Democracy." In *Athenian Political Thought and the Reconstruction of American Democracy*, edited by J. Peter

Euben, John R. Wallach, and Josiah Ober, 29–58. Ithaca, N.Y.: Cornell University Press, 1995.

——. *Politics and Vision: Continuity and Innovation in Western Political Thought*. Princeton, N.J.: Princeton University Press, 2004.

Wood, Gordon S. *The Creation of the American Republic, 1776–1787*. Chapel Hill: University of North Carolina Press, 1998.

Yeats, William Butler. "Under Ben Bulben." In *The Variorum Edition of the Poems of W. B. Yeats*, edited by Peter Allt and Russell Alspach. New York: MacMillan, 1957.

Young, Thomas. "To the Inhabitants of Vermont, a Free and Independent State, Bounding on the River Connecticut and Lake Champlain (April 11, 1777)." In *History of Vermont, Natural, Civil and Statistical, in Three Parts*, edited by Zadock Thompson. Burlington, Vt.: Chauncey Goodrich, 1842.

Ziai, Aram. "Development: Projects, Power, and a Poststructuralist Perspective." *Alternatives* 34 (2009): 190.

Zimmerer, Jürgen, Joachim Zeller, and Edward Neather, eds. *Genocide in German South-West Africa: The Colonial War (1904–1908)*. Monmouth, Wales: Merlin Press, 2007.

Žižek, Slavoj. *The Sublime Object of Ideology*. London: Verso, 1989.

Zupančič, Alenka. *Why Psychoanalysis?: Three Interventions*. Uppsala, Sweden: NSU Press, 2008.

CONTRIBUTORS

Gil Anidjar, "Blood," is Professor in the Departments of Religion and Middle Eastern, South Asian, and African Studies at Columbia University.

Étienne Balibar, "Exploitation," is Professor in the Department of French and Romance Philology at Columbia University and Anniversary Chair in Modern European Philosophy, Kingston University London.

J. M. Bernstein, "The Rule of Law," is University Distinguished Professor of philosophy at The New School for Social Research.

Akeel Bilgrami, "Identity," is Johnsonian Professor of Philosophy at Columbia University.

Jean L. Cohen, "Federation," is Nell and Herbert Singer Professor of Contemporary Civilization and Political Theory in the Department of Political Science at Columbia University.

Joan Copjec, "Sexual Difference," is Professor of Modern Culture and Media at Brown University.

Stathis Gourgouris, "Archē," is Professor in the Department of Classics and the Institure for Comparative Literature and Society at Columbia University

Andreas Kalyvas, "Constituent Power," is Associate Professor in the Department of Politics at The New School for Social Research, The New School.

Jacques Lezra, "Translation," is Professor of Hispanic Studies at the University of California–Riverside.

Adi Ophir, "Concept," is Professor Emeritus, Tel Aviv University, and Visiting Professor at the Cogut Center for the Humanities and the Program for Middle East Studies at Brown University.

Gayatri Chakravorty Spivak, "Development," is University Professor in the Humanities at Columbia University.

Ann Laura Stoler, "Colony," is Willy Brandt Distinguished Professor of Anthropology and Historical Studies at The New School for Social Research.

INDEX

IDIOM: INVENTING WRITING THEORY
Jacques Lezra and Paul North, series editors

Werner Hamacher, *Minima Philologica*. Translated by Catharine Diehl and Jason Groves

Michal Ben-Naftali, *Chronicle of Separation: On Deconstruction's Disillusioned Love*. Translated by Mirjam Hadar. Foreword by Avital Ronell

Daniel Hoffman-Schwartz, Barbara Natalie Nagel, and Lauren Shizuko Stone, eds., *Flirtations: Rhetoric and Aesthetics This Side of Seduction*

Jean-Luc Nancy, *Intoxication*. Translated by Philip Armstrong

Márton Dornbach, *Receptive Spirit: German Idealism and the Dynamics of Cultural Transmission*

Sean Alexander Gurd, *Dissonance: Auditory Aesthetics in Ancient Greece*

Anthony Curtis Adler, *Celebricities: Media Culture and the Phenomenology of Gadget Commodity Life*

Nathan Brown, *The Limits of Fabrication: Materials Science, Materialist Poetics*

J. M. Bernstein, Adi Ophir, and Ann Laura Stoler, eds., *Political Concepts: A Critical Lexicon in Formation*